To: Lisa

In order to succeed.
we must first believe
that we can.

Emilie Henriques

12/17/18

THE SECRET TO WEALTH

THE SECRET TO WEALTH

SECRETS FROM THE WORLD'S TOP LEADERS

The Secret To Wealth

Private Investment Club Corp. titles are available at special quantity discounts for bulk purchases for sales promotions, premiums, fundraising, and educational use.

For more information, please write:

Private Investment Club Corp.
#200 - 21 Queen St. East
Brampton, Ontario L6W 3P1

or call 905-488-4033
email: info@PrivateInvestmentClub.com

ISBN: 978-0-9938944-5-9

Published in Canada

BRIAN TRACY'S ENDORSEMENT

Congratulations on getting your copy of "The Secret To Wealth".

I'm so happy to be a part of this amazing book alongside of Sunil Tulsiani as well as all of the contributing authors to produce this masterpiece.

It's simple yet a very powerful book that will change your life.

In fact, I would highly recommend that you not only read this book, but study it to discover at least one secret in every chapter.

And then, take immediate, timely action.

Wish you massive success.

Brian Tracy

Best-Selling Author and a Professional Speaker

A SPECIAL NOTE FROM THE PUBLISHER

Dear Reader,

Congratulations on purchasing this book.

Writing a bestselling book sometimes seems like an individual's project, but it really takes a whole team of experts, designers, marketers, editors, planners, and a behind-the-scenes team.

Producing this bestselling book took over two years and well over 1,000 hours from my team.

I really encourage you to study this book, especially if your goal is to become wealthy...however you define your wealth.

Thank you.

Sunil Tulsiani, Publisher

Award Winning Best-selling Author

PRIVATE INVESTMENT CLUB
THE LARGEST REAL ESTATE CLUB IN CANADA

ACKNOWLEDGEMENTS

First of all, I would like to thank the contributing authors, Brian Tracy, Yury Petyushin, Cora Cristobal, Brian d'Eon, Michael Fielder, Til Lowery, Howard Lau, Sangita Tulsiani, Gwen Tewnion, Linda Pisani Elder, Senjey Joshi, Paul LeJoy, Mike Burgess, Lurline Henriques, Kuljeet Chouhan, Chai Harjo, Huong Luu, William Wong, Rinay Chand, Dennis Henson, Victor Quach, Nam Ratna, Tammy Smit, Shahzad Ahmed, Randi Goodman, Tim Bansal, Mark Kerwin, Ralston Powell, Naveen Sujan, and Robert Elder. Without each of your individual contributions, the Secret to Wealth could not be properly outlined for our readers.

I also would like to thank my staff, Sonia Sharma, Janet Singh, and Nav Sujan for their ongoing, behind-the-scenes hard work and dedication.

To my wife, Sangita, my son Dev, and my daughter Megha, thank you so much for being my "Why." Without you, all the wealth in the world means nothing.

I would like to thank the members of Private Investment Club, my partners, my mentees, my friends, and my coaches (including Jack Canfield, Robert G. Allen, and Brian Tracy) for their ongoing support.

Finally, I want to thank the buyers of this book, because you are the inspiration and the reason why we invested over two years to produce it.

Sincerely,

Sunil Tulsiani, Publisher - Private Investment Club
Award Winning Best-selling Author

CONTENTS

THE SECRET *to* WEALTH

CHAPTER 1

The Secret to Massive Wealth

BY SUNIL TULSIANI

"For a rich person, it's a rich world. For a poor person, it's a poor world. But it's the same world."
— Sunil Tulsiani

During my trainings, masterminds, and mentoring sessions, people ask me how I went from being a police officer to bringing massive amounts of wealth into my life and the lives of hundreds of my members. Is it truly possible to make massive amounts of money? What is wealth? How much money should one have to never again worry about money?

First, let's define wealth. You see, in the olden days, wealth meant only one thing. Money.

In my view, wealth means having so much money that you never have to worry about money, plus you're surrounded by true love, plus you have a wonderful family, plus you have lots of time doing the things you enjoy, plus you have true friends, plus you're healthy, plus you're really happy.

The important thing to understand is that you can have it all. You see, having huge amounts of money, but no one to share it with is no good. Having huge amounts of money but no time isn't wealth, either.

The most important word in the wealth formula is the word "Plus." Being wealthy means that you can have it all…you don't need to choose just one benefit over the others.

"The lack of money is the root of all evil."
— *Mark Twain*

Private Investment Club (PIC) Wealth Formula

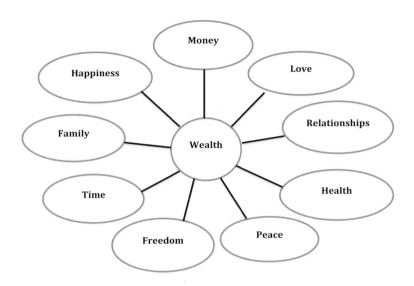

10 Million Dollars

I was on a stage, speaking alongside Jack Canfield, when one of the attendees asked, "How much money does one need to become wealthy these days?"

Obviously, the answer is very subjective, but in my view, one must aim to have a net worth of 10 million dollars in the next 5 to 10 years.

Of course, not everyone on this planet needs 10 million dollars to have a wonderful life. In your country, you may feel wealthy even if you have a million dollars or less.

But having 10 million would allow you to send your children to any school you want, quit your job (if you wish), do what you really want, go on vacations, hire mentors in your life, attend seminars anywhere in the world, spend quality time with your loved ones, give back more, and build your legacy.

Whether this takes you 2 years, 5 years, or 10 years, if you aim to be worth 10 million dollars, you would never have to worry about money.

"You become who you spend time with."
— *Tony Robbins*

$100,000 to $1,000,000 Positive Cash Flow

Whether you want to make one million or 10 million dollars, the idea is that you need cash flow to live.

They say cash is king, but I say <u>cash flow is king</u>.

For simplicity's sake, let's say you're able to make 10% ROI (some of my PIC members make a lot more than that). That means that a $1 million investment would give you $8,333 cash flow per month. $10 million would generate a cool $83,333 per month.

See the chart below:

Example PIC cash flow chart, calculated at 10% ROI:

Net Worth	Cash Flow
$500,000	$4,166 per month
1 million	$8,333 per month
2.4 million	$20,000 per month
4.8 million	$40,000 per month
10 million	$83,333 per month
12 million	$100,000 per month

Lots of people think it's not possible to make a million or more dollars or that a 10% ROI is unachievable. And that's normally the case for most people. But, I'm hoping you're not a "normal" person.

I'm hoping you're an "abnormal" person who wants abnormal, crazy results.

In my case, I don't invest in anything unless I'm making 15% to 25% ROI.

And, yes, it's doable right now in 2018-2019.

You need the right strategies, the right mentors, the right connections, the right team, the right masterminds, and (as Napoleon Hills calls it) a "burning desire" to make it happen.

In fact, you should become obsessed in growing your wealth and "do" whatever it takes to make it happen right NOW.

"Surround yourself with only people
who are going to lift you higher."
— Oprah Winfrey

Gun to the Head

In November of 2017, I was sharing a stage with Brian Tracy for the second time, when someone asked me, "If I hire you as my mentor, do you guarantee I'll make a million bucks?"

I smiled and said, "absolutely not."

You see, there are so many gurus who sell "Take this Pill" or "Push this Button" programs and make you think that you'll magically become rich while sleeping.

It doesn't work that way.

You do need to take action. It takes persistence, ability to move when you're <u>not</u> ready, risk-taking, and remaining focused on achieving your goals.

I occasionally have people who tell me that they're ready to do whatever it takes...nothing will stop them...and then, the next moment, they say things like, "It's not the right time for me," "My wife/husband won't allow that," "I'll do it someday," "I wish I could do it for free," "I don't want to take any risks," "I'll let you know later," "I'm too busy now," "I know that," and the big one..."I can't afford it."

This is a really important point. To make drastic changes financially, you'll need to do things that'll scare you.

Your mind's #1 job is to protect you and find reasons why it won't work.

It will almost always talk you out of taking immediate action. It will tell you to do it "someday."

During my training sessions, people swear that they want to make more money, they want more quality time with their spouse, they want to go on vacations, they want to pay off their debts, they never want to worry about money, etc.

Then they give me reasons why they either can't do it, or they'll do it later on.

They say things like, "I'll let you know next week," "It's too expensive," "I'll just do it myself," "I can't afford it," "I'll check with my spouse," "I already know all this stuff," etc.

I often say to people, "If there was a gun to your head and you were told you need to make $50,000 in the next 90 days – would you still find reasons (excuses) not to do it now?"

Of course not.

So, whenever you get scared or you fail to take the action that's going to take you to your one million dollars, 10 million dollars, or financial freedom, ask yourself, "If I had a gun to my head and I was ordered to make lots of money…would I still say things like, 'My wife won't let me,' 'I can't afford to get a mentor,' 'I'll do it some other day,' 'I don't have the time,' 'I've tried it before and it didn't work,' 'My parents told me I'll never be successful,' 'I was told that having too much money means I'm greedy,' 'I can't do it,' 'I'm not ready yet,' or tons of other reasons?"

"If you don't find a way to make money while you sleep, you will work until you die."
— Warren Buffett

"7 Simple Steps" Formula to Becoming Wealthy

1. Write down – What do you really want?
2. Educate yourself.
3. Pick a product or service to help others.
4. Who are your clients and where are they?
5. Build your list...now.
6. Find people who have achieved what you want and copy them.
7. Take action now.

> *"I don't think God cares if you are rich or poor. God loves you anyway."*
> — *Robert Kiyosaki*

Let's explore each of the above 7 steps in detail:

1. What do you really want?

My friend and mentor, Brian Tracy, says that only 3% of adults have written goals, and they earn 10 times as much money as the ones who don't write their goals.

So, please take the time to write down what you actually want and give it a deadline. Make sure to clearly indicate what you want.

The best way to do this is to find a 10-year-old child and tell that child your goals. Then ask them to repeat your goals. If they understand it… it's a great start.

Here's what I wrote over 12 years ago, which allowed me to buy and sell 77 properties in my first year alone after I left the police force.

> *"If you are born poor, It's not your mistake.*
> *But if you die poor, it's your mistake."*
> — *Bill Gates*

I, Sunil Tulsiani, will make 1 million dollars by _____ (date). Signed it. Dated it.

Then, I posted these all over my home, including washrooms, the kitchen, the basement, the living room, closets, the workout place… basically everywhere.

> *"Money isn't the most important thing in life, but it's reasonably close to oxygen."*
> — *Zig Ziglar*

2. Educate yourself.

During my coaching sessions, some people ask, "How did you learn this stuff?"

I learned it by:

- Attending seminars, workshops, and masterminds.
- Listening to audio books.
- Reading books (this was really hard for me when I started).
- Signing up for online courses.
- Watching training videos.
- Attending teleseminars, podcasts, webinars, etc.

Of the above, my favorite ways to educate myself are live events and audio books.

I basically listened to audio books of Tony Robbins, Robert Kiyosaki, Robert G. Allen, Jack Canfield, Brian Tracy, Napoleon Hill, Dr. Deepak Chopra, T. Harv Eker, Dr. John Gray, and other successful people.

I would listen to the audio books at least twice in a row (sometimes 10 times in a row) while driving and over the weekend. I basically got obsessed with growing myself, decided to reduce watching TV by 80%, and gave up listening to radio/news.

My biggest growth came from attending live events, trainings, expos, and masterminds, building relationships with potential clients, mentors, and JV partners.

I made a goal of hunting down at least 20 events per year and did whatever it took to find them and attend them.

I looked for real quality speakers and quality attendees by investing in myself consistently.

> *"The future depends on what you do today."*
> *— Mahatma Gandhi*

3. Pick a product or service to help others.

In my case, I chose real estate as a vehicle to help others.

I bought properties way below market value. I kept a few for myself and sold the rest to my PIC members at wholesale prices.

I also found ways to help members of the Private Investment Club to buy properties even if they only had $25,000, $15,000, or even $5,000.

In fact, some opportunities that I provided required no money at all.

I also ended up helping people with my mentoring services. I helped people become best-selling authors, speakers, and coaches, and I also helped bring paying clients to them.

In my view, you need to pick a product and/or service that you really enjoy doing. Then, study it. Become an expert, and then help others.

> *"Successful people rely heavily on their mentors. Ordinary people don't."*
> *— Robert G. Allen*

4. Who are your clients and where are they?

Most people are taught to go find their clients and sell to them. I help my Private Investment Club mentoring students find out who their clients are and how to <u>attract</u> them.

Attracting your clients means you set yourself up in such a way that your client hunts you down and wants to work with you.

In fact, if you offer great value, your potential clients actually insist that you take them on or they get upset.

I occasionally get nasty emails from potential mentoring clients who apply to work with me and don't get accepted.

I currently have a high-end, six-month, $25K mentoring program where I guarantee that if you're accepted, you'll make at least $50,000 or I'll keep mentoring you until you do.

To get into the program, there's a vetting process to see if they are suitable and if I want to work with them.

Here's what you should do to find your ideal people to mentor or work with:

Think about the best clients you ever had in your life. If you're starting out, dream about the ideal client(s) that you want to work with.

Then, take a piece of paper and write down what makes them your great clients.

For example:

- Are they male or female?
- What age group are they?
- Are they married or single?
- How much money do they make?
- What kind of profession are they in?
- How did they find you?
- What did they like about you?
- What did you like about them?
- Are they victims or leaders?
- Are they local, national, or international?
- Were they action takers or not?

Once you know the details of your ideal client, you can actually set up your marketing to attract the paying clients into your life who are perfect for you.

For example, you could do the following to attract the people you want to help:

- Write articles/blogs/ebooks
- Make educational YouTube Videos
- Make a simple website
- Become a coach/mentor
- Write a book
- Train people
- Write books with legendary leaders
- Speak on big stages

Remember, everything should be done for your ideal clients.

If you try to sell meat to vegetarians, it doesn't matter how good your product is. You'll fail.

> *"You can serve god and man in no more effective way than by getting rich."*
> — *Wallace D. Wattles*

5. Build your list...now.

During my exclusive high-end Millionaire Mastermind, one of the PIC members asked, "What's one thing I should be asking every morning (in regards to building a multimillion-dollar business)?"

The answer?

"What am I doing today to build my list?"

In today's world, it's important to have a list of potential clients whom you've built relationships with, people who would love to buy products from you.

At Private Investment Club, we have a big list. Every time I push the "send" button, I add huge value to the lives of my members and mentoring clients. At the same time, I make a lot of money.

Let me give you an example:

Several years ago, in Kitchener, Canada, we bought 28 condos at $90,000 each that were worth $120,000.

We sent out emails to my big list and sold all the condos within a week, just because we pushed a "send" button.

And, at the same time, I gave my PIC members an amazing deal…they bought the property for only $99,900 (20% below market value). This cash flowing property was rented, a professional management company was in place, and all the fixups were done.

And…get this…some of them bought it with nothing down.

How did they buy it with nothing down?

Here's how that took place.

The PIC members, whom I had great relationships with, borrowed 80% from the bank and I lent the remaining 20% (for their down payment) at a low interest rate. I even lent some of my mentees money for closing costs…so this became an absolutely no-money-down deal for them.

What's important to understand about this amazing value that I offered was that my members did not have to find a good deal, they did not have to negotiate a great deal, they didn't have to fix it, they didn't have to find the tenants, they didn't have to manage it (unless they wanted to) and they got it with either no money down or very little money down.

So, whether you're a real estate investor, agent, mortgage broker, coach, mentor, accountant, trainer, or any service-oriented businessperson, ask yourself, "What am I doing today to build my list?" and "how can I offer the best products/services to them?"

Want some ideas on building your list?

Here you go.

- Find someone who has a list and pay them to send out your offer.
- Write a report/ebook and give it away in exchange for the prospect's name and email address.
- Place ads to give away your report, ebook, or videos for free in exchange for their email address.
- Put up booths at expos and collect contact information from the attendees.
- Speak at events and give great value.
- Place Facebook, Google, or LinkedIn ads.
- Build your connections on LinkedIn – that builds your list.

"The act of taking the first step is what separates the winners from the losers."
— *Brian Tracy*

6. Find people who have achieved what you want and copy them.

In addition to sharing stages with Brian Tracy and Jack Canfield, I was fortunate to share a big stage with Robert G. Allen again this year.

The question from one of the VIP attendees was, "How do I find people who have what I want and get them to mentor me?"

My answer?

I attended as many events as I could and found the trainers who have done what they're teaching/coaching.

Then, I met the people whose lives have been changed because of the trainers.

Then, I asked what it would take to be mentored by them.

Then, I found a way to get the money to invest in myself.

Finally, once I decided to choose them as my mentors, I decided to completely trust them and do what they asked me to do…whether I was ready or not. Whether my family agreed or not. Whether I felt like it or not. Whether it was too cold or too hot. Whether my friends thought it was a good idea or it was a crazy idea.

I just did it.

And every time I started to have doubts and thoughts about delaying, procrastinating, or any kind of fear, I looked at my goals and asked myself, "Is this truly important to me?"

If the answer was yes, then I asked, "If I had a gun to my head, would I take immediate action?"

What I found was that I was almost never 100% ready, that I always had fears, and that I always thought, "I can't afford this," or "It's too expensive," or "I don't need a mentor," or "I'll do it someday."

7. Take Action Now.

There's one attribute that separates successful people from the regular people. That one thing, obviously, is taking immediate action.

My friend Brian Tracy says that when an amazing opportunity is presented to most people, they go to "Someday Island." "Someday I'll hire a coach," "someday I'll learn that skill," "someday I'll read that book," "someday I'll buy that property." Someday…someday…someday, And that "someday" usually does not come.

Here's the biggest takeaway…all opportunities come to you when you're not ready.

Any worthwhile changes require you to be bold and take action despite fear. Despite criticism. Despite not being ready.

It's so important for you to realize that taking massive action requires guts because it's not your mind's job to help you become wealthy, but rather to keep you in your comfort zone. You need to become comfortable being uncomfortable.

So, how do you become an action taker?

Realize that 95% of your thinking comes from being around the people you've associated with.

You dress like them, you think like them, you shop like them, you make similar amounts of money, you worry like them, you invest like them, etc.

So, let's find events, trainings, masterminds, and mentors where you find people who think like you want to think, people who'll lift you up, people who you can partner up with, and people who want to make millions or become massively wealthy alongside of you.

You need to become an action taker if you want to take advantage of the opportunities that come your way, if you want to attract the right relationships, and if you want to give back to the world. Whether you want to empower people, help people become wealthy, build churches, help the poor, or bring positive changes to the world...you need to become wealthy by taking immediate action wherever you are in life.

It is my true desire for you to become massively wealthy. As such, I would like to gift you this amazing audio book, Make A Million. You can have it by going to MakeAMillion.Net right now.

Also, if you want to know more about me or my real estate club (the largest elite club in North America), please go to: PrivateInvestmentClub. com or SunilTulsiani.com.

Lastly, please make sure you don't let anyone tell you that you can't be wealthy (not even your spouse, your family, your friends, or yourself).

Dream big, be persistent, and do your dreams now.

"Become so wealthy that you forget it's a payday."
— Sunil Tulsiani

SUNIL TULSIANI

Over the last 12 years, Sunil Tulsiani transformed from Police Detective to worldwide real estate mogul. In his first year alone, he invested in 77 properties.

The media nicknamed him "The Wealthy Cop."

He founded the largest elite club in North America, www.PrivateInvestmentClub.com, and has members across Canada, the USA, and around the world.

Sunil has been featured on *INC* magazine, CNBC, Fox Business News, CP24 TV, the *Toronto Star,* and has been on covers of many magazines, including Profiles of Success.

Sunil has shared stages with Jack Canfield, Brian Tracy, Ron Le Grand, Robert G. Allen, and many others across Canada, the USA, and India.

Now Sunil helps real estate investors, agents, coaches, mentors, speakers, and consultants to build their credibility by getting them on big stages; helping them coauthor best-selling books with legendary leaders; finding money-lending partners; and building their multimillion-dollar businesses.

If your dream is to become financially free, get on big stages, write books with legends, and get access to money for your real estate projects, then you need to connect with Sunil today by going to www.PrivateInvestmentClub.com or www.SunilTulsiani.com.

Lastly, here are Sunil's gifts to you: ***The 7 Most Expensive Mistakes I've Made in Real Estate Investing*** a $97 value at "http://www.7RealEstateMistakes.com". Also, a valuable audiobook called ***Make A Million***, which you can access at "http://www.MakeAMillion.net".

CHAPTER 2

Maximize Your Income

BY BRIAN TRACY

You have the ability, right now, to earn vastly more than you are earning today, probably two or three times as much, by changing some of the things you are doing each day. How do we know this? Simple. You are surrounded by people who are not as smart, as ambitious or as determined as you who are already earning much more than you are. And all of these people started off earning less than you are earning today. In this chapter, I will show you how to move to the front of the income line of life, and faster than you ever thought possible.

One of the qualities of the top men and women is that they are extremely self-reliant. They accept complete responsibility for themselves and everything that happens to them. They look to themselves as the source of their successes and as the main cause of their problems and difficulties. High achievers say, "If it's to be, it's up to me."

When things aren't moving along as fast as they want, they ask themselves, "What is it *in me* that is causing this problem?" They refuse to make excuses or to blame other people. Instead, they look into themselves, and seek for ways to overcome their obstacles and to make progress.

See Yourself as Self Employed

Totally self-responsible people look upon themselves as self-employed. They see themselves as the presidents of their own personal services corporations. They realize that, no matter who signs their paycheck, in the final analysis they work for *themselves*. Because they have this attitude of self-employment, they take a strategic approach to their work.

The essential element in strategic planning for a corporation or a business entity is the concept of "return on equity (ROE)." All business planning is aimed at organizing and reorganizing the resources of the business in such a way as to increase the financial returns to the business owners. It is to increase the quantity of output relative to the quantity of input. It is to focus on areas of high profitability and return and, simultaneously, to withdraw resources from areas of lower profitability and return. Companies that do this effectively in a rapidly changing environment are the ones that survive and prosper. Companies that fail to do this form of strategic analysis are those that fall behind and often disappear.

To achieve everything you are capable of achieving as a person, you also must become a skilled strategic planner with regard to your life and work. But instead of aiming to increase your return on equity, your goal is to increase your return on *energy*.

Most people in America, and worldwide, start off with little more than their ability to work. More than 80 percent of the millionaires in America started with nothing. Most successful people have been broke, or nearly broke, several times during their younger years. But the ones who eventually get to the top are those who do certain things in certain ways, and those actions set them apart from the masses.

Perhaps the most important thing they do, consciously or unconsciously, is to look at themselves strategically, thinking about how they can better use themselves in the marketplace; how they can best capitalize on their strengths and abilities to increase their financial returns to themselves and their families.

Your Most Valuable Asset

Your most valuable financial asset is your *earning ability*, your ability to earn money. All your knowledge, education, skills and experience contribute toward your earning ability, your ability to get results for which someone will pay good money. Properly applied to the marketplace, it's like a pump. By exploiting your earning ability, you can pump tens of thousands of extra dollars a year into your pocket.

And your earning ability is like farmland. If you don't take excellent care of it, if you don't fertilize it and cultivate it and water it on a regular basis, it soon loses its ability to produce the kind of harvest that you desire. Highly paid men and women are those who are extremely aware of the importance and value of their earning ability, and they work every day to keep it growing and increasing with the demands of the marketplace.

One of your greatest responsibilities in life is to identify, develop and maintain an important marketable skill. It is to become very good at doing something for which there is a strong market demand.

What Are You Good At?

In corporate strategy, we call this the development of a "competitive advantage." For a company, a competitive advantage is defined as an *area of excellence* in producing a product or service that gives the company a distinct edge over its competition. This "unique added value" enables the company to charge premium prices for its products and services.

To earn what you are truly worth, as the president of your own personal services corporation, you also must have a clear competitive advantage. You also must have an area of excellence. You must do something, or several things, that makes you different from and better than your competitors.

Your ability to identify and develop this competitive advantage, this special skill, is the most important thing you do in the world of work. It's the key to maintaining your earning ability. It's the foundation of your financial success. Without it, you're simply a pawn in a rapidly changing environment. But with a distinct competitive advantage, based on your strengths and abilities, you can write your own ticket. You can take charge of your own life. You can always get a job. And the more distinct your competitive advantage, the more money you can earn and the more places you can find to earn it.

Think Strategically About Yourself

There are four keys to the strategic marketing of yourself and your services. These are applicable to large companies such as General Motors, to candidates running for election and to individuals who want to earn the very most money in the very shortest period of time.

The first of these four keys is *specialization*. No one can be all things to all people. A "jack-of-all-trades" also is a "master of none." That career path usually leads to a dead end. Specialization is the key. Men and women who are successful have a series of general skills, but they also have one or two areas where they have developed the ability to perform in an outstanding manner.

Think About the Future

Your decision about how, where, when and why you are going to specialize in a particular area of endeavor is perhaps the most important decision you will ever make in your career. As the strategic planner, Michael Kami, once said, "Those who do not think about the future cannot have one."

The major reason why so many people are seeing their jobs eliminated and finding themselves unemployed for long periods of time is because they didn't look down the road of life far enough and prepare themselves well enough for the time when their current jobs would expire. They suddenly found themselves out of gas on a lonely road, facing a long walk back to regular and well-paying employment. Don't let this happen to you.

In determining your area of specialization, put your current job aside for the moment, and take the time to look deeply into yourself. Analyze yourself from every point of view. Rise above yourself, and look at your lifetime of activities and accomplishments in determining what your area of specialization could be or should be.

Keep Your Mind Open

You might be doing exactly the right job for you at this moment. You might already be specializing in an important area where people are eager to pay you a lot of money for what you do. Your current work might be ideally suited to your likes and dislikes, to your temperament and your personality. Nevertheless, you owe it to yourself to be continually expanding the scope of your vision and looking toward to the future to see what skills you will need in the months and years ahead. Remember, as Peter Drucker said, "the best way to predict the future is to create it."

You already possess special talents and abilities that make you unique and different from anyone else who has ever lived. The odds of there being another person just like you are more than 50 billion to one. Your remarkable combination of education, experience, knowledge, problems, successes, difficulties and challenges, and your way of looking at and reacting to life, make you extraordinary.

You Have Unlimited Potential

You have within you potential competencies and attributes that can enable you to accomplish virtually anything you want in life. Even if you lived for another 100 years, it would not be enough time for you to realize your full potential. You will never be able to use more than a small part of your inborn abilities. Your main job is to decide which of your talents you're going to exploit and develop to their highest and best possible use right now.

What is your area of excellence? What are you especially good at right now? If things continue as they are, what are you likely to be good at in the future—say one or two or even five years from now? Is this a marketable skill with a growing demand, or is your field changing in such a way that you are going to have to change as well if you want to keep up with it? Looking into the future, what *could* be your area of excellence if you were to go to work on yourself and your abilities? What *should* be your area of excellence if you want to rise to the top of your field, make an excellent living and take complete control of your financial future?

Keep Your Eyes Open

When I was 22, selling office supplies from business to business, I answered an advertisement for a copywriter for an advertising agency. As it happened, I had failed high school English and I really had no idea what a copywriter did. I remember the executive who interviewed me and how nice he was at pointing out that I wasn't at all qualified for the job.

But something happened to me in the course of the interview process. The more I thought about it, the more I realized how much I would like to write advertising. Having been turned down flat during my first interview, I decided to learn more about the field.

Back to School

That day, I went to the city library and began to check out and read books on advertising and copywriting. Over the next six months, while I worked at my regular job, I spent many hours reading those books and taking notes. Each week, I applied for a copywriting job to a different advertising agency in the city. I started with the small agencies first. When they turned me down, I asked them *why*. What was wrong with my application? What did I need to learn more about? What books would they recommend? And to this day, I remember that virtually everyone I spoke with was helpful to me and gave me advice.

By the end of six months, I had read every book on advertising and copywriting in the library and applied to every agency in the city, working up from the smallest agency to the very largest in the country. And by the time I had reached that level, I was ready. I was offered jobs as a junior copywriter by both the number-one and number-two agencies in the country. I took the job with the number-one agency and was very successful in a short period of time.

There Are No Limits

The point of this story is that I learned that you can become almost anything you need to become, in order to accomplish almost anything you want to accomplish, if you simply decide what it is and then learn what you need to learn. This is such an obvious fact that most people miss it completely.

Some years later, I heard about a lot of people who had gone into real estate development and made a lot of money. I decided that I wanted to get into real estate development and make a lot of money as well. I used my same strategy. I went to the library and began checking out and reading all the books on real estate development that I could find. At the time, I had no money, no contacts and no knowledge of the industry.

But I knew the great secret: I could learn what I needed to learn so that I could do what I wanted to do.

The Possibilities are Endless

Within six months, I had found an ideal piece of property for a shopping center on the edge of a fast-growing town. I then tied up the piece of property with a $150 deposit and a 30-day option. I immediately put together a proposal for a shopping center, as explained in the books that I had read.

With this proposal in hand, I tentatively approached several large potential anchor tenants, and several minor tenants, that together agreed to lease 85 percent of the square footage of this shopping center if I actually built it. Then I called on several large real estate developers with my proposal and my tentative lease agreements. On the 30th day of my 30-day option, I sold 75 percent of the entire package to a major development company in exchange for the company putting up all the cash and providing me with the resources and people I needed to manage the construction of the shopping center and the completion of the leasing. Virtually everything that I did I had learned from books written by real estate experts, books on the shelves of the local library.

In the years since then, I have successfully bought, developed, built out, leased and sold more than $100 million worth of real estate.

The Same Principles Work

As you might have noticed, the field of advertising and copywriting is very different from real estate development. But these industries, and every business venture I have explored over the years, had one element in common. Success in each area was based on the decision, first, to specialize in that area and, second, to become extremely knowledgeable in that area so that I could do a good job and get results if I got a chance.

In looking at your current and past experiences for an area of specialization, one of the most important questions to ask yourself is, "What activities have been most responsible for my success in life to date?"

How did you get from where you were to where you are today? What talents and abilities seemed to come easily to you? What things do you do well that seem to be difficult for most other people? What things do you most enjoy doing? What things do you find most intrinsically motivating? What things make you happy when you are doing them?

Increase Your Earning Ability

In becoming more valuable, in increasing your ability to get results that people will pay you for, your level of interest, excitement and enthusiasm about the particular job or activity is a key factor. You'll always do best and make the most money in a field that you really enjoy. It will be an area that you like to think about and talk about and read about and learn about. Successful people love what they do, and they can hardly wait to get to it each day. Doing their work makes them happy, and the happier they are, the more enthusiastically they do it, and the better they do it as well.

Become Different and Better

The second key to becoming more valuable is *differentiation*. You must decide what you're going to do to be both different and better than your competitors in the same field. Remember, you have to be good in only one specific area to move ahead of the pack. And you must decide what that area should be. What do you, or could you, do better than almost anyone else?

Segment Your Market

The third strategic principle in making a lot of money sooner is *segmentation*. You have to look at the marketplace and determine where you can best apply yourself, with your unique talents and abilities, to give yourself the highest possible financial return on the amount of time and energy you invest. What customers, companies, products, services or markets can best utilize your special talents and offer you the most in terms of financial rewards and future opportunities?

Focus and Concentrate

The final key to personal strategic planning is *concentration*. Once you have decided the area in which you are going to specialize, how you are going to differentiate yourself, and where in the marketplace you can best apply your strengths, your final job is to concentrate all of your energy on becoming excellent in that one area. The marketplace only pays extraordinary rewards for extraordinary performance.

In the final analysis, everything that you have accomplished up to now is a part of the preparation for becoming outstanding in your chosen field. When you become very good at doing something that people want, need and are willing to pay for, you will soon begin moving rapidly into the top ranks of the highest paid people everywhere.

BRIAN TRACY

Speaker – Author – Trainer

Brian Tracy is Chairman and CEO of Brian Tracy International, a company specializing in the training and development of individuals and organizations. He is among the top speakers, trainers and seminar leaders in the world today.

Brian Tracy has consulted for more than 1,000 companies and addressed more than 5,000,000 people in 5,000 talks and seminars throughout the US, Canada and 80 other countries worldwide.

He has studied, researched, written and spoken for 40 years in the fields of economics, history, business, philosophy and psychology. He is the top-selling author of over 80 books that have been translated into 42 languages.

To learn more about Brian Tracy, please visit his website at www. briantracy.com

CHAPTER 3

How to Generate Wealth and Meaning by Investing in Sustainable Homes

BY YURY PETYUSHIN

Part I. The Epic Flight of Dumbo and the Search for Meaning

"Dumbo! Dumbo! Where do you think you're flying so fast, you skinny rat?!"

A group of 9-year old kids shout at a young boy their age, who's dashing past them as fast as he can, pretending not to hear… He is clenching a grocery bag in his bony fist. His heart pounding. His palms sweaty. His skin feels the cold of coins hidden in his sock.

"Run, Dumbo, run!" – The kids hurl threats at his back. The boy switches to fourth gear and disappears behind an ugly-grey 16-story apartment building…

The year is 1993, and the boy is me. I am in the poorest neighborhood of the most criminal-ridden and polluted city in Russia.

My childhood memories are made up of dull high-rises, a railway station across the road, factory smokestacks that towered over my school's soccer field, and the news that yet another two dozen thugs were machine-gunned by a rival gang in a territory dispute. Also, you probably noticed that I am not very popular with the other kids in my neighborhood. In a word, I AM NOT A HAPPY BOY.

Fast forward to 2013. I'm a COO and partner of Allcorrect.com, one of the Top-20 translation agencies in Eastern Europe. I'm married to a smart and beautiful woman. Our household income is in the top 2% in Canada, and the bulk of it is passive. We just bought our first triplex in midtown Toronto, just 7 months after immigrating to Canada. We are financially free, young and healthy, with 24 hours a day to spend however we choose. Quite an ascent for little Dumbo, eh?

…There's only one problem: for some reason, I'M STILL NOT A HAPPY BOY!

I've experienced something that many people never will. I effectively retired at the age of 29. Most people invest most of their lives to achieving "success" to then become happy. My experience showed me that becoming financially free poses an even greater and more complicated question. "WHAT NEXT?!"

I do not intend to impart to you the secrets of life's meaning, nor do I claim that I have found them. I have, however, learned that my own anxiety and existential crisis is soothed dramatically whenever I do something that is bigger than myself; for true wealth is not just money, but meaning.

My intention in this chapter is to encourage you to generate wealth AND meaning by investing in "green" sustainable homes.

Part II. The Grand Myth of "Green" Sustainable Homes

When people think of green homes, they tend to imagine a sleek, modern dwelling, with floor-to-ceiling windows, solar panels on the roof, and a wind turbine in the backyard.

This popular notion is as widespread as it is false. A true sustainable building does not have a "smart" high-tech toilet that can be flushed remotely from your smartphone. Instead, it relies on smart design, the laws of nature, and sound building principles developed by our ancestors hundreds of years ago. There is, in fact, a reason that traditional dwellings in different cultures have different shapes - you're forced to be smart about building when you don't have cheap energy to rely on.

When I first arrived in Canada, I was surprised to find that this cold country chose to build homes with thin, flimsy walls and then equip them with oversized furnaces to compensate for it.

I then studied multiple green building standards and soon realized that the best way to generate energy is to not waste it. I found Passivhaus (Passive House), a building standard that cuts energy demand by up to 90% and is a great real estate investment.

Passive House was developed in Germany nearly 30 years ago, where it's been used so successfully that some European governments accept it as the standard for all new buildings.

Below are the differences between a conventionally-built Canadian home and a green sustainable home based on Passive House principles:

Attribute/ Feature	Standard House	Green Sustainable Home (Passive House)
Shape and size	Built without much consideration for energy efficiency. Large square footage per person, even though some rooms are rarely used. Shape reflects whatever became the "standard" look in that particular locale.	Simple compact shape. Layout is designed with actual USE in mind. No space is wasted, allowing higher density in the same square footage (greater ROI for investors).
Insulation	Follows minimum building code requirements. Poorly insulated foundation is a norm. Insulation layer is often penetrated by mechanical systems, creating gaps and "thermal bridges."	Continuous layer of super-insulation wraps around the house, including foundation and roof. This, along with a continuous air barrier, leads to 1,200% improvement in air-tightness.

Attribute/ Feature	Standard House	Green Sustainable Home (Passive House)
House orientation and windows	Little or no thought put into house orientation. Large and floor-to-ceiling windows often used on all sides of the house to create a trendy, "sleek" look (most of which are almost always draped to hide from undesired gazes and scorching sun – duh!).	House positioned to optimize solar heat gain and natural lighting. Bigger triple-pane windows on the south side with limited glazing on the north. Wide overhangs and external shading devices strategically block the high summer sun. Trees can also be used to provide summer shade and let the sun in during the winter.
Energy efficiency and heat recovery	Energy is wasted. Furnace, dryer, and water heater (usually oversized) are constantly pumping warmth and dollars out through their exhaust systems.	A low-voltage Heat Recovery Ventilation (HRV) system extracts heat from stale air before exhausting it and warms incoming air with it.
Indoor comfort	Overheats in the summer, with many cold areas in the winter. Noisy furnace and air conditioner work tirelessly to combat the design flaws above. Low airtightness means that you hear cars driving by, your neighbor's annoying dog, loud kids, and the late-night party three doors down.	House stays at the prescribed comfortable temperature throughout the year. No drafts or cold floors with plenty of fresh air. Heat and moisture from kitchen and bathrooms are spread throughout the house, making all rooms pleasant to be in. Always serenely silent.

"It's certainly the most comfortable house we've ever lived in!
Very quiet and humidity levels stay very constant,
so even in the winter you don't get dry air.
There are also no cold or drafty spots in the house."
—*Hart Jansson, owner of a Passive House in Oakville, Ontario.*

Thus, Passive House design eliminates the need for a traditional furnace and air conditioner, which **cuts your heating and cooling costs by up to 90%**. Most of the heat is generated by the sun, house appliances, and the warmth of your own body. You heard that right: you are what keeps your furnace-less house warm on those Canadian winter nights.

Part III. The Four Benefits of Investing in Sustainable Homes

A Passive House (PH) must be very expensive, then? No. In fact, it costs only 3-10% more to build a PH in North America, which means it pays off on many levels, providing a double-digit ROI and positive cashflow from day one.

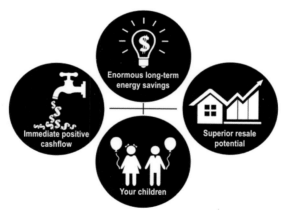

Let us examine the four main benefits and supporting numbers.

Benefit #1: Immediate Positive Cash Flow

With construction costs around $225/sf, the average cost premium of 6.5% to build to PH standard would amount to $24,863. Since you save around $15,000 on the cost of purchasing and installing standard heating and cooling equipment, the additional capital needed is only

$9,863. With current loan rates, this would cost an additional $49/month, including interest.

Cost to build a 1,700 sf house	$382,500
Cost premium to build green	6.5%
Additional cost to build green	$24,863
Savings on mechanical equipment	($15,000)
Net additional capital needed	$9,863
Current borrowing rate	3.5%
Additional cost to build green in $/month	**$49**

You're probably surprised by the low additional cost. However, creating a good building envelope does not require expensive technology or equipment – just knowledge, skills, and quality materials. Now, let's look at the savings:

Average monthly energy bill in Ontario:	$225
Cost of the heating and cooling portion	
(~75% of total energy costs or $225*75%)	$169
Energy savings in a PH	
(~90% of heating and cooling or $169*90%)	**$152**

With an average utility bill of $225/month, a typical single-family home in Ontario would save you $152 monthly, or $1,823 per year, lowering the bill to only $73/month.

> *"My 3,400 sq. ft. house consumes so little energy that the*
> *solar panels on my roof generate 1.5 times*
> *the amount of energy we use."*
> *—Lyndon Than, Certified Passivhaus designer and one of*
> *the first people to build a passive house in Toronto.*

Subtracting the additional monthly building cost ($49) from the monthly energy savings ($152), we get the cash flow of $103/month or $1,235 annually. Thus, the additional investment of $9,863 constitutes 13% ROI and pays off in eight years.

Bear in mind that if the money is borrowed, none of your own capital is tied up! There really is no "pay-off" period to wait for! You start making profit immediately, which means the ROI is not 13%, but infinite. You're free to start another project. It's like getting <u>immediate</u> positive cash flow. *For free*.

Benefit #2: Enormous Long-Term Energy Savings

While the calculation above is based on solid numbers, it does not account for future changes in energy costs. This is significant when you consider that the cost of electricity in Ontario increased by 108% between 2006 and 2016, which amounts to an 11% increase per year. [1]

Let's look at a couple of scenarios[2]. A very conservative energy cost increase of 3% per year amounts to total energy savings of almost $63,000 over the period of 25 years. This amount is 7 times greater than the initial investment into insulation and windows.

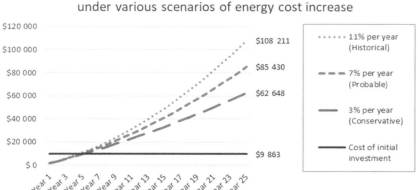

A more likely scenario of 7% annual increase would provide savings of $85,000, while the historical 11% would save more than $100,000.

---

1 http://globalnews.ca/news/3263787/how-much-have-hydro-bills-in-ontario-really-gone-up/
2 This diagram does not reflect that the government dropped electricity prices in 2017 and promised to artificially keep the rate increase below inflation for 4 years, because these costs are just pushed back to 2022. After this the government predicts rates to rise by 61% in 7 years.

It's worth noting that this forecast is based on historical data and does NOT factor in that worldwide energy demand that is expected to grow exponentially along with population and urbanization, as we've likely reached the peak of oil production capabilities. This demand-supply relationship will drive the cost of energy up and can lead to <u>dramatic price surges of unpredictable magnitude due to scarcity</u>. One thing is certain: PH provides enormous long-term energy savings.

> *"It is hard to predict how much the energy price will increase, but low-energy housing is certainly the answer to everything. Not just in terms of energy efficiency and security, but also thermal comfort and usability."*
> —*Senior Research Manager at Natural Resources Canada*

Benefit #3: Superior Resale Potential

A green home is insured against energy cost increases. Its superior envelope and simpler mechanical systems last longer and require cheaper maintenance; therefore, it appreciates better and provides greater value at resale.

> *"The concepts behind Passive House are not new. But coupled with solar panels, Passive House has opened the possibility of achieving net zero energy at cost parity with code-built housing. This appeal of being "off-grid" goes beyond just savings, it taps into a core human value — freedom. Independence from the fossil fuel industry and utilities is universally attractive regardless of political views or social class.*
> *— Rob Blakeney, owner at Local Impact Design, partner at SustainableDevelopment.Club*

Homebuyers don't just <u>claim</u> that they're willing to pay more for sustainability. Multiple data-based studies show that homes with green features sell 22% faster[3] and for a price premium of 2-9%[4]. With an average price of a detached home in Toronto at $1,283,981 (as of January 2018), this gives a significant profit boost.

---

3 http://content.usatoday.com/communities/greenhouse/post/2010/02/green-homes-sell-for-more-and-faster-than-rest-of-the-market/1#.WoqSgajibIW

4 https://southern-energy.com/high-performance-homes-price-premium/

Once MLS starts publishing energy ratings for all listings (potentially as early as 2019[5]), conventionally-built homes will look very undesirable, which will drive the resale potential of green homes even higher.

Benefit #4: Your Children

If you're under the impression that we'll be able to live the way we do now 10 or 20 years from now, you need to wake up. The U.S. Department of Defense listed climate change as the main threat to homeland security in their 2016 report. Global warming and depletion of natural resources will inevitably lead to unpredictable weather patterns, droughts, floods, and severe storms. This will cause low crop yields, lack of clean drinking water, environmental refugees, hunger, and violence.

Hart Jansson's Passive House in Oakville. Designed by Ed Marion and Hart Jansson. Photo by Yury Petyushin.

Buildings contribute to a third of greenhouse gas emissions worldwide, so we must revolutionize the way we build right now. Most of us are blessed to have never faced war and hunger. I wish my son and grandchildren will never see it either, but I suspect that even I may.

Our children are priceless, so there's your infinite ROI.

---

5 https://www.canadiancontractor.ca/canadian-contractor/heard-herd-will-change-way-build-renovate-houses/1003282416/

Part IV. Passive House in North America

If building green homes is such a great idea and investment, why don't we have more of them?! To find that out, I met and interviewed dozens of green building experts in Canada and the U.S., only to discover that there are <u>no valid reasons</u> other than general unawareness, inertia, and deep-rooted misconceptions about the cost of building sustainable homes.

During months of my research, I also discovered multiple documented cases where <u>passive houses are built at a 0% premium</u>. Using Lean Manufacturing[6] tools, prefabrication, and experience, Adam Cohen has built dozens of PH buildings at or below market cost. Adam explains, "The key to delivering an energy-efficient building on par with conventional build is a combination of creativity, building physics, and budget optimization."

During my quest, I formed relationships with several PH professionals who experience a steady demand for their services but often run into resource constraints. Limited operating capital prevents them from running more projects simultaneously and inhibits growth.

In order to bridge these gaps, SustainableDevelopment.Club was formed. Its goal is to bring together top green building experts and real estate investors to fund, design, and build energy-efficient, higher-density homes.

There are many ways to capitalize on this technology. If you would like to invest in a future-proof asset with superior ROI or just learn more, you can contact us at <u>Good@SustainableDevelopment.Club</u>.

If you would like to build a Passive House yourself, you can download our free step-by-step guide, which includes tips on choosing the best-suited lot, gathering a competent team, and avoiding the main pitfalls when building a passive house. Go to: <u>www.SustainableDevelopment.Club/Guide</u>.

---

6 "Lean Manufacturing" is a methodology for reducing costs and lead times and improving quality through observation, elimination of waste, and scientific problem solving.

Conclusion

My goals in this book were to show you an unconventional way to generate real estate wealth by investing in green homes and to debunk some myths surrounding the topic. Now you know that investing in sustainability is not a sacrifice, but a holistic decision that generates immediate positive cashflow and enormous long-term profit.

It also creates abundance on many levels other than mere personal wealth accumulation. For, if you're still pursuing strictly financial success, you are yet to face the "what next?" question that I started my story with.

If our values are aligned, I'd like to hear from you. In the end, the only thing necessary for the triumph of evil is that good men do nothing. And generating wealth by doing good is one thing that makes me a VERY HAPPY BOY.

YURY PETYUSHIN

Yury Petyushin is a serial entrepreneur, investor, process improvement professional, and Passive House consultant.

As a certified Lean Manufacturing expert, Yury has helped companies reduce costs and increase profitability in manufacturing, extractive industries, healthcare, legal and environmental services. In 2009, Yury joined Allcorrect. com, a small firm in Samara, Russia, which was then listed as one of the Top-20 Largest Translation Companies in Eastern Europe just three years later.

Yury had also made money as a firefighter, salesman, janitor, freelance translator, kitchen chef, project manager, working in Siberian coal mines, as well as diverting tons of office furniture from landfills and donating it to nonprofits.

In 2013, Yury pledged to only work on triple-bottom-line and socially responsible businesses. SustainableDevelopment.Club, his latest business project, aims to combat climate change through funding and building beautiful, highly-livable, and energy-efficient homes that represent a solid investment with superior ROI.

You can reach Yury at www.sustainabledevelopment.club, good@ sustainabledevelopment.club, or https://www.linkedin.com/in/ petyushin/

CHAPTER 4

How to Attract Wealth and Abundance Regardless of Any Situation in Life

BY CORA CRISTOBAL

"The journey to financial freedom starts the minute you decide you were destined for prosperity, not scarcity; for abundance, not lack.

Isn't there a part of you that has always known that? Can you see yourself living a bounteous life … a life of more than enough? It only takes one minute to decide. Decide now."
—*Mark Victor Hansen*

You might like to know that abundance is available for everyone. There is an unlimited and endless supply of resources and money for everybody.

Abundance within us and all around us is the secret of the Law of Attraction.

People pray or ask others for what they want when they're desperate. Or, they plead while believing (or fearing) that they have no chance. We tend to focus mostly on what we don't have, ignoring what we have.

The Trap of Poverty

This is a poverty trap that far too many people put themselves in, and it's because they simply don't understand the infinity of the Universe. We always attract what we focus on.

If you think you're focused on making money but you don't have it, ask yourself this: do you spend some of your waking moments noticing what you need, what you don't have, and what you wish you had? That's not focusing on abundance. And, if you don't believe it's possible to prosper, chances are you won't.

When you joke around with friends about how poor you are, it counts. What you think, what you say, what you write, and what you do are all manifested; in turn, your manifestations have momentum. They attract more of the same from the Universe, which doesn't know how to filter. In other words, if you say to yourself, "I'm so poor," the Universe doesn't say, "Oh, you're poor and unhappy, so I'll send more abundance."

The Universe just repeats back to you, "You're poor, you're poor." And, you'll look around and notice your lack. You get angry or hopeless, which doesn't attract investors, positive people, or millionaire mentors.

So, be very careful with your thoughts if you want good manifestations.

Important: You can shape your destiny, but you cannot control it.

Over the years, I've worked very hard chasing seemingly elusive wealth and abundance. Just like most of us, I've bet on lotteries to get rich quick, never work again, and enjoy the life of my dreams.

It took me a long time and some serious life challenges to discover that I can attract wealth and abundance.

It doesn't matter what circumstance or situation you're in now.

Too old? Too young? No money? No education? No experience? No spouse? No friends? No nothing? You can give all these alibis and excuses, but if you are really serious about becoming wealthy, you must find the key.

I've done many real estate deals and I wrote books sharing how I did it. But may I share my own personal experience about learning to attract wealth and abundance with thought? It wasn't easy to believe at first, but it definitely works if you follow these seven success principles.

1. **Discover Your Passion, Life Purpose, and Personal Purpose.**

   Passion is something you really have a strong fondness of and enthusiasm for. It's intensely positive.

   It's something you love doing because you believe in it, it resonates with you, and you feel like you were born to do it.

   When you have passion, you ignite energy that translates into enthusiasm and leads to laser-sharp focus.

   "If you love what you do,
   you'll never have to work a day in your life."
   —Confucius

   If you want to attract riches more easily, find two things: your life purpose and your personal purpose.

   a. <u>Life purpose</u> is the way you add value to people and planet Earth for this and future generations. How do you learn and grow? What do you enjoy on your journey? Everything in nature has a purpose. What's yours?

      What and how do you contribute in this lifetime? How many lives can you change today? Who can you help today?

   b. <u>Personal purpose</u> is your own mission. What do you want for your family? Which of your friends would you like to help the most? What leisure activities do you love the most? Do you enjoy a loud party, or quietly fishing in a secluded area?

   Purpose gives meaning to life. It gives us fulfillment, not just success. If you're aligned with your purpose, you have a reason to live. Fulfillment, worthiness, and motivation are yours.

   You can state your purpose in the form of a mission statement. For example, my Toronto Women's Club mission statement is, "To educate, inspire, and empower women and the men behind the women."

You can state your vision. What do you see ahead as you embody your purpose? Connect with your spirit for guidance.

My vision statement for the Toronto Women's Club is, "To be the preferred women's club in the greater Toronto area and the world, specializing in quality education, training, coaching and mentoring, branding, and wealth creation."

You have natural talents and God-given gifts. Don't be afraid to use them. In fact, stop blocking and denying them. You have them for a reason.

When you blend your passion, purpose, and profit, you create a blessing for everyone you help, not just yourself. Your life has a direction, and you attract wealth and abundance.

2. Learn New Skills and Never Stop Learning

Knowledge is power. Education is the key to attracting wealth and abundance. Life is continuous learning. Claiming you already know everything is a dead end.

> *"Once you stop learning, you start dying."*
> *—Albert Einstein*

You must commit to continuous learning and acquire new skills to be ahead of the competition. Pay any price, work hard, and make every sacrifice. Do it joyfully, because that's living your passion. Find and create your own niche and make a difference. Learn new skills like Internet marketing, email campaigning, speaking, writing, photography – whatever your heart desires or whatever will help you grow and improve your income.

When you know more, you make more money. People want to do business with you. When that happens, it will build your self-confidence and self-esteem. It will inspire you to accomplish more. Can you see that success builds on success, not on begging, praying, and pleading?

As you apply what you've learned, commit to excellence. People will come to you and throw money at you, without you even asking.

Give lots of value and deliver more, much more, than what is asked of you. The Law of Attraction automatically works because good deeds only attract good results!

I challenge you right now to:

- Write what new skills you need to acquire.
- Figure out where and how you can acquire them.
- Write down your natural gifts and talents.
- Figure out where you can build on them.

3. Hire A Good Mentor

Having a mentor is the safest, fastest, and easiest way to attain wealth, strategize your life or improve your results in business, real estate, health, fitness, relationships, and finance.

It's not only the elites who need mentors. Even a regular person, serious about bullet-proof success, should hire a mentor.

Yes, hiring a mentor costs money, but try ignorance and lack of experience. Good luck with that! Trial and error cost you more money and time in the long run.

You are your own best asset, so invest in yourself – get a mentor.

Make sure you hire a mentor who is highly successful and aligns with your dreams and goals. Pick a person you want to be like. I picked a mentor who is dynamic, energetic, consistently growing, and generous in sharing knowledge and wisdom.

Your mentor can influence you and open huge doors of opportunity for you.

I hired my mentor in December 2015. Within two years, I purchased five US properties; wrote three books (two award-winners and one Amazon bestseller); created the Toronto Women's Club; became a mentor, coach, and public speaker; and won the Woman of Inspiration 2017 award. And, I've shared stages with legends like Brian Tracy, Jack Canfield, and Robert G. Allen.

4. Build Credibility and Brand

Credibility is the heart of every business. If you want sustainable success, you must build, establish, and continually nourish your brand.

Let customers see that you deliver excellent quality. The more you give, the more you get. That's The Law of Attraction.

How do we produce credibility? Here are some basic ways:

- A great logo with a tag line
- Mission and Vision statements that exemplify your organization's values
- Verbal and written marketing

There are many other ways of building a brand and credibility, and here are my top three:

a. Association

We are known by the people we associate with. When I was younger, I always believed in the axiom, "Tell me who your friends are, and I will tell you who you are." That goes for income as well as other traits.

Choose the friends, partners, and relationships you admire.

"You are the average of the five people you spend the most time with."
—Jim Rohn

Here's another challenge for you: Write the names of the five people you spend the most time with outside of your family.

b. Appearance

How do you present yourself? Sloppy or elegant? Matching or mismatched? Polished or scuffed? Overweight or fit?

In test after test, the answers are always the same. The well-dressed, fit, smiling person always gets the vote, the nod, the hire, the contract, and the account.

c. Authority

To get extraordinary results, you must do extraordinary work. You can't be doing the same thing and expect different results.

For example, all 40,000 real estate agents give the same lines:

- "I give the best service," or,
- "I'm the best real estate consultant," or,
- "I'll sell your home in 30 days."

Get out of the sea of sameness and go to the island of differentiation!

For example, I help my members grow their credibility by helping them co-author a bestselling book by themselves or with legends. I also help my mentees become well respected public speakers.

I am amazed at the extraordinary results of my members and I got. The Law of Attraction seemed to be working. You give more, you get more. I immediately got more real estate deals, speaking engagements, interviews, new members in my Toronto Women's Club, and more students to mentor.

> *"What you think about, you bring about."*
> *— Bob Proctor*

5. Remove the messes in your life

Get rid of poisonous people and relationships.

I was once in a toxic marriage and had to file for divorce. It was tough. I also invested in business partners and lost a lot of money, time, and effort.

If that's what you're experiencing, you can get out. Learn from all your bad experiences and choose better in the future. Seek helpful, not hurting relationships, and be what you want to attract.

Physical messes also block the good energy! Welcome the Universe with clean, clear spaces, and it will bring you more wealth and riches. Clean up your home, office, car, and every surrounding you're in. Be organized in your personal life, business life, and work life.

6. Network, Collaborate and Cooperate.

Networking brings new clients, mentors, JV partners, suppliers, etc. You meet new people and make connections. You build new relationships. One connection snowballs to more connections, allowing you to have more success and happiness.

How do you network? Come to events that resonate with your goals, and not just the free ones. Investing in good events will likely take you to the next level.

At an event, look around. Is it good? How many people have you met, and how many leads have you generated? Call them or send them an email within one or two days. Connect to see how you can help them.

You can also become a member of a club with regular meetings. For example, I belong to the largest elite real estate club, known as the Private Investment Club (PIC), the 5 AM Club, and of course, my own club, the Toronto Women's Club.

> *"Your network is your net worth."*
> *—Tim Sanders*

7. Give, then Receive

I know you've heard this before. The more you give, the more you get. Give first before you get. This will make you feel really good and gives you a great source of happiness as well as a sure source of wealth.

During my coaching session with my mentee, she confessed that sometimes, giving feels like losing. How can I give when I don't have a lot?

I told her a story about a client who was moving back to her home country, the Philippines. So, I helped her sell her residential property. When she returned to Canada, I encouraged her to buy a house again. She didn't qualify, though, as she was just restarting life in Canada.

Without charging anything for my time, I found all the people who could help her get financed, rebuild her life, and get work. When she bought a house, I got a commission plus unexpected bonuses: a new venture with her mortgage broker, more clients, and much wider credibility as a person who helps people solve money problems.

I always start with, "How I can help you?" instead of, "What can I get from you?"

This is a key to success. Even if you're homeless, offer something to every person you see. "Can I pray for you?" or "May I give you words of encouragement?" This activates The Law of Attraction.

Those are the seven principles. We get the life we want by default, based on our thoughts. Thoughts affect our actions, decisions, and circumstances.

Unlock Your Future

It's time to start unlocking your success.

- Articulate your current life and situation.
- Do you love what you do now? What do you want to do?
- What are you doing differently to attract massive wealth and abundance?
- Who do you hang out with?
- What do you do to improve yourself?
- How are your personal and business relationships?
- What are your messes, and how can you clear them?
- What bad habits do you have, and how can you build new ones?
- What good habits do you want to amplify?
- Do you have a mentor to guide you in life or business?
- Do you want to accelerate your success?

Following these simple yet extremely powerful steps will help you attract your true calling, help you become wealthy, and be healthy.

And, I want to help you further by offering you two gifts: my award-winning book, *Journey to a New You: 12 Habits to a Happy and*

Successful Life, or a live, 1-on-1, private 45-minute mentoring session with me in person (or via phone/Skype).

Email me at cora@torontowomensclub.com or visit my site at www.TorontoWomensClub.com.

In the meantime, be happy, attract abundance into your life, and never give up on your dreams.

CORA CRISTOBAL

Cora Cristobal is the founder of the Toronto Women's Club, an award-winning and bestselling author, as well as a mentor, public speaker, and successful real estate investor/realtor. Her first book, *Journey to a New You: 12 Habits to a Happy and Successful Life,* was published in 2016.

Her whole life in the Philippines was hard work until she noticed some empty lots, bought them, and resold them for profit. She achieved a real estate license, moved to Canada, and successfully built a career.

When her husband deserted the family, she bounced back even stronger by finding a mentor, growing her business, and founding the Toronto Women's Club to share her knowledge.

Cora offers live events; education and training; mentoring; consulting; and investment collaborations for motivated individuals.

Get a free copy of Cora's book or a complimentary 45-minute mentoring session by visiting her website, www.TorontoWomensClub.com or emailing Cora at cora@torontowomensclub.com.

CHAPTER 5

Top Money-Making Strategies for Investing in Real Estate Without the Risk

BY BRIAN D'EON

It's well-known that real estate investing can be a very profitable way to make money. Passive income, big windfalls, cash-flow, generational wealth, retirement funding, rent-to-own, and no-money-down are some terms you've likely heard. Stories of mind-boggling profits and returns may seem irresistible–perhaps too good to be true.

So why isn't everybody doing it? The answer is fear of the unknown—the risk. You've heard the horror stories and decided that it's too risky. However, I've learned over the years that there **are** ways to invest in real estate virtually risk-free. Generally speaking, it's through proper education, training, practice, and making smart, well-informed, unemotional decisions.

I want to share my **Top Two Strategies** in this chapter. Your preferred strategy depends on whether you prefer to be:

1) An **active investor**, sourcing real estate deals on a regular basis.

2) A **passive investor**, with money to invest but not time to source and manage properties.

Thirteen years ago, I was reviewing my RRSP and investment statements, wondering why the previous ten years had produced almost no profit. I had sought professional help from multiple, highly recommended financial advisors. "Leave it to the experts," was the advice that I was always given. However, since I'd made so little money, I decided I had enough.

At that time, I knew real estate could be the solution and sought to learn as much as I could, so I attended seminars and read books like crazy. I read how "landlords make money in their sleep." But, after experiencing limited success on my own, I finally decided to hire a mentor. What followed would unexpectedly change the course of the rest of my life … in a good way, of course.

Together, we found a house in a decent, growing community that I could rent out for profit. I followed his plan to do "due diligence" and purchased my first cash-flow property. Within a few years, I used the equity to buy another house. I also learned how I could use my RRSP funds to invest in real estate, which allowed me to buy more houses!

While the cash-flow was nice, those houses needed to be managed and maintained—costs that eat away profits and can be aggravating.

For an active investor this may be no problem–and can make you a lot of money using just this strategy. With a few changes to this strategy, we can significantly reduce the risk and aggravation. Now let's explore my **Top Two Strategies**:

Top Strategy #1 - Active Investing

What if I said you could be an active real estate investor without the risk, and with little real estate knowledge or experience?

Active investors often seek joint venture partners (money partners) so they can do no-money-down deals. As an investor myself, the deal may look good on paper, but why would I trust them? Why would *they* trust *me*?

There is too much risk for both parties with so much unknown. What I might suggest instead is to *assign* the deal.

Assignments

Assignments are a fantastic way to make money, especially for the new investors. Rather than a joint venture and assuming risk, you can assign the deal.

This involves finding a property under market value and signing an Agreement of Purchase and Sale with a clause stating that it can be assigned. You then assign the contract to another buyer, still under market value. The assignee pays you an "assignment fee" for finding a great deal, which is your profit.

Example:

Current Market Value:	$560,000
Purchase Price:	$500,000
Closing Costs:	$10,000
Assignment Fee:	$20,000
Equity (value – costs):	$30,000
Purchase Price (for assignee):	$530,000

This is a "win-win" situation: there's value (equity) for the investor **and** you earn a nice assignment fee; you would profit $20,000, and the investor would get a house $30,000 under market value.

5 Steps to Assigning for Big Profit, Beginning Today

With a little effort, working only a few hours per day, you can be sourcing wholesale properties for assignment. Assignments can make up to $30,000 per deal, with the average being around $10,000. If you only did one deal per month, you could easily have a six-digit salary!

Realtors have the added bonus of already being "in the field" talking to prospective leads. Instead of offering only to list their property, what if you could offer to buy their property immediately, "as-is," at a reduced price?

Using the earlier example, you may offer to list their property for $560,000 or propose that you buy it now for $500,000 with a fast closing. There are multiple reasons why this might be an attractive offer to the seller, for example:

- Financial distress
- House is facing power of sale (foreclosure)
- House needs costly repairs
- House is generally "un-showable"
- Avoids agent commissions
- Property has liens
- Owner owes taxes in arrears
- Severed relationship, want quick sell
- Health issues
- Immediate need for relocation
- Loss of employment/income source
- Loss of household member

The reality is that unfortunate things happen, leaving people stuck and enduring additional financial stress. Be aware that some may view your position as taking advantage of the seller; however, I believe if you're able to assist them and create winning situations for all parties involved, then you are doing them a great service!

It is helpful to know their financial situation as well. Then you are in a much better position to assist them. What do they owe on their mortgage, and what other debts they are carrying? I usually help by paying off all their debts and giving them some extra money to relocate, rehabilitate, or just enjoy.

Here's one of the first deals I closed with my mentor:

> *A woman in her 60s was living out her last months as a cancer patient. She had no children, her husband already passed away, and her only surviving relative was her sister. She had a house on a beautiful lot on the Rideau Canal near Kingston, Ontario.*

Due to her health issues, she moved in with her sister in Ottawa over a year prior. Needing to sell her house, she listed it initially at market value, $725,000, but it did not sell and she was running out of time.

She contacted me explaining the need to sell. Her mortgage was $480,000, credit debts were around $10,000, and outstanding bills around $5,000. She was running out of money. Her biggest concern was that her sister, who was in her will, would inherit her debt and have to pay capital gains tax on her property. She also was paying $8,000 in funeral expenses.

I put a simple plan together to pay off her mortgage and debt, about $490,000. She nearly flew over the moon when I told her she would get $50,000 cash back after paying off everything. For me, I essentially got a $700,000 house for $540,000!

Within a few weeks (while still under a Purchase and Sale contract), I found a buyer who would take the house for $600,000, leaving me with a $60,000 profit!

Unfortunately, there was a big hiccup—the house had an oil furnace and during the inspection, they discovered the tank had been leaking. The Ministry of Environment got involved due to the house's proximity to water, and the estimated cleanup costs were $80,000. My total payout was now $620,000 ($540,000 purchase + $80,000 cleanup).

Fortunately, the buyer was still interested and agreed to pay $630,000; thus, I was still able to profit a $10,000 assignment fee. While not as much as I had originally thought, I estimated I spent 10 hours on this deal and had not even physically gone to see the property!

Ten years, and many deals later, I was able to quit my job and become a full-time real estate investor. Now I'm the one paying the assignment fees! The seminars, books, and mentorship really paid off!

You can start making money assigning properties following this five-step process:

1. Advertise to source below-market-value properties. Choose a neighbourhood. Place ads in classifieds and network with lead sources such as mortgage brokers, divorce lawyers and credit repair specialists. Spread the news that you are buying houses "as-is" with fast closings. You can go door-to-door, knocking or delivering pamphlets.

   Once, while sitting in a Toronto airport restaurant, a lady beside me revealed she lost her job and was moving back home to Nova Scotia. I indicated I could buy her house. The man on the other side overheard the conversation and said he was going through a divorce and needed to sell fast and part ways. Guess what? I bought both houses—well under market value!

2. Get the house under contract. This means signing an "Agreement of Purchase and Sale." Ensure that it includes an assignment clause.

3. Create a one-page prospectus. It should include the purchase price, market value, pictures, address (or neighbourhood), lot and house dimensions and details (beds, baths, living space, parking), comparables (list of similar houses recently sold in the neighbourhood), and rental rates if applicable.

4. Market to real estate investors – send out emails with your details; attend networking events (pro tip: Masterminds work best, if you're lucky enough to get invited to one).

5. Close the deal and provide exceptional value – see the deal through to its closing and offer to organize any and all services necessary, such as inspection, appraisal, lawyer, and preparing paperwork.

If you're serious about making money in real estate with *no money down* and *without the risk*, this is absolutely the best way forward. My mentoring students set a minimum for making $5,000 on their first deal, which they usually get within the first few months.

Top Strategy #2: Passive Investing

If you have money, but no time or desire to actively pursue sourcing deals, opportunities exist for passive income. Typically, this involves joint-venturing and splitting the income from a cash-flowing property. They provide the deal, you provide the funding.

This can be a fantastic way to invest, since annual ROI is typically 10-15%. Your profit split would be 5-7.5%, and you split the risk. The deal originator usually manages the property as well. However, there is still risk—the property could drop value, need substantial repair (such as new roof or leaky foundation), become vacant, or be vandalised.

I'm going to let you in on a secret I learned from wealthy investors: there is a way to make the same money without the risk. The cash still flows in regardless of whether the property is rented or vacant.

Investors with their own cash often seek additional sources of funds to finance their deals. You can loan them money in the form of a basic loan or even a mortgage. This is attractive for investors, who will pay higher interest rates because these loans aren't registered with the Bureau and therefore don't affect their credit scores or debt service ratios.

Are you holding investments that are not producing at least 5%?

Do you own a house with more than 20% equity? That equity can be working for you; if it's just sitting there, it's certainly not doing you any good.

- Move your equity into real estate or mortgages (even RRSPs). You can access the equity in your house to invest or loan as you see fit!
  - *You can even pay down your mortgage faster, if it suits you, by lending out your equity and applying the monthly cash-flow towards your mortgage!*

- You can use your equity to lend to a full-time investor. As an investor, I regularly borrow money to fund my deals:

For a five-year loan, I typically pay around 5-7% interest for five years before paying back the principal. This means that for every $100,000 you loan me out of your equity, you could make nearly $35,000 over five years.

Example:

Current Mortgage	$300,000	
Current Mortgage Payment:	$1,264	monthly (3% for 30 years)
Mortgage Refinanced to Access Equity:	$400,000	
Refinanced Mortgage Payment:	$1,686	monthly (3% for 30 years)
Increase in Mortgage Payment:	$422	
Cash-Flow from Loan:	$583	monthly
Profit from Lending Your Equity:	$161	monthly

(This does not include paying down your principal, which increases equity!)

At the end of the contract term, the loan can be paid back in full or refinanced for another term. In my experience, lenders are usually happy to refinance and continue to collect their monthly payments!

Ready to get your money working for you?

If you're still thinking about risk, these loans or mortgages are backed by legally binding contracts, like any standard loan. In the event of default, the lender can exercise rights as specified in the contract and ultimately recall the entire loan.

Five Steps to Start Lending Today:

1. Talk to your mortgage broker or lender to determine how much equity you have to work with, then refinance as needed.

2. If you already have funds or access to a large sum of low-interest credit (i.e. HELOC), make sure your money is accessible. DO NOT sell your RRSP or you will have to pay significant tax on it. You will, however, need to move it to a self-directed account, or transfer to an institution that can properly direct your funds.

3. Advertise your private loan to investors. Real estate events or Masterminds are a great way to do this. Use email distribution or classifieds.

4. Have a professional loan contract ready to sign and be prepared to transfer the funds to the borrower. For the monthly payments to the lender, I usually prefer to give postdated cheques for the duration of the loan (thus, 60 cheques for a five-year loan).

5. Sign the contract, collect the cheques, and transfer the money (wire or draft).

Profit … it's as easy as that!

Try My Top Two Strategies

As a seasoned real estate investor, I see investors falling into two categories, sometimes floating between them and sometimes even both at the same time. They are "Active," with or without investment money, or "Passive" with investment money. I have provided my top strategies and secrets for both.

I sincerely wish you the best in your real estate endeavours, and all the success, freedom, and happiness you deserve! Please feel free to contact me if you are serious about moving forward in your business and believe that I can help you achieve your goals.

To inquire about mentorship, or for investment opportunities, email info@canadianwealthmasters.com, or visit www.canadianwealthmasters.com.

To your success!

BRIAN D'EON

Brian d'Eon, "The Professional Real Estate Investor," was a successful independent management consultant for over 15 years. After starting a family, he was no longer willing to dedicate all his time to his job and started transitioning his career to real estate investing. Within two years, investing part-time, he successfully purchased 12 properties. The passive income from those investments gave him huge flexibility and much-needed life changes! By 2015, he left his full-time job to focus on family and real estate investing.

Although he agrees that the money is nice, investing successfully is mainly about quality of life and peace of mind.

Brian's Skills and Offerings in REI:

- Coaching and mentoring by phone, web conference or in person (for GTA).
- Mortgage brokering, refinancing through www.reimortgages.ca. Agent: M15001086, Broker: 12597)
- Creative funding for real estate deals, as low as 5% down.
- Long-term business planning for acquiring virtually unlimited mortgaged properties.
- Buying below-market properties and cash-flowing properties.
- Assisting professionals with transitioning into real estate investing.
- Providing solid, monthly ROI for your investment money or home equity.

To inquire about mentorship, or for investment opportunities, email info@canadianwealthmasters.com, or visit www.canadianwealthmasters.com.

CHAPTER 6

The Beginner's Guide to Part-Time Real Estate Investing

BY MICHAEL FIELDER

I'm just a regular guy looking for a bright future like everyone else, and that's why I started on the path to making six figures in real estate part-time.

Everyone gets started not knowing what to do. I'd like to encourage you – I'm proof that it can be done part-time. You see, people don't typically start by investing full-time. They start slowly, testing the waters. But what they do and the guidance they receive can make all the difference.

I focus on my target, go after my goal tenaciously, and look for solutions and answers regardless of the obstacle. When I don't know how to do something, I seek answers and even hire a mentor. I make a commitment to stay the course, adjust where needed, regardless of how long it takes.

The only reason people fail is because they quit. They need commitment and tenacity. The only difference is that I keep going despite obstacles.

Let me tell you how I got started.

Dreams and Motivation

There was a time when I had no idea how to earn a dime in real estate. I wasted lots of time and money trying to find out how to get ahead.

When I was a teenager, I used to love playing Monopoly with my family late into the night. If you've ever played, you know that the big payoff comes from owning hotels and other properties. When someone succeeded in cornering the market, it was impressive!

All my life, I wanted to own real properties: big houses, little houses, tall buildings, downtown storefronts, and sprawling businesses outside the city. I wanted homes with pools, and even imagined a ranch with horses. I loved them all. I even fantasized owning a few big, beautiful homes for myself along the way.

But, in the beginning, nobody I knew could show me how to invest in real estate. Nobody knew the secret that anybody who is willing to learn a few new things can discover how to become a successful real estate investor.

Late at night, I would often watch infomercials about real estate. The pictures of houses, expensive cars, and fast airplanes made me dream of the better life I had always wanted for my family. All those people on TV were living my dream.

Couldn't I do that, too?

The Learning Curve

One late night, it was raining hard outside and everyone else was asleep. I picked up the phone and ordered a single, complete, all-the-knowledge-I'd-ever-needed course that was GUARANTEED to teach me how to buy my first house as a real estate investor! Woo hoo! My success was assured.

I waited all week for that package to arrive. I knew just how much my life would change as soon as I discovered those hidden truths buried in the infomercial box of financial freedom.

Maybe you made a call just like that? And we're practical, right? We didn't really care about owning a jet.

When the box arrived, it was time to pass "Go" and get started!

Then came the reality. All the charts and slick pictures appeared to be exactly what was needed – until you read the manual.

What happened to the promise of running my business on auto-pilot, resting on the white sandy beaches of Hawaii? There were more questions than answers.

And I had no money to buy a house or hire a coach.

The Truth

Investing in real estate can be a rewarding, life-changing business for many people. Most people just don't know how or where to begin.

The big question is, *"How can I invest when I have no money?"*

The answer is, *"You don't need any money to get started in real estate."*

Sometimes it's easier to have a little money to put down, but you can learn how to invest with no money down. I've structured many successful deals that not only didn't cost me a penny, but put money in my pocket when the papers were signed.

You can learn that.

With our short time here, I can only focus on a few tried-and-true strategies, so I will focus on single-family homes, but I'll be sure to show you how to get more information when you're done reading.

Why Real Estate?

You must decide why you want to invest in real estate.

Real estate offers something tangible that you see. And, you choose who rents or buys your properties. Some of my tenants are almost like family. Very often, a family needs to rent, so I teach them how to improve their credit and help them purchase a home eventually.

I have many tenants who've lived in the same home for 6-7 years. Their children attended neighborhood schools and eventually left for college and/or got a place of their own. I've helped them purchase new starter homes and get financing. Those have been some of my most rewarding moments, which is why there's much more to real estate investing than just money and houses.

Types of Properties

Decide what kind of real estate to focus on.

- Single Family Homes (and Condos, Duplexes, Triplexes, up to Fourplexes); or
- Commercial Property (hotels, apartments, land, industrial buildings, offices, warehouses, and retail buildings)

I recommend starting with single-family homes because you already understand them, they're the most common, and there's always a market. They offer more flexibility, lower operating costs, and greater ease to buying and selling.

Increasingly, renters are paying for more repairs and improvements at their expense. I had one tenant who spent $10,000+ on improvements before moving.

How Do You Find Money If You Have None?

Each transaction requires cash, but not yours. The infomercial box failed because the best deals and cash are acquired via real estate investment clubs, networking and building valuable relationships. There are so many people who have money but do not have the time to find, evaluate and negotiate a great deal.

Here are some of the ways to find money:

- Safely use your IRA.
- Private investment money.
- HELOC (home equity line of credit).
- Your paid-off car as collateral.
- Credit cards to cover the down payment and rehab costs at 0% interest rates for 12-18 months. (Be disciplined, know your time limits and terms.)
- Bank loans.
- Joint Ventures (JV) or Funding partners.

How to build wealth right now?

You can't be a jack-of-all-trades in the beginning. Start by asking which type of return you want.

1. Quick cash? Then you should look at wholesaling.
2. A large, one-time lump sum? Then fix and flip.
3. Ongoing streams of income? Then look at rentals, owner financing, or passive investing.

You can do any of them part-time, like I do, but pick only one for now.

Imagine you bought a house for $40,000 that would be worth $100,000 when it's fixed up, and repairs are an estimated $20,000. What would you do to monetize that investment?

That depends on whether you want quick cash, a large, lump sum, or ongoing cash flow.

I'll give you a clear picture of how each method would work on a single-family home.

1. Quick Cash: Wholesaling

Here, you acquire a property at a deep discount and sell it to another buyer for a profit.

Often, you just sign a contract to buy a property from an owner needing and unable to sell. You then sell the contract to someone else at a higher price. You never actually own the property and don't need credit.

Wholesaling has a great return on investment (ROI) since most, if not all, of your investment is time, not cash.

I have bought and sold properties I've never seen in cities I've never visited. You can live in one city and do deals in another city, so you can do this anywhere.

Example:

You sign a contract agreeing to buy a house for $40,000. You then market the property and sell the contract to another investor for $50,000. You make a quick $10,000 profit. Repeat.

2. A Large, One-Time Lump Sum: Fixing and Flipping

In this method, you purchase a house that needs a lot of repair. Then, you renovate the property until it's like new and sell it for a nice profit.

There are a lot of details and hidden costs to do this, so I recommend you get the help of a mentor.

Example:

You pick a neighborhood, do your homework, and know home values. You find a run-down, but sound, home, let's say for $40,000. You work with your team to learn what you'll have to spend to raise the After-Repair Value (ARV) to full price.

You use a "hard money" loan to buy, meaning a high-interest, short-term loan from a private investor or company.

The loan of $70,000 covers 100% of the home price, $20,000 for repairs, and a reserve fund of $10,000 to cover loan payments until you sell the house.

After repairs, you sell the home for $100,000, as predicted. You'll pay 15% in selling expenses, leaving you with $85,000 plus $10,000 in reserves.

Use $70,000 to pay off the mortgage, and you've made a cool $25,000 on one house.

That's $15,000 more than you would get in our wholesaling example, but you've put a lot of time into it.

3. Generating Cash flow: Rentals, Owner Financing, or Passive Investing

    a. **Rentals** – Here, you purchase a property and rent it out for a monthly income. In my opinion, this is where true wealth is created, because your tenants are paying for your mortgage, you get to depreciate the home on your taxes, deduct interest on your mortgage, and enjoy appreciation on property values. (Consult your accountant, of course.)

Example:

In this scenario, you'd meet with two lenders beforehand, a banker and a hard money lender.

Initially, you'd get the same hard money loan for $70,000 described above and fix that $40,000 house. You'd then refinance for a better interest rate to pay off the hard money loan.

You can refinance $70,000 for 30 years at 4.5%. The monthly payment would be $354.68 plus estimated taxes and insurance of $325, so your total monthly mortgage expense would be $679.68. Typically, you have other expenses such as maintenance for $100 per month, and you may want to reserve 5% (or $50) for vacancies.

You should be able to rent the home for $1,000 per month, which means you now have a monthly cash flow of about $170.32 per month.

But you're getting much more.

i.   That $70,000 loan principal amount is reduced by $92 per month by the tenant. Essentially, your net worth increases by $170.32 + $92 = $262.32 each month.

ii. Also, you still have $10,000 reserve from an original hard money loan that you obtained.

iii. Rents typically increase by 3% a year, so your mortgage decreases faster as time goes on.

iv. You'll also enjoy depreciation, the only way to claim a deduction without spending money (check with your CPA about that).

v.   The property appreciates. Properties I bought 9-10 years ago have doubled in value.

The benefits of owning rental property are tremendous.

b. Owner Financing - You sell a property to a buyer, and the buyer makes mortgage payments to you instead of financing through a bank. The buyer is the homeowner and responsible for all maintenance. Use a third-party financing company to manage your note and simply enjoy the cash flow. Qualify the buyer, but you get the home back if he fails to pay.

Example:

When you owner-finance a property, you can sell as-is or fix it up. In this example, we're going to fix it.

As before, we have a mortgage on the house and our principal and interest (P&I) are $354.68. However, the buyer pays his own taxes and insurance.

Typically, an owner-finance strategy justifies raising the sales price to 10% above the ARV. In this case, we won't.

You've purchased the home for $40,000, spent $20,000 on repairs, and sold it for $100,000 with 15% down ($15,000). The buyer will mortgage $85,000 from you for 30 years at a 10% negotiated interest rate. The buyer's P&I (monthly payment) is $745.94.

So, you get $745.94 per month, and you pay $354.68 to your lender = a cash flow of $391.26 monthly.

You have no vacancies or maintenance expenses for 30 years. You don't have to manage the property or pay taxes and insurance.

I've bought and sold homes while on vacation. I love the cash flow that rental and owner-finance properties generate. It can create the same upfront cash as wholesaling and still generate streams of income for years.

I prefer cash flow over lump sums. Having cash flow gives you total freedom. I've surpassed a six-figure income part-time through real estate. I know you can, too.

c. **Passive Investing** – Here, you borrow or use your own cash to lend out for profit.

Example:

If you have $100,000 in savings, and you're only getting a return of 1%, that's $1,000 annually or $83.33 per month. However, if you let an investor with collateral borrow your money, you can get an average fixed return of 6-10%.

Let's say your return is 7%. Your annual cash flow is $7,000, or $583.33 per month. That's much better! If you could get 10%, then your monthly cash flow would be $833.33 per month, or a whopping $10,000 per year.

If you only lend 60-70% of the ARV, which is common, your money is secured in full by the property. If you lent $70,000 on a home worth $100,000, and weren't paid, you could get a house worth $100,000 and easily sell it for a huge profit (instant equity).

As you can clearly see, no matter what method works for you, great returns await you.

There are Seven Steps to Single Family Investing:

1. Find the deal
2. Find the money
3. Find the tenant/buyer before closing
4. Finalize the deal
5. Fix and Repair
6. Manage/Maintain
7. Rinse and Repeat

Some people define success as wealth, good health, happy family, freedom, contribution, and spirituality, and all these factors are part of the pie. Having an ample passive income gives you the time to enjoy whatever success means to you.

Where to Go from Here?

As I said in the beginning, I'm just a regular guy. I'm like anyone else without any extraordinary privilege or ability that you wouldn't have. If I can do it, so can you. In fact, I get people asking me for coaching because I'm easy-going and like to help people.

I do, however, have an awesome, super-simple system for cutting my vacancies, maintenance, and tenant-related fees and headaches by about 90%. It's so easy that it would blow your mind if you saw it, and you can get it as a gift right here: www.PartTimeInvesting.com/freegift.

I'm living proof that any reasonable person can succeed, even part-time. I hope you'll reach out via my website: www.PartTimeInvesting.com.

My best to you and your family.

MICHAEL FIELDER

Michael Fielder has been in the IT industry for nearly 20 years. Dreaming of retiring early so he could spend more time with his family, he discovered real estate. He built a six-figure annual income part-time; he enjoys helping others do the same.

Mr. Fielder is able to explain the nuances of all revenue-producing real estate strategies from the beginner's level to the most sophisticated. He can buy and sell properties sight unseen, profitably. He attributes his success to finding the right mentor and following a system.

He's also open to additional partners and students interested in all types of financing and real estate transactions.

As a gift to his readers, Michael's revealing his super-simple system for cutting his vacancies, maintenance, and tenant-related fees and headaches by 90%. Go to his website to access it: PartTimeInvesting.com/FreeGift. You can contact him at www.PartTimeInvesting.com.

CHAPTER 7

Making Mailbox Money with Real Estate

BY TIL LOWERY

What is mailbox money?

Well, in the old days, we got checks in the mail, and we took them to the bank to deposit them. That's physical – physical mailbox money.

Now, when you've got money pouring in on a consistent basis without even leaving the house, that's virtual – virtual mailbox money.

You can be sitting on a remote island beach, and "mailbox money" gets delivered straight into your bank account without you ever opening an envelope or driving to the bank.

The purpose of real estate investing is to make money, whether it's through hard work or via passive income. But, once you create mailbox money, I think you'll love it!

A New Way to Effectively Create Your Own Mailbox Money

I want you to know how to make mailbox money using very little effort, relatively little money, and some of your good credit.

What's awesome about this system is that its turnkey. It works month after month, year after year.

I call it the TL Global System, and this is another great part: you're going to be able to help a lot of good people.

*"You can get everything in life you want if you will just
help enough other people get what they want."*
—Zig Ziglar

So many people are getting robbed of their ability to own homes for reasons they can't control, like getting their identity stolen. My company, TL Global, Inc., helps them get their dream homes without going through a bank.

When you help someone else, you feel fulfilled and make a profit, too.

What's the Old Way to Make Money?

Normally, real estate investors have to find a discounted property before they have a buyer. Then they've got to bid on it, buy it, make repairs, and either resell it or rent it out.

If they don't do all this fast, they can lose money. Their cash is tied up, and they're still paying interest, upkeep, utilities, etc. I know from personal experience that this is costly and time-consuming.

Start with the Buyer, Not the House

With a revolutionary breath of fresh air, the TL Global System starts with the buyer, not the house. Every home is sold before you buy it! This eliminates holding costs, repairs, tax, insurance, interest, utilities, landscaping, commissions, vacancy, and maintenance costs. And, it's a great service for the buyer.

Let me explain.

After years of doing real estate transactions the old way, I discovered a new angle by accident. I had a family member who wanted to buy a home, but he didn't qualify for a loan. I have great credit and verifiable income, so he asked me if I would buy the home for him and let him make the monthly payments on the mortgage. He would then reimburse me for the down payment and closing costs and, ultimately, refinance the home in his name.

He believed that this was the only way he could be a homeowner.

Unfortunately, time went by, and my credit remained tied up for a long time while he tried to refinance. But, other people approached me asking for the same thing as a favor. I suddenly realized that there must be a new market emerging.

If good people with money couldn't qualify the usual ways, what could I do to help them? And how could I do it without tying up my credit?

My mentor and I brainstormed this topic over several mastermind sessions, and the outcome was life-changing, to say the least. We concluded that many people needed help, and we looked for a surefire WIN-WIN solution.

Then, I asked a powerful question. What if I started with the buyer instead of the house?

This unleashed all kinds of powerful answers. It flew in the face of traditional investing. We spent literally hundreds of hours designing and perfecting what I consider to be the most powerful "simultaneous close" strategy on the planet! We could have every home sold before we bought it!

Where There's Disaster, There's Opportunity

As of 2016, home ownership is at a 52-year low. In the last 12 months alone, we've lost over 400,000 homeowners and added two million renters. 90% of people can't qualify for a home loan. How is this possible?

Half of the married people get a divorce, destroying their credit. Every year, we have multimillions of new lawsuits, and half the people lose, sometimes getting fines and judgments. 30-40 million Americans have creditors chasing them for delinquent medical bills. Millions have tax liens. The USA's had 18 million foreclosures in the last several years, even more short sales, and 2-3 million bankruptcies every year. Those numbers are increasing.

Millions of people have non-verifiable income, and lots of people don't have social security numbers. Identity theft is impacting 15 million or more per year, and we have hundreds of billions in student loan defaults. Tens of millions of people have lost their jobs in the last several years, and if you miss bill payments, your credit score tanks. If you've had any kind of report or late payment in the last 12 months, that's a show stopper.

About 85% of all businesses fail within five years. When a sole proprietorship goes down, it takes your personal credit with it. Millions of self-employed people, who are the backbone of the American economy, get the short end of the stick when it comes to getting loans.

If your credit score is too low or your debt ratios are off, you can't get a loan. FICO reports that 50 million people lack the credit history needed to get credit. And, the net result of the Dodd-Frank Act was that 30% fewer people could qualify for a loan than the previous year.

It's amazing that anyone can qualify for a loan. It's a disaster. But where there's a disaster, there's opportunity. And the bigger the disaster, the bigger the opportunity.

So, what happens? People hit bottom and they suffer, but they don't give up. They try again and they keep trying. They get a new job, a new business, a new life, a new wife. (New husband?) They save money because they want security for their family, and they apply for loans.

Guess what the lender says? "NO! You need to suffer 7-10 more years!"

So, they resort to renting, which is like throwing money out the window. They continue to save (even though it's harder), and they dream of home ownership.

"Start with the buyers, not the homes."

—*Til Lowery*

The TL Global System: The Refreshing Revolution

Now, TL Global has found a way for you to help people get any home of their choice with the key requirement that they have a considerable down payment. And, you create mailbox money at the same time.

The key: Start with the buyers, not the property.

First, we find out what kind of cash they have for a down payment.

Now, let's assume we're going to help Sally and Johnny buy a home. We'll have a realtor help them search properties and choose. When they choose their own home based on their needs, tastes, limitations, and desires, whatever they are, it helps them bond with the house. Your extraordinary financial solution, the TL Global System, cements a very solid deal.

We're going to do what I call a simultaneous close, and you carry their loan.

You, the investor, buy the property at the par rate and resell it at the same price, on the same day, for a higher fixed rate with no balloon payment and no pre-payment penalty.

You just made an awesome amount of mailbox money for years to come.

The loans are serviced using a third-party note servicing company (very important). The homebuyer makes payment to the note servicing company, who then makes the payment on your loan and deposits your profit directly into your bank account. This equates to true passive income with no time consumption.

How the TL Global System Helps Homebuyers

This enables the buyer(s) to achieve their dream of home ownership with good terms. As a bonus, they don't have to get shamed by a mortgage lender, they're confident about the payments, and they get all the benefits such as pride, stability, and a neighborhood they enjoy.

Here are some other benefits they enjoy:

- The speed and ease of the process.
- The confidentiality of dealing with a private individual.
- The safety of working with licensed professionals
- The safety and convenience of a third-party note servicing company with monthly statements.
- An improved, positive credit rating.
- No balloon payment pressure.
- A loan good for up to 30 years.

- The possibility of refinancing with the FHA (Federal Housing Administration).
- 100% of the appreciation.
- 100% of the equity until they have no payments.
- Freedom and privacy – no landlord inspections, and they can make any improvements they want.
- The freedom to pay down the home early and save on interest.
- Possible tax deductions and benefits (they must consult a CPA):
    - For interest on their loan.
    - In tax-free profits, if they sell, up to $250,000 for a single person and $500,000 for a couple.
    - They can file a homestead exemption, which may lower their taxes.

How to Create Mailbox Money

All you had to do, as the investor, is qualify for a home loan and sign papers. You created a stream of mailbox money with little time consumption, providing yourself safety, stability, and a great return.

Since the payments are handled by a third party note servicing company, your payments are made on time every time, which positively impacts your creditworthiness, rather than tying it up indefinitely like I did the first time. What's more, your ROI is protected by strong collateral – the property itself.

The beauty of the TL Global System is that it is the same every time. When it comes to ROI, the purchase price doesn't matter – you always get the same rate of return if other variables remain constant. Because of this, investors like to do bigger deals to maximize their mailbox money.

Real estate investors love the program because it eliminates holding costs, rehab expenses, and any other unknown variables. This is what I call mailbox money: a stress-free, proven, rubberstamp process with a formula you can use over and over.

Once you've created one piece of mailbox money, what's next? Do it again, of course.

Security: The Magic of a Large Down Payment

Some of the most profound knowledge I've learned is, "The bigger the down payment, the less the risk." With the TL Global system, a significant down payment is one of the core principles.

On a typical deal with the TL Global system, homebuyers crank out over $40,000 to get into their dream home. Immediately, this already tells us a lot about the family. These people tend to have strong family values and value a nice place for their family to live. Additionally, the fact that they've responsibly accumulated that much money for a down payment shows that they are financially responsible. People who are financially responsible under-purchase what they can afford and responsibly save money. So, if a couple cranks out $40,000, do you think they'll make their payments? Absolutely. People don't let go of that kind of money without thinking long and hard. Once they've put that much down, their credit score is not important to us.

People who put 0-3% down can walk at the first challenge, especially if they're overextended.

By the way, have you ever experienced a tenant trashing a house? When you deal with people having a large down payment, you're dealing with a different caliber of an occupant.

Why It's Better to Be the Lender than the Landlord

Most heavyweights in real estate reach the same conclusion. You learn from repeated experience that it's better to be the lender than the landlord.

If it's a hot summer day and the AC breaks down, does the tenant call the lender or the landlord? The landlord. And they don't stop until it's fixed!

If someone falls and breaks their leg on the property, do they sue the lender or the landlord? The landlord, of course.

Landlords have many unknown variables that can devastate their return on investment. A major self-directed IRA custodian reported that 85% of investors lose money on their first fix-and-flip deal because they underestimate rehab costs and the resulting holding costs.

Lenders know exactly what their ROI is because lenders don't have expenses, responsibilities, liabilities, or unknown variables to contend with. Lenders have less stress, more fun, and they live longer!

Landlords often think that they get to maintain control. But if they fail to make payments, they find out very quickly who has control – it's the lender! If they don't get paid, lenders can foreclose! That's why lenders know that control is superior to ownership.

Success Stories Using the TL Global System

One of my clients did a transaction that created over $1,600 per month in mailbox money by helping a family that had just relocated from California. The family wanted a new home in the best school district for their children. They had just sold some properties and had a great income, but they couldn't qualify for the new loan. They were so grateful for the help.

Another investor made $1,200 per month by helping a family in a similar situation. One of my lenders watched the process, jumped on board, and is now enjoying $4,500 per month in mailbox money after only three deals!

I really love this system because everyone walks away so happy!

Profound Knowledge

When a family gets denied the opportunity to own the home they choose, it does terrible harm. When they're willing to pour their life savings into a home with a good school, they deserve a chance to improve their circumstances.

When you extend this opportunity to them, you make money. Everyone's happy. It's a win-win. And, the sooner you start, the better. Home prices are going up. Rents are going up.

The TL Global mission is to help people improve their quality of life by using life-changing, profound knowledge and enjoying the process.

If you're an investor with good credit, and you would like to start making mailbox money with real estate by helping a family get their home of choice, the next step is to contact TL Global, Inc. You can get in touch by visiting www.MakingMailboxMoney.com.

Or, if you're a homebuyer wanting your credit challenges to disappear, take action to acquire your dream home by visiting www.GetOwnerFinancing.com.

For a limited time, TL Global, Inc. is offering a free 15-minute phone consultation, which you can claim here: www.tlglobaltraining.com/FreeGift. Thanks for reading, and I'm excited to help you achieve your real estate goals by making mailbox money or buying your dream home!

Til Lowery

iCare@TilLowery.com

(832) 717-2600

TIL LOWERY

Public speaker, trainer, real estate investor, humanitarian, and mentor Til Lowery has been a licensed real estate broker in Texas and Florida for over 27 years.

She founded TL Global, Inc., and created the revolutionary TL Global System, a proprietary real estate investment strategy. She helps real estate investors create "mailbox money" while helping credit-challenged, aspirational homebuyers fulfill their dreams of home ownership, a truly socially conscious movement.

She's come a long way since escaping Vietnam as a child, floating for 17 days in a crowded boat and hoping to hit friendly land. She stayed positive despite her many struggles.

Today, she's proud to offer real estate training to prospective agents/ brokers, investors, and homebuyers in 26 different states. To sign up for a limited-time, free, 15-minute consultation, visit www.TLGlobalTraining. com/FreeGift.

CHAPTER 8

How to Create Generational Wealth by Buying Multifamily Real Estate

BY HOWARD LAU

Can you imagine a day when you didn't rush to your job in the morning? You enjoy your cup of coffee and take time to get ready. You take your child to school but drive back home instead of clocking in.

Can you imagine making money while you sleep?

Well, that's possible. You can achieve the lifestyle I describe above by buying real estate, and I'm here to tell you how.

Don't get me wrong. This is no get-rich-quick scheme. It is arguably slow, but many people have done it, as my wife and I have. Ten years ago, we started investing in real estate and generated great wealth that will outlive us. **Our net worth has grown from less than $10,000 to multimillions in four countries.**

> *"Stay away from the shortcuts. They are your farthest detour."*
>
> *—Howard Lau*

This chapter is about how you can use my systematic approach to create generational wealth through real estate. If you're looking for overnight success, you'll be disappointed.

I fortunately received my 10-step formula from a nationally-renowned real estate guru, Dave Lindahl. Like gravity, it always works!

1. **Pick an Emerging Market**
2. **Begin a Marketing Campaign to Generate the Deal Flow**
3. **Build Your Power Team**
4. **Analyze Deals Like the Bank Does**
5. **Make Two Offers Per Week Using Letters of Intent**
6. **Perform Due Diligence – Financial, Physical, and Legal**
7. **Finance Your Purchase**
8. **Close the Deal**
9. **Move on to the Next Deal!!**
10. **Take this Bonus Step if You're Extra-Ambitious**

If you follow these steps, you'll inevitably become rich.

1. **Pick an Emerging Market**

   Many times, I get asked by investors where they should invest. Immediately, they want to rush into whatever I tell them. But, it's better if I teach them how to pick the emerging markets themselves. There are five action steps:

   a) Determine the cities with the highest job growth rate. I use a minimum of 2% over the last two years.

   b) Make sure to enter the right market with enough tenants in the population pool. My favorite is a population of 150,000 or more, a sustainable population that will support multifamily buildings.

   c) Contact the local Economic Development Department (EDD). Get a sense of what the city is doing to attract investment and growth. You really need a diversified economy and an abundant creation of various types of jobs, such as manufacturing, high tech, engineering, white collar, and biotech. Every professional job creates three service jobs, such as bakery, convenience stores, and dry cleaners.

   d) Research the number of construction permits the city issued over the last year, as this affects the housing supply. New construction provides more rental choices, and overbuilding yields high vacancies. You need jobs drawing population and creating an adequate housing demand. I like a job growth rate of at least 1-2% higher than the housing growth rate.

e) After that, make a final decision on a market and stick to it.

2. Begin a Marketing Campaign to Generate Deal Flow

Once you've decided on a market, the hard work begins. Multifamily buildings are not like your typical homes listed online MLS.

Pocket Listings

Many brokerages save these multifamily listings only for their select, well-known clients who have the money ready, buy frequently, and make purchase decisions quickly. Competition is high in a commercial real estate.

That's why we say these listings are in the "pockets" of the realtors, brokers, and agents.

90% of all good commercial deals (if not all) come from pocket listings. If they're private and not available online, how can you find them? Through a broker relationship.

"The quality of your deal will be determined by the quality of your broker relationship. And that's something you can easily build."

— Howard Lau

Broker Relationships

Almost all the great deals you can get as an investor will be determined by how good your relationships with the brokers are.

We have at least 5-10 good brokers in any market that we're consistently working. That keeps the deals coming often, even daily. If you don't have good broker relationships, chances are that you get bad deals or no deals at all.

How do we make good broker relationships? We call brokers directly and daily. We fly to the area to visit and get to know them personally.

We have drinks or meals with them, go to a game, or play golf. If we can get to know their families, we do that, too.

We take the time to nurture the relationship. A lot of times, they become good friends. The essence is that the quality of your deal will be determined by the quality of your broker relationship.

We habitually call as many brokers as we need to **create a deal flow**. We locate brokers online, by referral, on LinkedIn, and here:

a) www.Loopnet.com

b) www.CCIM.com

c) Marcus and Millichap

d) Hendrick Partners

e) RE/Max Commercial

The quickest way to get quality leads is to locate possible contacts from these places, make a list, and call them.

For us to buy 150-250 doors (apartment units) in the emerging market per year, we need to be crystal clear and focus on what needs to be done. I contact 5-10 new brokers each week, and here's my formula:

a) Go to loopnet.com and get a list of brokers' contact information.

b) Make a habit of calling brokers every day.

c) Build relationships by talking about local market conditions, non-business local events, and more importantly, join a community such as a local investment club.

d) Make a follow-up call at least every week until a deal is found.

e) Go to the market and tour available properties.

While going through the list, the key is to build great rapport. It's just a matter of time until your broker sends you a deal. The better the relationship, the sweeter the deal!

3. Build Your Power Team

Whether you invest in a local or remote market, you need a great team. As I said in my book, 9 Millionaire Secrets on Real Estate Riches, real estate is a team sport. You cannot do it alone!!

We cannot successfully invest in a market by wearing all the hats. You would not have the skills and the time required to do everything yourself. For deals to go through successfully, you need most, if not all, of the team members listed below.

Most importantly, make sure you intend to give the right compensation. Build the team like any other relationship – treat them with respect (both in manners and with enough compensation) and set yourself apart from competitors who don't.

"We control our own destiny. One way or another."

—Howard Lau

Here is the Power Team I **develop for each market**:

a) Brokers

Make sure you have a minimum of five brokers at each emerging market. If you follow Step 2, you'll have no problem contacting at least 20-30 brokers. Your key job is to nurture the five broker relationships with the best potential and keep the relationship warm.

b) Property Management Companies

Property management is the single biggest factor in whether your investment is profitable. It can make or break your success. Property managers do many things for you, like walking through a building for you (if you're not in the market yet) and performing due diligence for you, physically and financially. **If you don't have a great, honest, hardworking property manager, your property will soon bleed cash and turn from an asset into a liability!**

c) Lenders

Lenders will lend you money on the right properties by checking the deals that you do. Unfortunately, they won't lend you money on a property that doesn't satisfy their lending guidelines and is likely to lose money. This protects you, too. Treat them respectfully as key partners.

I always say that banks are your best partners! Who else would lend you hundreds of thousands (or millions) of dollars with a 4-5% return, especially when you only need to put 25-30% down?

d) Attorneys

A great attorney is an absolute must. A good one will not only draft the P&S (purchase and sale) Agreements, but also recommend the best holding structure for the purchase.

e) Appraisers, Insurance Brokers, Accountants

These are the other professionals you'll be dealing with on a regular basis. Look for high personal standards such as honesty, competence, and fairness.

4. Analyze Deals Like the Bank Does

You really need to be a master at analyzing and underwriting your deal. It's the most important way to keep you safe. If you can't do this well, you won't be in the game for long.

I'll give you three key parameters to follow and reduce your risk. That is how I do it when I invest:

Three Key Parameters for Analyzing Investments:	
1. Cap rate > 8%	
2. COC (cash on cash) > 12%	
3. DCR (debt coverage ratio) > 1.6	
Cap rate =	The ratio of the net operating income vs. price. The rule of thumb is the higher the better when you buy, and the lower the better when you sell. **Cap rate = NOI (net operating income) / Sale Price**
COC (cash on cash) =	Investor's return on investment. The higher the better. COC is the most simplified way to look at the return and screen deals. Cash on Cash Return = (NOI - Capital Expenditures - Debt Service) / Total Acquisition Costs
DCR (debt coverage ratio) =	The ability of the property's net income to pay off the mortgage of the property. DCR = NOI / DS (Annual Debt Services)

You must be a good investigator. Look at the income and expense, but more importantly, look beyond the surface and dig into the details of anything that may make the property a bad investment.

The more conservative you are, the safer you are. But, being too conservative might cost you some great deals. So, it comes down to underwriting accuracy. These numbers are only the first set of parameters for screening deals.

How does the bank see your deal? For example, they probably won't lend you money if your debt coverage ratio is under 1.2-1.3.

Why do I use 1.6%, then? Because my deal will be much easier to approve, and I'll always be able to pay the debt services.

5. Make Two Offers Per Week Using Letters of Intent

Put out two offers to buy every week. Why two?

Sellers won't accept 90% of your offers because your competition is less conservative, and chases deals that don't meet our cap rate, COC, and DCR requirements.

There are legit reasons for this. They might be using institutional money with lower requirements on returns, such as a cap rate of only 4%.

Regardless of their practices, we need to make enough return to provide for our investors. We might miss some deals, but we decrease a lot of the risk. That's why you need to make a lot of offers before you get a deal.

In life, many things are a numbers game, and investing is one.

6. Due Diligence – Financial, Physical, and Legal

Once you get an offer accepted, the due diligence clock starts ticking. You negotiate the actual buying contract (P&S Agreement). You normally have 45-60 days, but it's negotiable.

Financial Due Diligence

Request these from the listing broker:

a) The last three years of operating statements on a 12-month trend report.

b) Profit and Loss Statements **for the last two years**.

c) A current balance sheet **of the property's assets and liabilities**.

d) The last 12 months' rent roll, **ideally broken down by each rental unit**.

Proper financial due diligence verifies that the income and expenses are as the seller stated. Don't simply trust the seller's numbers; really discover the true story, like any investment. The best buyers always assess financial viability correctly.

Physical Due Diligence

The other word for physical due diligence is property inspection. Typically, you hire a competent engineer to check all major building systems (electrical, plumbing, heating, A/C, roof, etc.) and give you a report detailing the condition of the building. With the report in hand, you (yes, you) go to the property and physically walk every single unit with your property manager or maintenance person.

Legal Due Diligence

You need to hire a competent attorney to do the title work. A clean title is critical: no lien, no ligation in the process, and no outstanding property tax.

7. **Finance Your Purchase**

   You can use local banks, national lenders, or conduit lenders to finance your deal, and they should be part of your power team.

   More importantly, you want to finance your deal with a mortgage broker. It will typically cost you 1% (one point) of the loan, but they can save you money by financing the deal with the right lender, product, and terms for your deal.

   The wrong types of mortgages (due to rates, terms, pre-payment penalty, etc.) can easily cost you more than 1%, which is why I **choose** mortgage brokers.

8. **Close the Deal**

   Now that you've finished the first seven steps, complete the transaction and sign all the required paperwork at the title company's or attorney's office.

9. **Move on to the Next Deal!!**

   Repeat step 1 to 8 and buy more units.

10. **Take this Bonus Step if You're Extra-Ambitious**

    Now that I've shared my success formula to help you hunt down these big properties, you'll immediately spring to work if you're a hard worker who wants to expand what you do. There is a huge profit in investing in multifamily properties.

But, the bonus step is to make sure you have the right mindset.

You can do all the right things mechanically, work hard, persist, and follow all the rules, and you'll succeed. But when your mindset is right, your profits and opportunities increase exponentially. Adding a coach who's seen all the nuances can help you enormously because they understand and know how to deal with them.

***

Partner with Me and Do More Deals.

Like the advice in my book, 9 Millionaire Secrets on Real Estate Riches, I recommend that all investors build a powerful team. Real estate, like any business, is a team sport built on relationships.

It's critical that you partner with an experienced, successful investor whose skillset you can trust. After creating a portfolio of over $4 million in four countries, I have a wealth of information to give, and can't give it all in one chapter.

However, thank you for your time in reading and your initiative in improving your life. Here is a copy of my book, 9 Millionaire Secrets on Real Estate Riches, a $197 value, absolutely free. This book is stuffed with tried-and-true strategies, examples, and principles that will help you create your own generational wealth. Go to this website, where I give regular talks to my coaching students, www.hay2brick.com.

It's been a pleasure serving you, and I hope you'll let me know what you liked and what questions you have. You can reach me at howard@hay2brick.com or 1 (866)-991-1336.

HOWARD LAU

Howard Lau, author, public speaker, and founder/president of the Hay2Brick Real Estate, has successfully invested in commercial and residential real estate for more than 10 years. He is frequently featured as a Success Story on the Keyspire portal.

Buying and managing single family properties in his local Canadian market led to investing in multifamily properties internationally. His multi-million portfolio includes properties across Canada, the United States, China, and Hong Kong.

Howard employs a systematic approach to real estate investing, concentrating on investments that generate double-digit returns. He continues to grow his portfolio and educates other real estate investors by hosting seminars on the real estate cycle and proven investing techniques.

More questions about real estate?

For more information about Hay2Brick Real Estate and a free copy of Howard's book, *9 Millionaire Secrets on Real Estate Riches,* visit www. Hay2Brick.com, send an email to howard@hay2brick.com, or call 1 (866) 991-1336.

CHAPTER 9

Nine Things that Could Invite a CRA Audit: More Insider Secrets

BY SANGITA TULSIANI

These powerful, unknown CRA audit-proofing techniques are almost guaranteed to keep you out of the "Audit Pile."

1. **Are You Working, But Not Paying Yourself? Employment Insurance Issues**

    As we all know, there are a lot of people losing their jobs due to numerous factors: the economy, wage increases, financial burden on employers, the market, etc.

    In these situations and after leaving a job, an individual may incorporate a business or invest all their time in one that they already have. The individual may then decide to leave all the money in the business or corporation and take no wages. They may do so because the business is not making enough money or revenue to pay a salary to themselves.

    Since the individual does not receive any personal wages, he or she may be motivated to apply for EI unemployment benefits? It sounds simple, right? Wrong!

    In a Feb 6th, 2018 federal court judicial review, it was established that whether one is employed or not is a matter of work performed rather than the wages received. In this case, the individual was working, but did not receive any personal income. Therefore, the individual was not considered unemployed and was not eligible for EI benefits.

The court went on to note that the right to receive income from a business is sufficient to establish employment, even if the income is not actually received.

In situations such as the above, the individual will be audited and may be required to pay back EI benefits received in addition to interest. Watch out for these scenarios!!

2. Taxi Drivers Must Register for GST/HST

Most businesses must register for a GST/HST account if they earn revenues from worldwide taxable supplies greater than $30,000 within the previous four consecutive quarters or exceed the $30,000 threshold in a single calendar quarter.

A special rule applies to self-employed "taxi businesses," which requires them to register regardless of the quantity of revenues.

There has been some uncertainty as to whether drivers of ridesharing services, such as Uber, are considered "taxi businesses."

The 2017 federal budget ended this uncertainty by proposing that ridesharing services will be defined "taxi businesses" for GST/HST purposes and therefore will be required to charge and remit GST/HST.

More specifically, the term "taxi business" will now include all persons engaged in the business of transporting passengers for fares by motor vehicle within a municipality and its environs where the transportation is arranged for or coordinated through an electronic platform or system, such as a mobile application or website.

In conclusion, drivers of ridesharing services should consider registering for GST/HST.

3. Business Loss or Personal Venture? Deducting Losses Against Other Income

The taxpayer must be able to prove that they're truly running a business before applying their business losses to another source of income such as employment earnings, thereby reducing the overall tax liability. They have to show that the undertaking was in the pursuit of profit.

An April 28th, 2017 Tax Court of Canada case considered whether a practicing lawyer had a source of business income in respect to her law practice from 2011-2014.

The taxpayer incurred losses in all the years in question ranging from $4,000+ to $12,000+, and she reported annual revenues ranging from $0 to $3,800+.

The taxpayer reported that the time she spent on the proprietorship was diverse; however, on average she worked about 5 to 10 hours per week. The taxpayer testified that she did no pro bono or volunteer work, but rather charged clients depending on their circumstances. In some cases, the client did not end up paying for the services.

The court found that the lawyer's work was very commendable; however, the practice did not have a view to profit. For example, the gross revenues per hour for the years 2011-2014 were $5, $1.70, and $7.70 (assuming 50 weeks at 10 hours/week for the year). These amounts were not even minimum wage, much less amounts that could sustain a law practice operating with a view to profit.

Although the taxpayer's work was not strictly volunteer, it was very close. As the venture was not carried out with a view to profit, there was no business, so the losses were not deductible against other sources of the taxpayer's income.

Action: If your proprietorship is in a loss position, be sure to document evidence to support your efforts to be profitable.

4. The Underground Economy: Contractors, Online Sales, Farmers Markets, Etc.

In recent years, the CRA has particularly focused on tracking underground economy activities. One way they are doing this is by obtaining information from key third parties. For example, recently the CRA obtained details from contractor credit applications submitted to the well-known home improvement store, Rona.

Assuming the details would include names, addresses, and other specifics that would help determine whether the credit should be given, the CRA could presumably compare that information to the contractor's tax returns.

The CRA has also recently obtained information from mobile card reader Square Canada. Through a Federal Court Order issued to Square Canada, the CRA obtained identifying vendor information and sales details associated with individuals or entities using the app. The information requested primarily focused on those with annual revenues of $20,000 or more for the tax years 2012-2015 and part of 2016.

It would not be unreasonable to expect that the CRA could obtain similar information from other websites, web-based apps, and organizations.

Action: Make sure to bring in all related sales information for discussion at tax time. Sales may or may not be taxable, depending on the specifics of your case.

5. Income Sprinkling, AKA Income Splitting, Pending New TOSI Rules

Income sprinkling or splitting is used by higher-income small business owners or incorporated professionals to redirect their income to other, lower-taxed family members. They do it through the payment of private company dividends, capital gains, and certain income from partnership trusts.

To limit the practice, there are rules currently in place known as TOSI (Tax on Split Income). For example, currently, the rules require applying the highest marginal tax rate (33% federally, plus provincial tax) to the split income of certain family members under the age of 18, which also makes it known as the kiddie tax.

New rules are scheduled to roll out in 2018. Even with TOSI in effect, there are often a host of discretionary ways people can choose to distribute (or sprinkle) their income to family members, and some of these new rules may actually help.

If you are at least 18 years old in the year you receive the split income, and it came from an "excluded business," you're in good shape. The TOSI rule taxing at 33% won't apply to you.

An excluded business is one in which you were "actively engaged on a regular, continuous, and substantial basis in the activities of the business," either in the tax year in question or in any five prior tax years which need not to be consecutive. To be considered actively engaged, you must have worked in the business at least an average of 20 hours per week.

If you are 25 or over, you can also be exempt from the old TOSI rules if you hold "excluded shares." These are shares in a private corporation that give you 10% of both the votes and value. This exception will not be available for either professional corporations or service businesses.

If none of these exceptions apply, you are permitted a reasonable return on your shares, taking into account a variety of factors, including the work you performed, the property you contributed, and the risks you assumed.

If you are between 18 and 24, the only factor taken into consideration in determining the reasonable return are capital contributions made with "arms-length capital," meaning that the two parties involved in a transaction have no other relationship with each other.

One must keep records to satisfy the CRA in case of audit. For example, keep track of the 20 hours per week you worked in a business by maintaining timesheets, schedules, and logbooks. The

CRA will consider the information contained in the payroll to support the number of hours the individual worked.

The new rules, if enacted, are proposed to apply to 2018 and subsequent tax years. Therefore, take advantage until the end of 2018 to satisfy the 10% ownership test under the definition of "excluded shares."

Some of you may not take this seriously and think, "What if the rules aren't passed until later in 2018? Will the CRA administer the new income sprinkling proposals before the law is actually enacted?"

The CRA has clearly stated that it expects taxpayers to file their returns on the basis of this proposed legislation, a longstanding practice. To assist taxpayers in calculating their TOSI for 2018 and later years, Form T1206, "Tax on Split Income," will be updated by January 2019 to reflect the proposed legislation. With all the complications, you'll need qualified professional help to deal with the changes and prevent an "invitation to audit" from the CRA.

6. **Real Estate Transactions is a Very Popular Subject for Audit by CRA:**

An individual must determine and properly record their real estate transactions. Some types of real estate can be considered as business income or capital gains income, depending on the nature of the transaction, the amount of time the real estate was held for, etc. Fix and Flips, Assignments, Real Estate Investment Rentals, Primary Residence Renting, operating a business from your primary residence, and deducting more than 35% of the house to generate income may all meet the criteria of inviting an audit by the CRA

Many flippers or renovators are confused with the tax implications of flipping a house. Many people are under the impression that if you sell a house, only 50% of the profit is taxable. This misconception comes at a huge cost. If you are truly renovating a property for a quick flip, and there was no intention to rent the property out, the profit is considered income and 100% taxable.

If you report the flip incorrectly as a capital gain, the CRA may even impose a penalty on top of the taxes due, increasing the tax liability. Some renovators/flippers even decide to move into the property to avoid tax liability, hoping to live there for a couple of months, move back to their own home, and then sell the property. They think that they can shelter the gain using the primary residence exemption, but qualifying for primary residence exemption is a two-step process:

1. The property in question must be "capital property," which means any property that can create capital gains or losses when you dispose of it. To determine this, the CRA considers "intention." The problem is that intention is subjective, so how do you prove that your intention is to truly move into the property?

2. The other criteria are whether the transactions form a part of your regular business, the frequency of your transactions, etc. If your true intention is to flip, chances are you would not even pass the first test.

Sometimes, transferring the property to a family member may or may not be a taxable transaction. The taxable event would occur when a change of "beneficial ownership" happens. Usually, a beneficial change and legal change are one and the same, but not always.

In a June 14, 2016 technical interpretation, the CRA examined a situation where a married couple transferred the title to a property and the mortgage into a parent's name because they no longer qualified to refinance the original mortgage. Once their financial position improved, they transferred the title and mortgage back. The original taxpayers continued to live in the dwelling throughout the legal transactions and made all the mortgage payments and other house costs.

The CRA opined that despite the legal ownership changes, no beneficial ownership change occurred. Therefore, there was no taxable disposition.

Since the taxability of such a transaction is a matter of interpretation, caution should be taken when relying on such a position. Discuss your fact pattern with a professional and be sure to document appropriate support.

7. **Foreign Tax Credits: Invitations for Audit**

Prior to 2015, the CRA often accepted copies of U.S. tax returns as support to claim a U.S. Foreign Tax Credit (FTC). The CRA recently changed its requirements to accept proof of payments made or refunds received in lieu of a notice of assessment, transcript, statement, or other document from the applicable foreign tax authority (county where the income is earned and taxes paid), or FTA. The FTA has to provide all the following information:

- The payment made to or received from the FTA
- The amount of payment or refund
- The tax year to which the payment or refund relates
- The date of receipt of payment

Before you even receive a CRA pre- or post-assessing review letter, you should always request these documents to expedite your FTC claim.

8. **Are You Mixing Personal and Business Expenses? This is Popular for Audit by the CRA**

If you counted your tuition payments as business expenses rather than credits, and you haven't registered as a real estate agent yet, CRA will have an issue with that. You're trying to deduct expenses prior to establishing a business.

As a business, you can deduct any expenses that help you generate income, courses being one of them. That being said, early in your studies, you didn't know whether you would get through all the courses or whether you'd ever get to the point of registering with a brokerage as a real estate agent.

It's very important to deduct expenses according to the CRA's guidelines.

The expenses may vary from one self-employed individual to another. For example, a popular musician may deduct the cost of clothing and hairdos as part of their business expenses if he or she is required to appear on TV or stage frequently.

9. **Claiming Expenses Without Meeting Industry Standards**

The CRA has set industry codes that enable the tax man to know what the average relationship between expenses and income will be in certain types of businesses.

In my last 22 years in a tax-related career, I have seen many audits due to individuals claiming expenses on the basis of guessing. I advised them that they needed to have receipts for backup, and the answer I often get is, "The receipts are at home, and once I add them up, they will be actually more than the figures I'm guessing."

After all, a client is always right! At the end of the day, they are signing their tax return, and they reassure me that they're correct. And some are.

But, sure enough, after one or two years, they get an audit letter from the CRA wanting to see the receipts. The clients panic and contact me to handle the situation, but at this point they do not have enough receipts to sustain the expenses claimed, so now we try to get expenses off the bank statements and the credit card statements, which the CRA will accept sometimes, but not always.

At this point, we also need to make adjustments, as the expenses are either more or less than what was claimed. This is a trigger point for the CRA. They may start asking for several years of backup. So, always claim expenses that you have proof and receipts for.

Most of these audit-proofing techniques are not understood well by most Canadians, and some of them are quite new, but having this information and taking the appropriate action will almost guarantee to keep you out of the CRA's "Audit Pile."

I help my clients with planning, reducing taxes, getting money back, audits, or even with just a second opinion when needed. Please feel free to contact me at (1) 905-915-3399. I only take on a small number of new clients every year at a fair price.

SANGITA TULSIANI

Did you know that 90 percent of all businesses pay too much tax? Sangita Tulsiani knows. She's been in the tax industry since 1995.

Today, she's a best-selling author, real estate investor and a highly sought-after accountant. Her tax tips have been published in newspapers, in best-selling books and other formats.

Sangita and her team specialize in helping individuals, business owners, and real estate professionals to legally keep more of their money in their own pockets and out of the hands of the tax man.

It's no wonder that she has more than 500 returning, loyal clients from all over Canada who trust her with their tax planning, cross border taxation, getting a tax id number in the USA and legally taking advantage of tax deductions.

For a limited time, readers can get access to her exclusive report *"The Top 10 Mistakes Business Owner Make When Doing Their Taxes,"* by going to PayLessTaxes.gr8.com

CHAPTER 10

Property Management: Protecting Your Investment

BY GWEN TEWNION

Real estate is one of the most powerful wealth-building tools that is available to everyone in Canada and the United States. With over 13 years' experience in real estate, I realized early on how much wealth was possible from acquiring rental properties. Not just one or two, but multiple properties.

Let me ask you: Would additional cash flow from rental properties each month change your life? For most people, the answer is yes, but there's an obvious problem with having one or more rentals – the tenant headaches.

This chapter will assist in walking you through the process of determining whether you have what it takes to manage rental properties or whether you're better off leaving it to a professional. I also cover the pitfalls of renting and attempt to make the entire management process smoother to provide you with a peace of mind.

Many years ago, while purchasing additional rental properties for my portfolio, I was searching for a trustworthy property manager that would care for our properties and protect our investment. This proved to be a difficult task - my husband and I found a cash-flowing triplex, but the seller was an out-of-province owner. The current property manager was unethical and billing the out-of-town owner for repairs – garage roof replacement, basement sewer pipe, and floor repairs – that were NEVER completed. Receipts were produced by the seller, and we sent photos back to show that the work was never completed.

We did purchase the triplex in the end. However, we did not turn our properties over to a property manager and resolved the problem by continuing to manage our properties ourselves. Over the years, we evolved into a successful property management and contracting company, currently managing hundreds of doors and caring for owners' properties like they're our own.

As an industry leader, here's another story we hear all too often. Someone read a few books, researched some information on the Internet, and got the voice in their head that says, "I can take care of the property myself! Really, how hard can it be?" Sooner or later, they flash back to that other old saying, "Famous last words."

Once you have purchased your rental property, the most important question you need to ask yourself is, "How am I going to sustain and protect my Investment?"

The answer is **MANAGEMENT.**

Let's face facts: you work hard for your money. So, what does a great property management company do? A great professional company cares for your property like it is their own, knows the rules and regulations, utilizes the correct forms, sends photos of repairs, is accountable, returns your telephone calls and emails within 24 hours, and has your best interests in mind. That company is worth its weight in gold.

There are good property management companies out there, someone you hire to deal with all the tenant issues and headaches, and the best way to locate them is through referrals. Make sure to ask for references, and speak with some of their long-term property owners, so you get the true story. Also, find out how long they have been in business.

Managing rental properties isn't for the faint of heart, but it can be rewarding for the right person. If you have managed your properties successfully to date, maybe it is time to consider turning your properties over to a trusted, honest, and respectful property manager, so your time can be better utilized finding more deals and you can continue to grow your portfolio.

Avoiding the Pitfalls - 7 Costly New Landlord Mistakes (Plus Three Bonus Mistakes)

1. Not Obtaining Insurance

Obtain homeowner's insurance, third-party liability coverage, and rental insurance. Most landlords forget to advise their insurance company that it is a rental property. If a tenant or their guests are injured on one of your rental properties, you may face a lawsuit. It is important that regular maintenance is completed at the property to prevent any liability issues. It is also important to notify the insurance company if the property is vacant for more than 30 days.

2. Rents are Too High

If you have completed your renovations and asking top dollar for rent, unaware that the vacancy rate is three percent, you have not researched comparable rentals in your area. Your rental property is sitting vacant and costing you money. If you lower your rents to fair market value for the area, you may get a longer term tenants and have less vacancies, allowing your property to flow cash. Another option is to offer incentives, for example, $100 off the first month's rent or a ½ month free.

3. Improper Screening of Tenants

A poor-quality tenant can cost you a year's worth of cash-flow profits. When speaking with the current landlord, find out if the tenants have given notice and why they are moving. See if the information matches their application. Any bed bugs? You do not want to endure the costly treatment process. In addition, you want to perform a thorough background check (courts, residential tenancies branch, current landlord, employment, references, etc.). The person you really want to speak with is the previous landlord to their current one. They have nothing to lose and are not just trying to move along with a poor-quality tenant. They will give you the real story regarding the applicants and tell you if they paid rent on time, etc.

4. **Security Deposit and First Month's Rent – IMPORTANT**

Do not accept a personal cheque for either the security deposit or first month's rent. This is non-negotiable. What happens if the cheque is returned non-sufficient funds three weeks later by your financial institution? What if the tenant then decides not to pay? You may have trouble getting the tenant out of the property. Save yourself the headaches. Accept either cash (give a receipt), money order, certified cheque, or money transfer for the security deposit and first month's rent. After the first month, you can accept postdated personal cheques.

If a tenant does write an NSF cheque at any point, do not continue accepting cheques from the tenant unless certified by a bank and make sure they pay the NSF and late fees as well. **Important:** Do not turn over keys until the security deposit and first month's rent are paid in full and the Move-in Condition Report is completed.

5. **Tenancy Agreements (aka Leases)**

These are legal documents. Do not place a tenant in a rental property without having a signed Tenancy Agreement. Use the correct forms supplied by the governing body for the province or state of your rental property. This will assist in proving your case if necessary. Be sure to complete them correctly and make sure both parties initial any changes. Be sure you are charging the correct amount for the security deposit.

6. **Not Completing Move-In or Move-Out Inspections**

It is imperative that you complete a move-in inspection for the rental, list the condition of the rental, and test that the smoke alarms are operational upon move-in. It is also a good idea to take photos during the move-in and especially during the move-out so you can prove your claim if necessary. During the move-out, you must document any damages, cleaning needed, furniture or garbage left behind, or keys not returned. Otherwise, you will have problems justifying retaining the security deposit for cleaning and repairs.

7. **Not Recording Utility Readings (Move-in and Move-Out)**

Take the meter readings and photos of the meter during the move-in inspection. Write the utility meter numbers and their readings at the bottom of the Condition Report. Write down the utility information for the tenants and have them call the utility companies to set up the applicable utility accounts in their names within 24 hours. You then email the utility companies with the information and the tenant's name, address, and telephone number. Within 36 hours, you should email or call the utility company again to ensure that the tenants have set up the accounts in their names to prevent you from getting charged for their utility usage.

8. **BONUS MISTAKE #1: Lack of Property Inspections**

Too many new landlords or property management companies do not perform quarterly inspections on their properties. If they don't, who is protecting the investment? Initially, some of our owners questioned our quarterly inspections charge, but came around when we explained the reasons for wanting to protect their investment.

Quarterly property inspections allow us to enter the rental unit to check for some of the following: Possible additional occupants living in the suite who are not listed on the Lease Agreement; tenants smoking in the suite or using illegal drugs; pets at the property without the tenant paying a pet deposit; lack of cleanliness; damages at the property; maintenance issues that, if not taken care of, could lead to costly repairs; smoke alarms not operational or removed by the tenants. After knowing this, our owners are thankful we take such good care of their rental properties.

9. **BONUS MISTAKE #2: Being Too Lax on Late Rents and Other Issues**

Ever heard the saying, "Give an inch and they will take a mile"? Yes, that applies to tenants also. Late rent is just that, late rent! Rent is due on the first of every month. Keep the tenant on track and charge late fees conforming to the rules of your province or state.

If the tenant is paying past the fifth of the month, set up a Mediated Agreement including the landlord, the tenant, and the governing authority for your province or state. The Agreement should include the date and amount the tenant will pay, including the rent and late fees. This can usually be completed over the telephone. Also, have the tenant agree to pay the next three months' rent in full and on time. If the tenant breaches the Agreement, a day late or a dollar short, you have the option of enforcing the Agreement and getting the tenant out of the rental very quickly. These little tricks will not only save you time, but will also save you money.

As issues arise, deal with them immediately. For issues other than nonpayment of rent, issue a notice to correct it within five days or within one rental period. If not corrected, a Termination for Cause may be necessary.

10. BONUS MISTAKE #3: Not hiring a Property Management Company Earlier

What is your time worth? It is all too common for landlords and revenue property owners to attempt to save a dollar and manage their own properties. When they realize they do not have the time or are faced with a situation that is now out of control, they discover that they may be stuck because they did not seek assistance earlier.

Often, it is not due to inability, but lack of education with respect to the vast amount of rules and regulations. This is often the case when our office receives a call for assistance from the property owner. It is important to seek assistance from qualified individuals who are not your friends and family and who can legitimately assist you in resolving the issue at hand. We can resolve numerous issues daily.

Important Note about Tenant Files

Create a separate tenant file for each new tenancy and document everything: dates, times, and events. You will be glad you did when the time comes to refer to your entries.

Approximately 90 percent of our tenants are great quality tenants, but there is always the 10 percent rule. It is true, those unreliable 10 percent of tenants will take up 90 percent of your time dealing with various issues, like chasing rents, issuing notices for lack of cleanliness, reminding them to cut the lawn, and the list goes on. We have specific processes in place to prevent most of these issues, which makes the entire process smoother.

Nine Properties

One of the secrets to wealth with rental properties is acquiring nine or more cash-flowing rental properties instead of just one. This should provide the income to sustain the properties through the many problems that can come up. One property is a great place to start; however, when you have nine or more rentals, this starts to increase your annual income and move you forward, providing of course that your cash-flowing rental properties are being managed correctly. Owning only one rental property may cause you some headaches and you may not have the revenue to sustain it. In addition to owning rental properties, we also buy/fix/sell various properties to create an additional revenue stream, and we split the equity with our joint venture relationships. This ensures that we always have sufficient revenue available at all times.

Final Note

Purchasing and acquiring rental properties is a great way to make money. Just remember that it can be a lot of work if you are not running your properties like a business. You will encounter challenging tenants and may be faced with adversity on occasion. Make sure you have a contingency fund to cover those unexpected emergencies and repairs.

Purchasing rental properties is not for everyone, largely because of management issues. If you cannot manage the property yourself, then you should consider hiring a trusted, professional property manager who has your best interests in mind. Happy investing.

If you have questions for Gwen about these issues or any Certitude Enterprises services, please email certitude.enterprises@gmail.com or call 1 (204) 272-9165.

GWEN TEWNION

Gwen Tewnion is the Vice President and a CEO of Certitude Enterprises in Winnipeg, Manitoba, a company specializing in property management and care, 24-hour tenant services, renovations, repairs, buy/fix/sell, and additional landlord and coaching services.

Gwen's goals are to help as many people as possible, to create win-win opportunities, and to provide peace of mind to both revenue property owners and real estate investors.

Prior to founding Certitude Enterprises in Winnipeg, Manitoba, Gwen had a successful career in various management roles within the hospitality industry as well as numerous years of experience in the day-to-day operations of successful businesses, customer service, and client satisfaction. She has always strived and continues to strive for excellence in all her endeavours.

She realized the kind of wealth that is possible from acquiring rental properties, which inspired her to over 13 years of leadership and experience in buying, fixing, holding, selling, and managing properties. She is an active, successful real estate investor, revenue property owner, and care manager for hundreds of revenue properties.

To learn more about Gwen and Certitude Enterprises, please visit www. certitude-enterprises.ca

If you have questions for Gwen or about any of the Certitude Enterprises services, please email certitude.enterprises@gmail.com or call 1 (204) 272-9165.

CHAPTER 11

How A New Immigrant Bought over 100 Doors in 18 months: A Success Story

BY LINDA PISANI ELDER

Go ahead! – "Tell me to quit 999 times, and I'll start again 1,000 times!!!"

I have a story that you will love… and in the process, it will ignite your dream, your passion, and your knowledge!

How badly do you want to reach your dream? How much passion do you have to chase after it? How much information and knowledge do you have about it?

If you could choose the people around you, would you like to be surrounded by positive, happy, healthy, and successful people or by negative, unhappy, unhealthy, and defeated people? Which of these will contribute to a better world?

Millions of people like to visit the United States for fun, education, and business. I came to the US with a three-month tourist visa wanting to become wealthy and successful.

Where to Start?

When I arrived in the US, I researched statistics and learned that 80% of the wealth in the US starts with *REAL ESTATE.*

I had three months to come up with a plan that would work, due to my visa! So, I started running the numbers and looking for markets with affordable pricing for single-family homes and robust activity in the market. Although I searched many markets such as Texas, Oklahoma, Mississippi, Tennessee, and Kansas, I decided to invest in Dallas, Texas.

In Dallas, in spite of my very limited English, I started talking to realtors, contractors, and brokers. Their questions were, *"What are your experiences in this market? How many properties have you already bought? What is your farm area? Which counties are you looking for?"* My dream screamed louder than my insecurity.

I had no idea what a county, school district, or farm area was. I didn't even have a Social Security Number or credit score. I had a heavy Portuguese accent that made it hard for anyone to understand. And, my answers shocked them, because I think outside the box!

People told me how difficult it would be for me to buy houses in the US. They said, "It's impossible!"

One by one, they shut me down. They didn't know about my passion to reach my dream; they didn't know about my healthy habits to achieve my goals.

Positivity and Persistence

How determined are you to reach your dream? Are you willing to realize all your dreams? How many "no's" can you take on the way?

I was very determined to pursue my Dream. Nothing or nobody could change my mind or convince me I couldn't do it.

I kept a positive mindset and thought, "PLEASE don't tell me how difficult it can be! Just give me one chance to start, and I'll show you what's possible!"

My Childhood and My "Why"

Most people see Brazil as beautiful beaches, landscapes, great food, and parties everywhere. True, we have all that; but we also have poverty and slums everywhere you turn. My town was quite poor and so was my family. We grew up without toys, money, and not much food.

My parents struggled a lot, and I thought, "If I don't work hard, I'll have the same life." So, I put money away from my childhood jobs, and thought about becoming a pirate. Instead, I moved away at age 14 to work my way through college. Every minute I wasn't studying, I worked.

My passion was to change the world, and it had to start with me.

I studied Spanish, which led me to a job where I could travel for my company. It was the first step into a different world. I lived in Argentina, France, Italy, Spain, England, India, and Thailand before coming to the United States.

Over the years, problems to me were just another maze, a new challenge to solve and I could easily see a way out. It was a gift. I learned that I was born to use it and could help others succeed.

Climbing My Mountain

In Dallas, I went to all the meetings: REIA (Real Estate Investors Association), workshops, and seminars. I did all the free educational stuff available in the area. I said to myself, "I don't need to pay for these classes. I'm smart enough to figure it out on my own. "Yet, I was still lacking the right knowledge.

Many contractors and realtors turned me down, until I finally met a contractor who was willing to listen to me. He soon became my partner and contractor. We worked together and did a few deals, and I made little money from it. Yet, he made three or four times more than me because he was charging me more than double the market price for every repair. Soon, I realized that wasn't the partnership that I expected.

I needed more knowledge and it was time to be humble and to get it from the right sources. I sought a mentor to give me the best education possible. Yes, I was willing to be taught, to be humble, and to be the mentee.

I found two wonderful mentors, Dennis Henson and Robert Elder.

"If you think education is expensive, try ignorance."

—Derek Bok

I found Dennis in the Dallas area and decided to take his full-year program, one that would teach me the rules for the American Real Estate Market and eventually change my life. He is such an amazing Teacher and Mentor that I ended up extending my visa.

The Risk

How bad do you want to reach your dream? Is your dream bigger than your fear?

I realized that Dennis's program cost me everything I had. I mean it literally cost me everything.

I agonized about how much I could do with that amount of money and how much I could make with the right knowledge and his coaching. I was determined to get this mentorship.

I'm glad I did, because that was the day that changed my life.

Within my first year, I did at least 10 times the money that I paid for the coaching, because I followed his advice.

There is a saying in India: ***"When the disciple is prepared, the Master will show up."*** I decided to be prepared, to recognize the masters that life presented me, to learn with them, and to accelerate my development in every area of my life.

I kept on working hard, even harder than before. I had lots of homework, classes, meetings, and seminars to attend while I was also working out deals. It was all worth it! **It completely changed my life!**

In one year, I closed more than 30 deals in three different states (Florida, Texas and Oklahoma). I also did overseas deals. I remodeled and held properties as rentals as well.

My Mountain Top

How big do you want to grow?

I'm really proud of my team. They understand very well my criteria and bring me very good deals every day. Because of them, I can evaluate a deal fast, send offers, put them under contract, close, add value by making repairs, and decide if I want to sell for a profit or rent for cash flow.

It's a win-win situation. We solve the sellers' problems, and the team makes money. My business grows in size, equity, knowledge, networking, and value.

Still at the Top of My Mountain

After all that hard work, **I can now see this amazing outcome that just keeps growing.** It is exciting, challenging, and very rewarding, because it reflects the seeds I'm planting as I mentor others to reach their dreams.

Allow me to share a little bit of what I do:

These are two examples of **how I put money to work for me instead of working for money** (all examples are in US dollars):

Example 1: Fix and Flip

I found this house that met my exact criteria: 1,600 square feet, 3 beds, 2 baths, 2-car garage, and built in the 60's or later. The starting price was $110,000. The seller marketed it for four months and could never close the deal because it would not pass inspection. I explained to the seller that it was impossible to sell the house under such a condition. They wanted to move fast, so they agreed to sell the house for $90,000.

I remodeled and updated the entire house with $26,000 in 30 days. Then, I put the house back on the market and the house was sold for $165,000 in ten days. I made $34,000 profit. Not bad for a Brazilian rookie with a thick accent and dreams bigger than the obstacles!

Numbers!!!

Fix and Flip Breakdown:		
Expenses		
Price of House	$90,000	
Finder's fee	$2,000	
Closing costs	$1,500	
Renovations (updating kitchen cabinets, granite countertops, appliances, AC, electrical, landscape, and front yard, all in 30 days)	$26,000	
Total Expenses	**$119,500**	
Selling Price		**$165,000**
Closing cost	**$11,500**	
Total investment	**$131,000**	
Net Profit	**$34,000**	

My mentor invited me to his mastermind, which I thought was too soon for me and too expensive. But, I went anyway. And, I'm glad I did. I met an experienced real estate investor from Oklahoma named Robert Elder, who had 600 rental units. He became my mentor, and we got married soon thereafter.

I ended up getting a long-term visa and learned from Robert how to invest in rental houses. I used all his information and coaching and ended up buying 10 rental houses and one apartment building with 84 units.

Here's an example of one of the properties in Oklahoma:

Example 2 : Buy and Hold

I found a house in poor condition priced at $50,000 and bought it for **$43,000**. I spent $20,000 on repairs so my final cost was $63,000. **The appraisal after repairs came to $107,000.**

My bank offered to lend me 80% of the appraised value, $85,600. But I only took the amount that I invested in the house $63,000. So, I ended up buying this property with no money down plus some cash in my pocket, including $440 per month in rental income.

See below breakdown:

Buy and Hold Breakdown:		
Expenses		
Price of House and closing cost	$43,000	
Repairs	$20,000	
Total Investment	**$63,000**	
Monthly Expenses		
Monthly mortgage payment (Principle and interest, 5.5% for 15 years)	$510.00	
Other expenses (tax, insurance, vacancy, maintenance, and management)	$250.00	
Total Monthly Expenses	**$760.00**	
Monthly Income		
Rents	$1,200.00	
Total Monthly Net Income		**$440.00**

Mentoring

I learned so much through my mentors.

Dennis Hanson saw big potential in me as a mentor and offered me to teach his program. My husband is a real estate coach; together, we created one amazing coaching program and masterminds that can lead people to a very successful life.

Here's one example that motivates me even more as a mentor. I was teaching about real estate, and this young lady came to me and said, "I had a dream to be a doctor, but I couldn't go to college because I need to work. Now that I know that I can substitute my active income for passive income, I'm buying houses and studying hard to go back to college."

A good mentor is someone who is successful now in the same business that you want to grow: Someone who can show you the way, save you time and effort, and give you some fun in the process.

Yes, Yes, Yes!

I am living the American Dream, because I had and have dreams and passion to do what I do. *"Yes*, it is possible!" *"Yes*, I make lots of money," and *"Yes,* I want to help others to achieve their goals and financial freedom."

How to Be a Good Learner

Are you motivated to reach your goals through using a mentor to increase your opportunities? Do you think a mentor is absolutely necessary to bring financial freedom? Do you want someone to help bring passive income to your life? Do you want to do it safely?

Here's what you need:

1. Be prepared to invest in yourself and take action. Yes, a good mentor's fee is high, and yes, it's hard to part from your money. Having a mentor is the safest and cheapest way to safely become wealthy.

2. Be willing to try the unfamiliar things. Be willing to take action, even if you're scared. Be willing to follow your successful mentor and take action, despite what others say.

3. Be willing to manage your time in order to improve your skills and step out of your comfort zone. It is important to understand that you must be willing to follow someone who has done what you want to do and to carefully manage your time.

So, let me ask you this.

How much money do you want to make?

How do you define financial freedom?

What kind of life would you like to have?

If you truly want to be financially free, here are your next steps:

1. Write down your goals…be very clear. For example, I want to make $100,000 in the next 6 months.

2. Educate yourself by reading books, attending events, seminars, and masterminds.

3. Connect with like-minded people.

4. Find yourself a mentor who is experienced and who has helped others in the past.

5. Put offers on as many properties as possible and learn to do your own due diligence.

6. Buy properties below market value that give positive cash flow.

7. Don't wait for tomorrow. Take action now.

> *"Don't tell me what happened in your life, tell me what you plan to do with it."*
> —*Linda Pisani Elder*

My mission is to help many men and women **rewrite their stories until their lives become their dreams. I often see people with a dream of making a million dollars so they can better take care of their families, but for whatever reasons, they just don't take action.**

Generally, it's the fear that stops them. Well, I have fears, I have doubts, and I have the "I can't afford it" syndrome. But the difference is that my dreams are much bigger than my fears. I take action when I'm scared to fail.

I know it's not that easy, but if you take action, if you follow your dreams of becoming wealthy, and if you truly persist, I'm here to tell you that you can do it.

I mean, if a new immigrant with a 3-month visa, little command of the English language, and no connections can buy 106 doors, so can you.

All you have to do is take the first step.

As I end this, I want to give you a special gift. It's an e-book called *7 Simple Steps to Your Real Estate Success*. In this book, you'll learn how to begin and grow your real estate business starting right now.

To grab your exclusive copy, go to www.millionaireinvestmentclub.com.

And, please feel free to contact me at Linda@MillionaireInvestmentClub.com.

Now, let's work on your dream.

Go ahead! – "Tell me to quit 999 times, and I'll start again 1,000 times!!!"

LINDA PISANI ELDER

Linda is passionate about life.

She was born in a small, poor town in Brazil and lived there until graduating with a degree in International Business. Afterwards, she eagerly traveled and invested abroad in Argentina, France, Italy, Spain, England, India, and Thailand, and now speaks five languages. A former financial planner, she currently lives in the USA, where she's a celebrated real estate investor and coach for groups and individuals.

Her passion is helping driven individuals achieve their dreams in finances, health, and happiness. She proves that investors can replace their working incomes with passive ones when given top-notch coaching in recognizing and leveraging opportunities.

Linda's background inspired her worldwide philanthropic efforts to bring opportunities, exposure, and knowledge to the world. She embraces big causes such as building ecofriendly high-rise housing.

She's eager to hear from you at Linda@MillionaireInvestmentClub. com. And, check out her e-book, *7 Simple Steps to Your Real Estate Success*, your special gift for reading Linda's chapter, available at www. millionaireinvestmentclub.com.

Peace, wealth, health, and happiness to all.

CHAPTER 12

Real Estate: The Fastest way to Retire Rich

BY SENJEY JOSHI

Everyone has a desire to retire rich and retire soon. We want **financial freedom**.

We'd all love to go on vacations and experience different countries, cultures, and people. We'd love to work on our own schedule, do things that makes us happy, and not be working at a dead-end job.

But, how many of us can realistically do what we want? Do we have enough money? Is there any reliable way to earn that money without being tied to a job we don't really want?

> *"Winners don't do different things,*
> *they do things differently."*
> *—Shiv Khera*

Benefits

Ask any self-made millionaire or multi-millionaire, and they'll tell you that investing in real estate is their secret to massive wealth.

I have decided to lay out 7 reasons as to why learning and investing in properties can be a life changing, especially if you're looking to become financially free with little risk.

1. Dependable Income Stream

One of the biggest benefits to income-producing real estate investments is that the assets are generally secured by annual leases. If done correctly, this can provide a regular and dependable income monthly. One needs to do careful due diligence prior to buying any properties to ensure they've taken into account all the expenses, such as mortgage payments, insurance, taxes, management fees, vacancy allowance, and upkeep. Also, ensure you've properly understood what the potential rents are going to be once you close.

2. Leverage

One of the most important characteristics of real estate investing is the ability to place debt on the asset that is several times the original equity. This allows you to buy more assets with less money and significantly multiply asset value. For example, you can buy a $5,000,000 property by putting down $100,000 or even less. Try that with your stock or mutual funds.

3. Debt Reduction by your tenant

If your rental property has a mortgage, your debt on the property will be reduced by the property's net operating income (NOI). This essentially means that within 25 years (or whatever the mortgage amortization is), your renter is going to pay you enough cash every month to pay down your mortgage for you. The trick is to never find a negative cash-flowing property.

When I deal with my clients or investors, I advise them to make sure that they are putting money into their pockets every month after paying all the expenses.

Of course, I've seen people who bought a break-even property or worse, a negative cash-flowing property.

WHY REAL ESTATE?

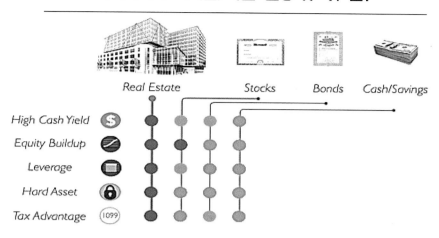

4. Inflation Hedge

Studies have shown that real estate investments have historically shown the highest correlation to inflation when compared to other asset classes such as the S&P 500, 10-year treasuries, and corporate bonds.

As countries around the world continue to print money to spur economic growth, it's important to recognize the benefits of owning good, income-producing real estate as a hedge against inflation.

Generally speaking, when inflation occurs, the price of real estate will also rise.

5. Physical Assets

Income-producing real estate is one of the few safe investment classes that has meaningful value as a hard asset. The property's land has value, as does the structure itself. And, the income it produces has value to future investors. Income-producing real estate investments do not have red and green days, as does the stock market.

Generally speaking, it doesn't matter whether people make a living by working as an employee, having their own business, or any other way…but most self-made millionaires make money by investing in properties either full time or part time. It is estimated that 80% of the wealth generated by successful people around the world is due to real estate.

6. Tax Benefits

The tax code benefits real estate owners in a number of ways, including no-limit mortgage interest deductions. It also offers depreciation accelerations that can shield a portion of the positive cash flow generated and paid out to investors.

When a home is bought, the Canadian Revenue Agency allows the buyers a provision to designate it a "like kind" instrument and defer all taxable gains into the future. (*See your tax advisor for a full explanation of all tax issues.*)

7. Appreciation of Asset Value

Although real estate has an up and down cycle, property prices go up in value historically. One of my clients who was worried about the real estate crash recently asked me if 2018-2019 is still a good time to buy properties. My answer is simple: Buy properties that give you monthly cash flow, and if the market were to soften, just hold on to the property and collect rental income.

Also, if you look at a couple of "real estate crashes" and just did what I'm suggesting (buy rental properties), today you would be wealthy. Whether you went through the 1990 crash or the 2008, if you had a mentor, he or she would have helped you get 3-4 properties. You would be a millionaire or more and making some amazing cash flow. Remember, you don't buy properties just based on appreciation. Although this is a great benefit, you buy it because it's a good deal and it produces income for you.

Questions

Hopefully, you're convinced that investing in real estate is a great idea for anyone. Whether you're a stay-at-home mom, single parent, young person, someone who's starting out, or a sophisticated business person, the time to start or buy more properties is right now.

Make sure to ask the right questions and do your due diligence prior to making any decision. Make sure to have a trusted team, including a professional agent, lawyer, inspector, financier, contractor, property manager, coach, etc.

Some of the questions that I get asked by my clients are:

Q. How Can I Invest in Real Estate Without Much Knowledge or Experience?

An older couple came to me and wanted to buy a second property, but other than single-family properties, they had no idea what multiplexes, triplexes, five-level back splits, or any other kind were. They had no experience investing in real estate and were naturally nervous.

I looked at their financial situation and found out that they could invest in a property with 3-5 apartments in the same unit because they would generate a lot more cash flow that way with no more paperwork or stress than buying another single-family home.

We found one that looked extremely promising, but the couple had no idea how to manage a rental, and weren't wanting another job, anyway. I knew of a great management company that would do most of the day-to-day dealings with renters, including advertising for renters, screening tenants, collecting the rent money every month, evicting tenants if necessary, doing maintenance work, getting repairs done when needed, inspecting the property, maintaining a good relationship with the tenants, etc.

The couple liked the idea that all the work would be done by the management company. (Who wants to get those 3 a.m. calls about toilets?) Of course, they really love the idea that their money would be deposited into their bank account every month.

Q. How Can I Invest When I Don't Have Much Money?

I like to educate people so they're very clear on the benefits of real estate, what the pitfalls could be, and how they can pick a plan that suits their individual needs.

I've had people approach me and say that they don't have any money, but wish they could invest somehow in real estate. I asked one couple how much they had, and they told me they had $10,000.

I told them, "I know another guy who has $10,000 – why don't you do a joint venture?"

They thought it was a good idea, so I connected them and told them to discuss it and let me know. They clicked, and the idea worked out. I brought in financing and had them sign. They split the title and the income. They were perfect strangers, but they loved the outcome so much that they came back to me and asked if they could do it again!

As time goes on and they grow in knowledge, they'll continue to invest, as many others have done who got started this way.

Q. I Can't Invest with Zero Money, Right?

There are several ways to invest, even if you don't have money. For example, if you have good credit, find a down payment partner and do joint ventures with each other.

If you can find a property considered to be a good deal, you may be able to assign (or transfer) it to an investor and make a profit.

You may be able to find a property owner who wishes to make a steady monthly income, but is fed up with his property or renters. He might do a 100% vendor take back (VTB) mortgage.

The most common one I usually come across is that people actually have money, but they don't know it or don't know how to structure it.

One time, a man told me that he really didn't have any money. I asked him, "Do you have a house, and do you have equity?" He did.

We got his house appraised, he refinanced his house, and he got a lump sum of money. I then helped him get qualified for an investment property. I was able to find a great property with good returns. After doing his due diligence, he bought the cash-flowing property and decided to use my property management company to help make the property a turnkey. He tells me how happy he is to collect a cheque every month while building equity. That too, without dealing with any tenant issues.

Q. Can I Acquire Commercial Property Without Buying the Franchise?

The short answer is yes.

I do a lot of work with commercial properties. There are three main kinds of buyers, and you have to know what they're looking for. Some of them want to buy the land or the property without buying the business, some want to buy the business without buying the property, and some want to buy both. And, some of them want to lease the property with an option to expand after 20 years of regular, predictable rent hikes every five years.

Q. Are Reverse Mortgages Good for Our Golden Years?

Well, I'm sure they're working for some seniors, but if you're thinking about a reverse mortgage, I have some questions for you.

What attracts you? Is it the idea of getting money every month, hands-free?

If that's what sounds good to you, real estate investing is by far is the best market-proven product, whether in commercial or residential.

I have other questions, too. Did you want to leave something for your kids? Also, what happens if you live a long time, which hopefully you will, and you run out of equity?

Let me make a suggestion for you. Instead of taking money out of your home in small, monthly drips, try taking a chunk of your equity and investing it in property. You can choose smaller rental properties or small commercial properties.

If you choose a good mentor, you can earn enough money, hands-free, to provide for your retirement without draining your home of equity. That way, if you live a long time (and I hope you do!), you'll still have something to leave for your kids. And, you'll have a steady flow of income so you can enjoy life, especially if you have a reputable property manager and advisors to help you.

There's one more advantage I want to reveal to you, and this is a tightly-kept secret. Investing in real estate can be fun! It might provide a second career for you, and one that you can put as little or as much work into as you want. It's freedom.

A reverse mortgage is good, but only for you. If you have kids or want to leave something for charity, consider the idea of investing in something real.

Always be careful, of course, and check with your CPA, but there might be tax benefits for investing that you wouldn't get with a reverse mortgage.

Your money is always either growing or shrinking, but it never stays the same.

Freedom and Energy

Financial freedom is one way to experience success.

Some think that retiring by age 60 from a good job and getting a gold watch is a success. Some think that being debt-free is a success. Others think that you have to have a certain set amount in assets or income to be successful.

To me, success means freedom. If I have enough income to make any choices I want, I'm free.

I know I have a certain number of gifts. I'm a good public speaker. I'm a coach and presenter, with the gift of convincing people as long as I know the subject. I love connecting with people so they can experience my energy.

Too often, we get trained out of our authentic gifts very early in life. If someone asks you, as a child, how you are, you'll answer honestly, "I'm sick." Then your parents and teachers tell you it's not polite. And you lose energy that way, trying to figure out the right and wrong of every move. You used to have enthusiasm, but now you have a caution.

When you're financially free, you get that energy back. But you can't become financially free if you have no energy, because money is energy.

When you have the right mentor to help you tap your own inborn energy, your world starts opening up. Since I know how to tap into my own energy, one of my gifts is being able to get other people excited about their financial freedom. It isn't really that hard to attain if you have the energy behind your desire. You can do it.

Whether you just want to be a private citizen with investments or you want to join a very enthusiastic team, I can assure you that you won't be disappointed in me. Whether you're looking to purchase your second, third, or multiple properties or to learn to be a professional investor, I can help you.

I want to give you plenty to think about in this chapter, but there's not enough room to tell you everything. So, I've created a cheat sheet of the 5 Most Pressing Real Estate Problems, and I want you to access it by going to Senjeyjoshi.com/freegift.

You can also reach me at SenjeyJoshi.com or email me at senjey.joshi@gmail.com

SENJEY JOSHI

New Delhi native Senjey Joshi moved to Canada in 2004 and became an accomplished, award-winning real estate broker, investor, community leader, and motivational speaker.

Senjey's multi-faceted, professional, and corporate experience includes business process outsourcing, construction, sports, and public services.

As a part-time realtor, he facilitated over 50 real estate transactions worth $40 million. As an investor, he owns seven properties and teaches investors how to buy below-market-value properties, renovate them, and rent them as a path to financial freedom.

Senjey's a featured real estate expert and was interviewed alongside of Jack Canfield (Chicken Soup for the Soul) in a Canadian Real Estate Wealth TV segment.

Senjey's definitive "Answers for the 5 Most Pressing Real Estate Problems" is free to readers at: SenjeyJoshi.com/FreeGift.

You can reach him at senjey.joshi@gmail.com or SenjeyJoshi.com.

CHAPTER 13

Always Play to Win: Never Give Up

BY PAUL LEJOY

"The number one skill in life," Bryant McGill said, "is not giving up." So true! Yet, how many people start, and how few finish?

The fact of the matter is that life is not easy. Not everyone was born with a silver spoon in their mouth. And even those who were born that way suffer from one setback after another. The key to real living is never giving up.

Life is like a marathon. And marathons have become popular these days. What do you see at the starting point? Throngs of people. Halfway through the race, the numbers start to dwindle as some people begin to give up. At the finish line, only a handful of the contestants make it. Why?

Why did most people give up? They knew that it was going to be a 26-mile run. Were they already defeated in their minds, even before they set out to run? What was it that made them fail to reach the finish line?

"In this world, you will have tribulations," Jesus told His disciples, "but be of good cheer, for I [and you] have overcome the world." Even God knows that we will have obstacles in life.

Parents birth children, knowing fully well that they will face obstacles in life. Yet, that doesn't stop them. You and I will face obstacles from within and without. Obstacles from our mindset and obstacles from our environment.

I love to watch basketball. Living in the San Francisco Bay area, I have taken a keen liking to the Golden State Warriors. Every year, a total of 82 games are played in the regular season. During the 2014-2015 season, they won a record of 73 games. But they also lost 9 games.

No team goes into a game to lose. They all want to win.

In the game of basketball, the teams that make the most wins are the teams that go on to play in the playoffs. During the playoffs, the teams that win the best of 7 games are the ones that go to play the next round. A total of 16 teams take part in the playoffs. At the end of the day, only the best team from the Eastern Conference will face off the best team from the Western Conference. Since 2015, only the Golden State Warriors and the Cleveland Cavaliers have reached that top spot.

The tougher the opponent, the more exciting the games.

In the game of life, you play to win. You will lose in some ventures and win in others. The key is to have more wins than losses.

No one applauds the loser. On the other hand, when you succeed, the whole world conspires to see you succeed even more. That's so true. Since the Warriors started winning BIG from 2015, they have become the darlings of basketball. Now, fans are willing to pay an arm and a leg to watch them play.

The number one skill in life is never to give up.

Here's a classic example: In the 2016 championship, the Cavaliers were down 3 games to 1 against the Warriors. They had lost to the Warriors in the 2015 Championship and could have easily been demoralized and given up because of that loss. Led by the venerable LeBron James, they equalized with the Warriors and indeed, went on and won the championship. That was the first time in 50 years they had won that coveted trophy, and James became even more popular and respected in his homeland.

History is replete with heroes that never gave up. These people knew what their purpose in life was, the reason they were born, and the goal they were brought to earth to accomplish. They never wavered from that goal.

Jesus is one classic example. He knew what His mission on earth was. He healed the sick, raised the dead, gave sight to the blind, fed thousands. Yet, His purpose was more than that. His purpose was to die on the cross and bring salvation to all mankind for generations to come after Him.

He faced immense obstacles. Here's someone who performed miracles such as no one before Him or thereafter had. He was revered and worshipped only to be denied, humiliated, and rejected by the same subjects that gave Him all the adulation before. Talk about obstacles, both internal and environmental! If He were an average Joe, he would have given up and abandoned His plan, but because He knew what His purpose was and embraced it even to the bitter end, He accomplished His mission, and today He remains indelible in the annals of history.

The problem is that many of us have virtually no clue what our purpose in this life is. We have not sat down to think why we were put here on this planet. We are merely existing, and that's not good.

Martin Luther King, Jr. (MLK) knew what his purpose in this life was. He witnessed the wickedness of racism and segregation and lived and died to abolish this sin for good. And boy, did he face a multitude of obstacles and tribulations! He could have given up, just like a lot of us do when faced with a daunting task.

How many people have given up on their spouses just because of one obstacle or the other? The divorce rate in America is sky high.

Life is tough, and the tougher the challenge, the more glorious the victory. Then how come we give up so easily? How come we don't try to work out a solution? How come we don't play to win?

Imagine if the Cavaliers had given up when they were 1-3 down. They could have looked at their loss in 2015 against the Warriors and mentally given up. They did not. Instead, they produced some of the best games and entertainment the NBA has given the world of sports lovers.

"Our greatest weakness," Thomas A. Edison once said, "is giving up." If Edison had given up, we'd all still be living in darkness today. Edison made 1,000 unsuccessful attempts at inventing the light bulb. When a reporter asked him how it felt to fail 1,000 times, Edison replied, "I didn't fail 1,000 times. The light bulb was an invention with 1,000 steps." A lot of us would have given up at the third attempt.

In his classic, *Think and Grow Rich*, Napoleon Hill tells the story of R.U Darby's uncle. He had a passion to mine gold. After he raised the funds to buy the machinery for this, he and Darby returned to the mine with the machinery, worked very hard, and had some success. But they faced some obstacles: the supply of gold soon stopped. They kept working hard, digging, but not finding. So, they sold the machinery for pennies to a Junkman, who then hired a mining engineer to examine the mine. The engineer calculated that there was a vein of ore only 3 feet away from where the family had given up. The Junkman went on and became one of America's richest men in his time.

The number one skill in life is never giving up.

Like Martin Luther King, Jr., Nelson Mandela also witnessed the injustices in his society and took upon himself the role and purpose of eliminating such wickedness. "Greater love has no man than one who lays down his life for others," Jesus once said.

Mandela laid down his life for all South Africans. He was imprisoned for standing up for what is right, 27 years in absolute isolation. Many of us would have given up when beaten once or twice, let alone taken to jail and knowing that we'd be spending the rest of our lives there.

27 years later, he was released from jail and went on to become South Africa's first black President. At his death, hundreds of dignitaries attended his funeral and today, he is revered as one of the most admired statesmen the world has ever known.

What's your purpose in this life? What's the one thing you could die for? Have you identified your raison d'être? If you have, live for it. Never give up.

Your purpose does not have to be as lofty as Jesus', Edison's, MLK's, or Mandela's. It could be just serving your community, your family. Not all body parts are the same. What's important is that all of them play a key role.

"Never give up," admonishes Jack Ma. "Today is hard, tomorrow will be worse, but the day after tomorrow will be sunshine."

Discover your purpose and how you can enrich others and live for it. That, my friend, is true wealth.

MLK delivered one of the greatest speeches in history on August 23, 1963 in Washington, D.C. Hundreds of thousands of people were in attendance.

His success did not start overnight. I am sure he faced enemies within. I am sure that, at some point, he looked at the daunting task at hand and doubted if he had the guts or whatever it'd take to end America's darkest era. But he would not listen to the naysay in his own head. He had to win that battle first. And we all know what external battles he had to fight to win the war.

Today, because of his vision, resolve, and tenacity, all Americans now have sunshine, regardless of one's race, color, or creed. And today, there's only one person whose birthday is a national holiday in the USA.

"Don't quit," says Eric Thomas. "You're already in pain. You're already hurt. Get rewarded for it."

What was MLK's reward? We'll all die someday, but how many of us will be remembered the way King is remembered, even if not to his scale? How many people will say about us, "This man, this woman, touched many lives and made a BIG difference in his/her community"?

Remember that success takes time. "Good things come to those who believe," someone said. "Better things come to those who are patient, and the best things come to those who don't give up…Giving up (therefore) is the best way to tell your worrywarts they were right all along."

Is that what you want to hear?

Isn't that's what is happening to thousands of Americans?

In 2012, I published my first book in the USA, entitled, *It's Impossible to Be Poor in America*. The book received mixed reviews. Some people loved it. Others loathed it, pointing to the millions of poor Americans they see every day. I see them, too. I see them living under the overpasses in San Francisco, Oakland, San Jose. I see them even in the smaller cities in the Bay area. How come? This is, after all, the land flowing with milk and honey. This is where kids can get jobs easily.

How come, then, these adults are living like this in the same society where others are mega-rich and in their 20's and 30's? How come some agents in my real estate firm are earning over a million dollars a year while others hardly make even $34,000 a year? They are all in the same company headed by me. They are given the same opportunity, yet they produce different results.

The key to success is never giving up in the face of challenges. Some of my agents have not identified real estate as their passion or made it one. They are simply existing. They are not living. They have given up.

Never give up.

I like this quote by Inspire99: "Never give up on something you really want. It's difficult to wait, but more difficult to regret." Some of my agents will live to regret. They will retire without any savings. Yet, those who seized on the opportunity and made it a passion will retire wealthy. In fact, my top two agents are only in their early 30's, and they can retire comfortably in their mid-30's if they so desire.

Never give up. "Weeping may last for a night, but joy comes in the morning." Faith, hope, and love are the intricate ingredients to success. You've got to know your calling, fall in love with it, and have faith that you can do it; hope will make it happen for you.

I know this for sure. Born in a poor, poor, super poor village in Cameroon, Africa, I find myself here in Silicon Valley, where the best of the best learn, live, and work. I find myself the founder of one of the most successful real estate firms in the area. Did this happen overnight, and did I face daunting tasks? You bet.

My first office was broken into and a ton of important stuff was stolen. At one point, I was a victim of fraud and my bank account was frozen. I have been circumvented by some of my agents. Some borrowed money from me and left my company. Others caused so much unbelievable pain and left me in huge debt. Besides these external/environmental forces, there's also pain that I brought upon myself because of poor due diligence on my real estate investments.

At the end of 2016, I felt like my skin was coming off my face. I had never been that stressed in my life. I know of people who have been in my position and killed themselves. Not me. Not when I have an entire village counting on me to make their lives better. Not when I see thousands of African youth dying at sea trying to cross over to Europe. I must live to make their lives better. To create a viable company that's profitable and can channel some of the profits to help educate and employ them and keep them in sunny Africa.

I have discovered my purpose and must live it in spite of the odds stacked against me. I must let the world know what my purpose is. I must work hard for it and see it come to fruition. Like MLK, like Mandela, I will not sleep until I see this happen. If I have to die doing it, so be it, but work hard, love it, and live I must.

That's how I want to be remembered, and I will be remembered as such.

Just say it. Just dream it, and it will come to pass.

Life is not easy. It's not for the faint-hearted. But we must never give up. Help is always on the way. "Never give up," says Harriet B. Stowe, "for that is just the place and time that the tide will turn."

"If you're going through Hell, keep going," said Winston Churchill.

"Fall seven times, stand up eight," said Albert Einstein.

Remember that "nothing worth having comes easy," per Theodore Roosevelt. Remember that "Winners don't quit, and quitters don't win," per Vince Lombardi.

Discover your purpose, live for it, and never give up.

You can reach me by calling 510-299-0093, emailing lejoy@lejoy.com, or visiting www.paullejoy.com.

PAUL LEJOY

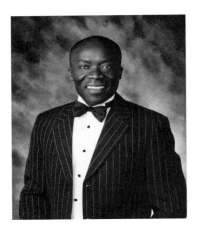

Born in a poor village in Cameroon, West Africa, Paul LeJoy is now the founder and managing broker of Pacific Realty Partners, a tech-heavy, investment-oriented real estate brokerage located in Silicon Valley, California. Paul's goal is to take his company national and create a firm that offers investors highly attractive returns and affords real estate agents predictable incomes.

Paul LeJoy is the author of It's Impossible to be *Poor in America, From a Mud Hut in Africa to Mansions in Silicon Valley,* and *The Top 7 Most Costly Mistakes I Have Made as a Real Estate Investor.* He is also a real estate wealth consultant, speaker, and mentor.

Paul has a burning desire to help those he left behind in Africa to attain the basic standards of life that bring dignity to the human spirit.

You can reach him by calling 510-299-0093, emailing lejoy@lejoy.com, or visiting www.paullejoy.com.

CHAPTER 14

Passive Income from Your House

BY MIKE BURGESS

Introduction

If you are reading this book, it's safe to assume you have a strong desire to generate wealth. Understand that money is not to be hoarded but rather used as a tool and provides choices. By having the right attitude and implementing the correct strategies, more money will come.

The majority of the population works an hour and gets paid for an hour. If they don't work that hour, they don't get paid. The wealthy have learned that true wealth is achieved through leverage. This often means a combination of leveraging their time, their money, their resources, other people's time, and other people's money to create their wealth. They have figured out how to invest an hour to be paid for 10, 100, or 1,000 hours.

Think about your dreams, or more specifically, all your goals. Will extra recurring income help you achieve them?

This chapter offers one scenario on how to begin building a foundation for achieving wealth. My first hand experience proves that this is a powerful strategy when starting out in the financial world. Also, what I'm about to show you can create a solid asset base and an income stream that can continue into retirement. Just building a rental suite in your house will not make you wealthy, but it can be an important component in achieving your goals.

This was a strategy I used in a couple of my homes when I was in my twenties. I understood and shared with others that the monthly cash flow from one additional rental suite equalled an additional week's pay each month. I chose to share my home with a tenant rather than try to find a fifth week in each month. This taught me early in life the true value of leverage.

Building a Rental Suite

I assume you are at a point in your life where you may have limited resources, but you have a burning desire to be wealthy and financial security is important to you. To save money, you may choose to invest a portion of your time in sweat equity rather than contracting out all of the required tasks. You may have to search for a property if you don't currently have a house that can be modified. At the same time, you have to plan and design renovations and search for your tenant. Remember that it is time well spent, because by choosing this path, you are creating a recurring monthly income stream for yourself.

Adding a self-contained apartment to a single-family home can be a vehicle for wealth creation and a powerful strategy for a first-time homeowner.

For those with a larger real estate portfolio, this can be another sideline where you can purchase a single-family house, renovate it, and collect an income from all the units.

This chapter describes an owner-occupied scenario but can be duplicated in numerous ways in which all units can be rented out. An example of this is a house I purchased in an R-4 zone, meaning it allowed up to four units. I remodelled this single-family home into three units. By simply installing a fire door, I created a large two-bedroom unit on the main level and two separate apartments in the basement. These three units created a dependable income stream.

This chapter will review the benefits and drawbacks of adding a suite to your home. You will learn the advantages and disadvantages of creating this income source and the important aspects of design. You will also learn some essential facts on criteria and structure and what to consider in choosing your ideal tenant.

Benefits

This is a great strategy to make a first home affordable by living in one part while renting out the second suite as a source of income or as a supplement to the mortgage or other housing expenses. Understand that for every monthly mortgage payment made, a portion is going towards building equity and adding value to your home, which helps to generate wealth.

Having a rental unit in your home may have some positive impacts on your income tax deductions. If this is new to you, I recommend that you seek the advice of an accountant.

If you follow through with this strategy, you will learn and develop useful skills and attitudes that you can draw upon when generating wealth in the future. Be careful – this can be addictive.

Challenges

The first impact you may feel is that when you use part of your home as an apartment, you forfeit personal space that you may have used for a family room, laundry, additional bedrooms, or storage. If parking is provided, then it may mean giving up or sharing some of the driveway.

Another disadvantage of creating a second suite within your home is that it may affect your privacy. If it is an owner-occupied situation, compromises often needs to be made with privacy and noise. This impact is to both indoor and outdoor spaces, as your backyard may need to be shared as well as your home.

Privacy and noise goes both ways. You may also have to modify your activities to respect your tenant's well-being. Make sure you protect your private space. Make and keep clear friendship and tenant rules from the start.

Remember that this is your home; you probably don't want to have an open-door policy. If you define rules and expectations from the beginning, things have a much better chance of running smoothly. It's much easier to establish rules in the beginning compared to taking away benefits from your tenant later.

Neighbours may not appreciate that your home has changed from being a single-family structure to having a rental unit with a second family living in your home, as it can change both the neighbourhood image and impact the density in the area. If you talk to your neighbours and have a good, established relationship, they are more likely to bring an issue to your attention rather than involve the authorities. It's often easier to solve problems when neighbours feel that you care about their concerns.

Tenants don't always respect property that is not theirs, so care of your home or pride in ownership is lacking.

Being close to your asset can cause some problems in that you are "living with your job." Tenants can feel that you are available 24/7, so they approach you without regard for your personal time.

The possibility of an increased insurance premium could be another disadvantage, but the income that you collect in rent will far offset this additional cost.

Structure

For many people, an unfinished basement is the ideal canvas to start a renovation. However, I recommend that the appropriate professional trades are consulted before starting any project.

For example, you may have a better understanding than others on identifying loadbearing walls, while others may have more knowledge of heating/cooling systems, ventilation, electrical, carpentry, millwork, etc.

Your own knowledge and experience will dictate if a general contractor should be hired to oversee the entire project or just portions.

Zoning and Codes Criteria

One of the first questions to ask is, "Do I have the necessary square footage in my basement or home to allow for an additional suite?"

Whether you already own a home or will be purchasing one, there is a variety of criteria you will have to meet. Zoning is an important one. Some municipalities recognise the benefits and allow homes to be modified with basement apartments. Other municipalities will not allow these apartments and can force you to remove any modifications you have made at your expense. It is critical that you follow the zoning bylaws and act within the scope of the law.

Additionally, there are building codes you will have to follow. One example of these is the egress. Egress is a specific minimum size requirement of the openable portion of a window. This allows a person to escape during an emergency. The dimensions (height and width) of the openings are specific and will need to be confirmed with your local authorities.

Here are some other building code examples, which may vary by jurisdiction:

- There are minimum floor-to-ceiling height restrictions.
- Entrance doors between the units must have a fireproof door tagged with the appropriate fire separation rating. These ratings are often 20-minute or 45-minute time frames of fire protection. The direction of the door swing, whether it swings inwards or outwards, may also be covered under the Code.
- Smoke detectors are required outside the bedroom doors.
- Carbon monoxide detectors may be required by code
- An exhaust fan in the bathroom may be required, but even if it isn't, it is a logical option to help reduce excessive moisture in bathrooms.
- Any stairs in place, whether they are interior or exterior, will require hand railings. Check the code for railing height, as this has changed over the years. Previously, lower heights were acceptable.
- Check HVAC (heating, ventilation, and air condition) systems to ensure the airflow is independent within each unit. This is a safety requirement to limit fire or smoke from travelling between units.

Adding insulation or a sound barrier between units is an additional expense and although it's probably not required, you may want to have it installed.

Design

When designing a basement apartment, many factors have to be considered. Unless you are prepared for an expensive extension to your house, you must work within the existing space or footprint.

Think about the type of tenant you are targeting, as a family may have different needs than a couple or one or two single people living in the same space.

Determine the optimal layout while considering how to take advantage of existing infrastructure such as plumbing. In laying out the design, determine where the kitchen and bathroom will be located. Once these are in place, then the number of bedrooms and the location and size of the living area can be determined. Note that the windows are not necessary for kitchens and bathrooms, but they are required for bedrooms and living rooms. Consider that the more bedrooms can generate more rent.

Cost

Earlier it was discussed that leveraging is an important tool in wealth creation. Consider your own skills and resources and leverage them to help you tackle this project and move you towards your goals.

Determine how your skills, knowledge, and hands-on work can reduce labour costs. What can you do yourself?

A general rule of thumb with most projects is that expenses are normally 50% material and 50% labour. Calculate what an hour of your time is worth and what an hour of time would cost you if a professional were hired to do the required tasks. If you calculate that you can hire someone to do the job for less than what you could make spending your time on another job, you should hire out that task.

Target Tenants

So, you've built a bachelor, one-bedroom, two-bedroom, or three-bedroom apartment. Who is your target market? If it's a bachelor suite or one-bedroom you've built, you are probably looking for a single person or a couple. If you build a two-bedroom, you're probably looking for a couple with a child or a single parent with a child. Consider that for every additional person living in your suite, there will be an increase in your water and hot water consumption, which means increased utility bills.

Decide if pets will be allowed. If they are, understand that they can create more damage and wear and tear. If local tenancy laws allow, charge a pet deposit.

There are different approaches to renting out the apartment:

1) Contact a leasing company who will advertise, co-ordinate viewings or showings of the apartment, screen potential tenants, and coordinate the lease and signing. The cost of this service is usually between a half and one month's rent.

2) The second option is to do all of these jobs yourself. Consider how knowledgeable and fluent you are with these duties. What advertising, people, and screening skills do you have?

Once the unit is ready and the tenant is found, the lease must be prepared and signed. Make sure the lease includes the name of the tenant, the rental terms, the amount of the damage or security deposit to be held, the amount and date the rent is due, and notice timelines. A boyfriend or girlfriend moving in can increase utility charges and noise levels and cause other problems. Are you knowledgeable with the local tenancy laws in your area? They do vary from one jurisdiction to another. What is the allowable damage deposit that can be charged? What are the laws in your area for a tenant paying their rent late, and what is the process to have them evicted?

There are a wide variety of real estate investor groups both local and national, that you can choose from and join. These can be found by Googling real estate investor Meetup groups. These groups meet monthly or quarterly, often organized by investors or agents who focus on income properties. The members generally consist of people ready to acquire their first property to investors with a large real estate portfolio. The networking can be invaluable and there is always something to learn.

Conclusion

This chapter covers the many benefits of investing time and resources into adding a rental unit to your home. The increased monthly cash flow will not only help pay down the principle on the mortgage but will also produce a forced appreciation in the value of your home. More importantly, it will increase your comfort level in leveraging the income as a landlord. Once this process is done and in place, you will be well-positioned to grow. You may wish to acquire multi-unit properties or branch out into other areas. You will be closer to generating multiple sources of income and realising your goals.

I wish you all the best in your wealth creation.

MIKE BURGESS

Mike has had the real estate bug for over 30 years. He has renovated countless properties and has focused on a buy-hold-rent strategy throughout his career.

For over 30 years, Mike chose to focus on buying, renovating, and renting apartments, and he currently manages his portfolio of multi-unit buildings in Nova Scotia. He's actively involved with various organizations within his community and contributed significantly to a positive cultural change within the neighbourhood.

He's repositioned and increased the value of his investment properties by stabilizing his buildings and improving the caliber of his tenants. Over the past few years, Mike has extended his investments to the USA and has acquired several Florida properties, where local property managers handle the day-to-day operations.

Mike has been found giving talks to real estate investor groups and has co-authored in best-selling real estate books.

If you wish to benefit from his experience, Mike offers coaching services for a limited number of students. Use the keyword "apartment" when applying.

For more information, contact Mike at mike@successbyburgess.com.

CHAPTER 15

The Hidden Gems in Real Estate

BY LURLINE HENRIQUES

Why Should You Invest in Real Estate?

The main reason you should invest in real estate is because it is a wealth creation tool that can take you to your 7 Figure Retirement.

You must define, however, where you want your real estate investment to take you financially. If you don't know where you want to go, you will not be able to foresee where I am taking you.

If you can't foresee where I am taking you, you will never get there.

First and Foremost

There are two concepts that are mentioned regularly in the successful investing world. Those concepts are diversification and asset allocation.

Both of these involve spreading your investments around to mitigate risk while trying to get a higher return that might normally be associated with safer investments. Real estate is often mentioned as a portion of a well-diversified portfolio.

When you own and operate a real estate investment business, you are in a position to do something that almost no other investment can do. Namely, you can reap higher than average returns with lower than average risk.

Before I get into the reasons, let me define very specifically what type of real estate investment I mean and what type I do not. There are three characteristics that must exist to meet my definition of high return/low risk real estate investing:

1. You own property directly or have an ownership interest in specific properties.

2. That property produces a regular income that exceeds your expenses.

3. You provide some level of labor or management necessary to run this as a business rather than as a pure investment.

Let's look at a rental property, for example. Depending on the size of the property, it can be purchased with 5% down and, in some instances, no money down, depending on your creativity.

While the renters are paying down your mortgage, your property is increasing in equity and at the same time you are gaining cash flow each month, which means that your income stream will also be growing over time. (This depends, of course, on how and where you purchased the property).

All of these factors act as a hedge against inflation.

Unlike the more typical items offered as inflation hedges, such as gold, real estate gives you an income while you wait. Gold just sits there.

Passive Real Estate Income Stream

Real estate is known to be far more passive than running a traditional business. If you hire outside management it will reduce your income stream somewhat, but that can make it even more passive. It is important to note, however, that it should never be 100% passive. If you have no idea what is going on with your real estate business, you've lost the safety buffer the business is designed to provide.

The income stream real estate produces tends to be extremely stable and predictable. Rents tend to rise over time and, even during tough economic times, they tend to be fairly stable. You won't find yourself wondering how much income your properties will produce next year. They should produce higher than they produced last year with the increase in rent or property expansion. If they don't, they are being poorly managed, and this must be addressed.

Rental properties, when purchased correctly, can generate significant cash flow. If purchased with 100% cash, the cash flow should be approximately 10-12%. These are very strong numbers. Remember that this doesn't take into account the appreciation of the property. This is just cash that you put into your pocket every year. If the property is purchased with 20% down, the approximate cap rate can be 8% and higher, again depending on the area of purchase.

The cash flow a property generates is the single most important thing about real estate investing. If an era of real estate investing offered no properties that could generate good cash flow, such as in the early 2000s, I would simply not be a buyer of any additional real estate in that environment. Keep in mind, however, those properties you already own will continue to perform as they always have, regardless of the inability of new properties to do so.

The reason this is so critically important is because real estate investing can be both stable and low risk. Refusing to buy properties that do not offer strong cash flow will keep you out of investment trouble. I cannot stress this enough.

Safe real estate investing revolves around cash flow. You should never purchase properties with appreciation as your primary objective. Your business runs on cash and cash flow, not on appreciation.

Cash flow is king!

Freedom of Time

Time is money; it's also one of the few things in life that can't be replaced once it's gone. Real estate allows you the freedom to enjoy your life while your properties are appreciating and providing you with cash flow.

One of the first things I will teach you as an immigrant investor is to create your business plan and then create an action plan.

Remember, you must change your actions in order to change your results. Your business plan will save you time because it will help you to avoid big mistakes. The last thing you want to do is work on your start up for a year, only to realize you were doomed to fail from the start.

Many real estate investors learn the hard way; they did not have enough money and did not seek out how to allocate additional funds prior to starting the business, or they took on partners with the wrong skills and resources.

Your business plan will help make you into a real estate investor and not a speculator. Your emotions should be counter-balanced. At times during your start up experience, you'll be manic, so passionate about your ideas you lose sight of reality. At other times, you'll be overwhelmed by doubt, fear, or exhaustion.

When your emotions get the best of you, having a business plan lets you step back and take an objective look at what you are doing and why, what you know for a fact, and what you are trying to figure out. Your business plan will make sure everyone is on the same page if you are working with partners, which helps to launch your business faster and smarter. Ideally, you'll have partners, so you can launch faster, smarter, and with less need to pay employees or suppliers. Even if you don't have partners, you may have family, friends, and advisers involved.

Your business plan will act as an action plan. At start up, execution is everything. That means you have to set priorities, establish goals, and measure performance. You also need to identify the key questions to answer, like:

- "What features do customers really want?"
- "Will customers buy or rent our properties, and how much will they pay?"
- "How can we attract customers in a way that's cost effective and scalable?"

Your business plan will indicate how you'll raise capital. If you raise or borrow money - even from friends and family - you'll need to communicate your vision in a clear, compelling way. A business with a business plan will raise twice as much capital as a business without.

Your action plan, on the other hand, will be focusing on where you want real estate investment to take you financially. Be specific about how this success looks. For example, how will you be spending your time? What exactly will your financial picture look like? Will you continue to work in your field, or will you live off the cash flow from your properties?

As with any successful journey, you need to know where you are going in order to get there, and that destination needs to be very specific. Set a realistic timeframe in which to achieve this success. Ask yourself:

- How long do I realistically believe it will take me to get there?
- What buffer of time do I have in case of unforeseen detours?
- Will I be disappointed if I get to my financial destination later than expected?

Leverage

If you don't overleverage your real estate investments, they will make you wealthy.

One of the greatest advantages of investing in real estate is your ability to use leverage. In finance, leverage is a general term for any technique to multiply gains and losses. In real estate, leverage allows you to achieve a much higher return on investment than you could without it. Real estate investing allows you to use leverage when you buy. It allows you to use it when you operate. It also allows you to use it across multiple tenants.

More than any other alternative investment, real estate is designed to take advantage of leverage.

Can you imagine what your banker would say if you came in and told him, "I want to purchase $1,000,000 worth of XYZ Company's stock. Will you finance 80% of it? I'll bring 20% to the closing table." Most likely, the banker would laugh and politely ask you to exit his office. However, that is exactly what bankers agree to every day when making loans to real estate investors.

When I first started in real estate investing, a wise investor told me, "If you use leverage to your advantage, it will make you very wealthy. However, if you take out too large of a loan on your properties, you will lose them."

I think that advice still rings true. If you use financing responsibly, you will be rewarded. The properties will produce positive cash flow and grow in value. However, if you take on too large of a loan on your properties and take all your money out, you run a high risk of losing them.

Let's take a quick look at how leverage can be used successfully in real estate investing. It is used three ways to create wealth and massive income:

1. **Financing Your Purchase**

    Real estate is one of the few places that if you buy something for $100,000, you need only a small fraction of the purchase price. As an immigrant, the banks will still lend you a significant percentage of the purchase price. They will finance it and allow you to pay them back over time. For example, if you had $150,000 to invest, you could buy a duplex for all cash that produces $12,000 a year in income. However, if you take the same $150,000 and use leverage, you can buy property valued at as much as $750,000. If the bigger property generates $6,000 a month in income and you subtract the loan payment of $4,000, you would make $2,000 a month. That is double what you would have made without using financing.

2. **Income Property Valuation**

    Investment real estate is valued by the income that it generates after subtracting expenses. So, if you raise income or lower expenses, you raise the income and value of the property. If you do both, it raises the value and cash flow even more. Depending on the property, this can increase the value 10- or even 12-fold. For example, an increase in income or a decrease in expenses of $10,000 in a year could increase the value of your property by as much as $100,000-$140,000. Small changes to the performance of the property over time can make you huge amounts of money.

3. **Multiple Tenant Principle**

    Investment in real estate with multiple tenants, like an apartment complex, office building, or retail center, allows you to maximize leverage. You can maximize your return by making small adjustments across multiple tenants, such as small adjustments in rent. With one apartment it doesn't make much difference to your income. However, when applied across multiple tenants, small changes can add up to create big results. For instance, let's say you own a 100-unit apartment complex. If you raise rents $10 per month, per unit, you actually create $1,000 a month in extra income. Just imagine what happens when one day you have 1,000 apartment units. You make the same $10 rent increase, but this time it increases your income by $10,000 per month. Making small adjustments across multiple tenants can increase your investment dramatically.

As you can see, leverage is one of the biggest advantages to investing in real estate. As long as you use it responsibly and avoid taking on loans that are too big for your properties, it can be your greatest asset. It can be accentuated by making small changes in income or expenses over time. These changes can dramatically increase your income and net worth.

My advice to you is that there are four things you must have to create wealth in real estate investing: (a) the mindset; (b) a system that works; (c) affiliation, and (d) the ability to take action.

Exit Strategy

The next step for you is to decide on your exit strategy, some of which are:

1. Buy-N-Hold – rent it out
2. Buy, Fix & Flip
3. Buy & Flip
4. Wholesale
5. Lease to own (rent to own)
6. Student Rentals
7. Etc. (There are many!)

The Hidden Gems

There are gems in real estate, but the Hidden Gems are the ones that I have been investing in for the last couple years. Why are these Gems hidden, you may ask?

They are hidden because you have to go out and find them. These are not listed on the MLS, they are not on Kijiji, they are not on Craigslist, they are not listed in the newspaper, they are not listed for auction, and there is no for sale sign. You simply have to go out and find them, so there is no competition and no bidding war.

These are properties that are discovered by "bird dogs." They're properties that are abandoned with no pride of ownership, properties that are left unattended for reasons such as divorce or death in the family, owners who have been moved to a nursing home with adult children who have no time to repair the property for sale, properties that are neglected, homes on pre-foreclosure, and the list goes on and on…

Another reason why these properties are Hidden Gems is because there is no other person placing an offer on such properties since they have not been advertised. When I find the properties, I place my offer below market price (maybe 50% below) based on the condition of the property. Then the negotiation starts. With properties such as these, all of the exit strategies can be applied. It is your decision.

Remember, real estate investing can be extremely profitable with the right coach, mentor, and/or joint venture partner who is experienced. Make sure to do your due diligence and buy cash flowing properties only.

To reach me for more valuable information on how to profit from real estate investing, please email me at lurline@TT&Tpropertiesinc.com or call me at 1-800-746-0449.

LURLINE HENRIQUES

Lurline Henriques left Jamaica at the age of 21 in search of more opportunities.

While in Canada, she put herself through school, raised three professional daughters, and built a great career with the federal government. She became a successful real estate investor, the award-winning author of 7 Figure Retirement: Real Estate Investment Strategies for Immigrants, and a real estate investment coach. A few years later, Lurline expanded her real estate business to Orlando, Florida.

Today, as she settles in to retire with a real estate portfolio worth over seven figures, she's helping you set yourself up for a wealthy retirement at any age.

Lurline volunteers with Kingdom Covenant Ministries, Junior Achievement of Central Ontario, and the Canadian Diabetes Association. Lurline is a member of Toastmasters International, Mississauga Board of Trade, Toronto Board of Trade, Central Florida Real Estate Investors Group, and several Meetup groups. Lurline is also a past member of the Real Estate Investment Network and Rock Star Inner Circle.

To reach Lurline for more information or assistance in purchasing cash-flowing real estate, email lurline@TT&Tpropertiesinc.com or call 1-800-746-0449.

CHAPTER 16

Passive Income: A Small Step Towards Wealth

BY KULJEET (KC) CHOUHAN

The most prevalent and earliest memory I have of my childhood is my parents always working, especially my father. He was an auto manufacturing worker, breaking his back doing 12-hour shifts up to 7 days a week. I never saw him, but we had money. Although we weren't rich, we weren't deprived of anything. I have observed their lifestyle for years, going to work, coming home, going to work again. Never had any time or energy to enjoy life.

> *"Whatever the mind of man can conceive and believe, it can achieve."*
>
> *—Napoleon Hill*

As a child, I knew I didn't want to live that way, but didn't know of any other option. My parents taught me to go to school, get a job, and work until retirement, which was the same concept taught to them. I didn't want to work all my life, but how would I keep money flowing in?

All throughout school, I took business courses. I knew I wanted to work for myself, but what would I do? Start a business? A retail store? A franchise?

At age 15, I was given an assignment by my high school entrepreneurship teacher. It was about how money, savings, interest rates, compound interest, and dividends work. I remember being very overwhelmed and a little angry because I had to do something that I had no interest in.

I realize today that I had no interest in how the money worked because I knew nothing about the topic. That assignment was the beginning of my journey to wealth. I began to realize that my money can make money without me doing anything.

Education: The More You Know, the More Powerful You Are.

At this point, I knew that I needed to learn more, but what, exactly? I didn't know. Someone recommended a book to me, *The Wealthy Barber*. I learned the fundamentals of starting to create wealth.

The first and simplest step is to start saving money by paying yourself 10% per paycheque first. It is a crucial step in creating wealth through a retirement fund, life insurance, and an emergency fund. It's the hardest part, because most people like to spend. It's hard to skip a vacation when you have $5,000 in the bank.

Becoming wealthy requires you to have good money habits and think of the future.

> *"I realize today that I had no interest in how money worked because I knew nothing about the topic. That assignment was the beginning of my journey to wealth."*
>
> — *Kuljeet (KC) Chouhan*

Learn How Finances Work

There are many kinds of passive income:

- Bonds and GICs (Guaranteed Investment Certificates)
- Mutual funds, stocks that pay dividends — Be sure to inquire about their DRIP

(Dividend Reinvestment Program)

- REIT's (Real Estate Investment Trusts)

- Annuities
- Book sales
- Rental income
- Revenue from being a silent partner in a business
- Vending machine rentals
- Storage facility ownership
- Licensing your intellectual property to others
- Royalties

I thought I had a plan. I would keep paying myself monthly, slowly creating that passive interest income, until I ended up rich, and then I'd spend the rest of the cash however my heart desired. I had a head start on my parents, and I'd set. Then, late one night, I stumbled upon a book, *Rich Dad's Guide to Investing: What the Rich Invest in that the Poor and Middle Class Don't.*

It changed my frame of mind, allowing me to see money from a different perspective. You never know when something will inspire you to change.

It helped me see that I was stuck in a rat race and that real estate can create passive income, wealth, and an escape. I got an understanding of how to handle money wisely and turn it into passive (residual) income.

What's passive income? It's an income stream that initially requires an upfront investment, a bit of nurturing, and a lot of hard work until it sustains itself and brings you consistent revenue without much effort.

From the book, I realized that paying myself was not enough. I could only put away a certain percentage of what I made without big sacrifices.

> *"Don't turn your hard-earned cash into trash."*
> *—Robert Kiyosaki.*

I continued to read other real estate-related books and attend free seminars to further my quest for passive income and overall wealth. I realized I still had a lot of learning to do before buying a property.

Know Before You Buy

When you get ready to purchase a house, there is a lot you need to know. For example, you'll need to know:

- The correct way to purchase a rental property and the legal clauses required.

- How to analyze the financials of an investment to see if you'll make a profit each month.

- How to read and create income and expense statements.

- How to keep track of money coming in and going out.

- Basic tax laws pertaining to rentals.

- Where to find tenants.

- The art of screening tenants.

- Where to get leases and applications.

- The art of keeping tenants in line and dealing with issues.

- The local landlord and tenant laws and procedures.

- The eviction process.

- Government-supported and other income sources such as disability, spousal support, and child tax credits. You'll need to know how they work because you'll rent to people who rely on these programs to pay their rent (and your bills). What happens if your tenant stops receiving them?

- Human rights and privacy laws, including what you can ask of potential tenants and how to properly reject their applications without infringing on their rights.

- Rental laws and bylaws in the local area: what's allowed and what requires licensing.

- How to maintain and repair your properties and all their components.

- Key items to look for when purchasing a rental property, like mandatory repairs (such as the furnace) and which cosmetic improvements will bring up rental rates (such as new flooring or paint).

When I first started investing, I didn't know these items, and I won't be able to teach you how to do them all in one short chapter. But, I can tell you this: Life taught me the hard way. You should get training so you don't make the same mistakes I did! (I'll show you how to get excellent, free training later in the chapter.)

My First and Second Properties

I had saved up a small down payment and was ready to buy a rental property. I told my father, and he was against the idea, predicting I would lose my money and go bankrupt.

He was scared; I was fearless. I didn't care if I lost – I wanted the experience. I took advantage of being young, and I knew I had time to recover.

My father wouldn't help me purchase the property, so I sourced out a realtor, a lawyer, and a mortgage broker. Together, we found a property. I crunched the numbers and signed the papers. At the age of 24, I had bought an 80-year-old house that needed work, but it had a separate basement apartment.

TIP: To increase cash flow, look for properties that have basement apartments or separate units to maximize your rental income from that property.

The ground level needed cosmetics, which was within my scope, and I rented to students. The basement needed help, so I kept it for myself. My mortgage broker helped me get extra cash at financing for repairs and upgrades.

Did you catch what I did? Because I lived in the basement, I was able to purchase the property as a principal residence, so I only put down 5% instead of the 20% required for rental properties.

After all the renovations were done, I had the mortgage broker refinance my mortgage, which allowed me to pull some money out and put it into a second property. I got another property with a separate basement, moved in, and rented the first property out completely. Again, I claimed the new property as a principal.

This strategy works great, but requires you to move every time you purchase another property.

I sold the first property about 2½ years later. I ended up making $30,000, not even counting what I made monthly in rent, which also paid down my mortgage. Not bad for my first investment!

The Motto for Acquiring More Properties: Be Brave

I never had this much money before! Mind you, I made quite a few mistakes along the way. But, I got to learn, an opportunity I would not have had if I'd held back. I was hooked.

Over the years, I continued to purchase properties. My criteria were sound properties that needed cosmetic work to bring up the value, and preferably single residential houses with side entrance basement apartments, duplexes, and triplexes. These properties maximize your cash flow.

TIP: Don't give into fear. If I had listened to my father's fear and advice not to buy, where would I be today?

Focus on a certain geographic area and become a specialist. Make sure the properties are within walking distance to amenities, shopping, transportation, schools, youth centers, and parks. Get info from realtors. Visit the EDD (Economic Development Department) at the local city hall. Specializing will help with travel time because your regular visits will be in the same town. Every market is unique, so get to know what's happening and changing.

My Power Team

I didn't do this alone. I had a great power team, which is definitely something you need.

Here's who you need to include in your power team:

- Real estate agents and brokers.
- Mortgage agents, brokers, and private lenders.
- An accountant and possibly a tax specialist.

- Lawyers for real estate matters.
- Paralegals for tenant matters and evictions to save money. Most people don't know this! Paralegals can save you fistfuls of money because you don't need a lawyer to do it.
- Contractor or handyman that can provide repair estimates & do the work.
- Other investors.

There is a difference between agents who are investment savvy and those who sell pretty homes with white picket fences. For your team, source out investment savvy people who work with investors.

When I Needed a Mentor

I got to a point where I could not come up with the down payment I needed. I was leveraged very high, and according to bank lending criteria, my employment income was not able to support more debt.

I didn't know that there are mortgage specialists who can use your passive income and other products to help you continue purchasing properties. I didn't know how to move forward at the time. Keep learning!

TIP: Put together a "power team" of professionals who will be there along the way to help you purchase the type of properties you're looking for.

Remember those free seminars I would attend? They're a good place to start, but I finally paid for a course that covered some simple, helpful techniques that I probably never would have learned without that course. This type of knowledge is not out there for the general public.

Another good thing about paid courses is that you get to meet like-minded people who want to invest. Imagine having your own network of like-minded people who have your interest in mind. They'll become your eyes and ears and help you find what you're looking for, so do the same for them.

I would get creative and look for tired landlords who would help me buy their properties in the form of a VTB (Vendor Take Back). They helped with a small part of the financing, usually the down payment, and that allowed me to get a mortgage easily.

Another strategy is to get the landlord to rent the house to me with the option to buy in three years. I would then rent-to-own it to someone else, who would purchase it from me.

Once you become more sophisticated, you learn to find good rental properties, put together a package, and do joint venture deals. My partner(s) put up most of the money, I did all the work, and we split the profits. It's a great way to increase your passive income.

Mentors Help Avoid Costly Mistakes

Do you really want to go to the next level?

The next step I took was to align myself with mentors, other successful people who have done what I want to do, but have gone A LOT further. I got as many successful people as I could to teach me the tricks of the trade.

I learnt important lessons like:

- The importance of networking and building relationships, and how to do it.
- Not to use your savings and how to source other people's money.
- Creative ways to unlock money that you might not think you can. You can even use retirement funds safely with the right mentoring.
- How to form strong power teams to get your results fast and securely.
- How to do "no money down" deals.
- How to buy properties with pennies on the dollar.
- How to find people who beg you to buy their properties.
- Advanced techniques that are not known to the general public, trade secrets that many lawyers are not even familiar with.

After working with mentors, I realized:

- Who better to guide you than someone who has done it already?

- Mentors also become your lifelong friends and emotional and spiritual pillars.

TIP: You can be creative in finding properties and financing when you have a great power team to advise you of legal work-arounds.

How to Learn More

I realize that even though a lot of material was covered in this chapter, I can only cover so much detail in the space provided to me. However, please visit my website at www.AleetInvestmentGroup.com, where you can find free reports designed to help you create massive wealth through passive real estate income:

There's a virtual bonanza of material waiting for you to claim:

- How to analyze the financials of an investment.
- How to read and create income and expense statements.
- Where to find and screen tenants, and the art of keeping them in line.
- How to evict legally.
- Due diligence needed to purchase a rental property, what items to avoid, and what items increase rent and value.
- Where to go for credit checks.
- Sample rental lease and application.

My students love these reports because they teach the art of passive income!

This journey of passive income gets as crazy as you want it to get. For some, it's enough to have one or two rentals to support their retirement fund or kids' education while they hold down regular jobs. Others may want to create $10,000 a month in passive income.

Remember: success lies within you. Don't limit yourself.

Thanks for reading!

To access your gifts, please visit www.AleetInvestmentGroup.com and select the ones you want. Also, you can reach me anytime at AleetInvestmentGroup@gmail.com.

Thank you in advance for reaching out!

I wish you all the success, and may you achieve the wealth you desire.

KULJEET (KC) CHOUHAN

KC's father was sent from India to Canada with $20 and a mission: support the family back home. And, while KC's parents were great role models, their rat race inspired him to dream of passive income.

KC defied his father's advice to avoid real estate, buying his first rental property at 24 and becoming a real estate investor.

When KC married in 2012, his loving wife shared his passion for real estate. In 2014, they combined their first names to creatively spell "Elite," forming the Aleet Investment Group, Ltd.

Their real estate investment company specializes in rent-to-own properties and creating passive income. They've grown to include wholesaling and property management services. They actively seek to help and work with buyers, sellers, and investors in a variety of opportunities.

To thank you for reading, KC created some in-depth, how-to articles to help you generate massive wealth, available at www.AleetInvestmentGroup.com; or contact AleetInvestmentGroup@gmail.com.

CHAPTER 17

5 Ways to Get Wherever You Want to Be

BY CHAI HARJO

This chapter comes from my mind, since I want to give you wise strategies and the things you need to know as you undertake your own real estate career.

It also comes from my heart, because it's an expression of something I genuinely love doing. I love real estate investing. That's where I made my mark, and for me, it's not only a vehicle to get me where I want to go, but a great way to have fun, too.

After all, my family and I sometimes spend our weekends visiting open houses for fun!

"When you think of it, you probably know where you want to go, but you really don't want the road to be a constant struggle."

— Chai Harjo

I simply can't get enough: the transactions, the inspections, the excitement that comes with that final closing. This energy and enthusiasm is what ultimately led me to begin my real estate mentoring and investment career – and, of course, my desire to provide a stable retirement for my wife and myself.

How I Unwittingly Became a Mentor

I started with one rental property, and had a small hiccup or two along the way, but ultimately, I was adrenalized by the whole thing. I couldn't wait to invest in another. Perhaps other people sensed my positive energy.

When friends discovered how well I was doing in real estate, they started asking questions. I started with discussions on how to do real estate investing with several close friends at my home and my rental properties. Then, more and more people were asking me how to start, so I had an idea to have a gathering in my basement. The first gathering was attended by 60 people, including seven speakers. The second gathering was attended by 80 people, including six speakers. I started thinking that I needed to find another, bigger, meeting room.

Strangely, I'm an IT professional by trade, but here I was, hosting more and more people and coaching them on my true passion, which is real estate.

From one property, my houses grew in number. The tenants kept coming, and for the most part, they were amazing tenants. I found that I was not only successful at this endeavor, but inspired. I was helping others grow successful in their own real estate investments as well.

People came to me for two primary reasons:

1. I had hands-on experience and added homes to my portfolio each year. This is what budding investors want. They want to know that you've been there, that you've walked the walk and not just talked the talk.

2. I gave everyone with whom I consulted unbiased, to-the-point advice. If I made a mistake, I would tell you and help you avoid the same one. If something works really well for me, I'll certainly let you in on the "secret."

This wasn't some marketing ploy or get-rich-quick scheme for me; it was simply sharing what I loved to do and my experiences with the people I mentored.

As the mentoring gathered momentum, I felt in my heart and in my soul that the next step was to write a book about these experiences, about what I think you need to do as you invest, and about some of the downfalls and victories that you can expect.

Shortly thereafter, I decided on a catch phrase to describe who I was – the Down-to-Earth Mentor.

Teaching people about real estate investing, truly comes from deep inside my brain and my heart.

Where Do You Want to Go?

In real estate, I'm often delighted with win/win/win situations. The homeowner is happy (whether buying or selling), the investor is happy, and I'm happy.

What brings me even greater joy is to mentor people who really want to go someplace special, but have no detailed idea of how to do it.

I don't know how you can get where you want to go if you don't already know where the destination is, so planning is key. Do you know what your goal is? Are there markers along the way?

If you have a goal of being happy, for example, you can get there immediately. Just look outside and enjoy watching a bird sing or a cat sleeping in a tree. Eat some cake. Cuddle your child. There's nothing to it – except for the other 24 hours in the day.

That's why we set goals. If we don't, then our moments of happiness are elusive. When you have goals, you have a way of measuring how happy you're going to be when you get there. Also, whenever you reach a marker, you already feel happy even though you're not there yet.

I'll give you my destination in the next section. Do you know yours and how to get there?

The Ritual of Creating Markers

I've been in real estate over seven years, and I've done many transactions representing multimillions of dollars. I create markers along my road, a plan, before I start the journey. Following this ritual is very simple, and very simple actions, repeated with intelligence over time, lead to massive wealth.

> *"Take breaks, meditate, and sip some tea. This may be the best advice I've ever given!"*
>
> *— Chai Harjo*

No matter where you're starting, highly successful or don't have a clue, this ritual will sharpen and simplify your focus. There's nothing sexy or mysterious about it, and having a mentor or a support group will help you stick to it.

I follow this five-step ritual faithfully, because I know it's the fastest way to get to my destination without going down side roads and getting lost.

1. Write down your goal.

State clearly what you want when you get to the end of the road. My statement was, "I want to have 10 detached single-family rental homes that are located within 70 kilometers from my principal home, all mortgage-free, by the time I reach 55 years of age."

As you can see, this statement doesn't have to be complex. It's just a way for you to keep from forgetting where you want to be by a certain age. It doesn't matter if you want two homes or 50 homes, and they don't necessarily have to be paid off.

> *"I don't know how you can get where you want to go if you don't already know where the destination is."*
>
> *— Chai Harjo*

In fact, you might not want any real estate at all so you can live on a boat. This is a very individual process, and I suggest you take some time and think about it.

You may have to revise your plan from time to time, but make sure you make your goal bigger, not smaller, so you don't fall into the trap of quitting before you reach the finish line.

2. Write a plan so you have markers along the road.

This is where a lot of people fall down in the process. I might want 10 properties, but if the first two are very difficult to get, I'll be tempted to downsize my plan or give up after I get the first two! You really don't want to do that.

When you create a plan, you create an immediate way to tell if you're on the right track or not. If you're not well on the way to reach the first marker, you'd better ramp up your efforts until you are, or the whole plan will go downhill.

This is a really good time to have support, as it's often the hardest part of getting started. Get a mentor, join a mastermind, or find some other support system. NEVER share your goals with someone who's going to beat them down.

If someone doesn't agree, acknowledge their input, but never discuss it with them again. This is not to say that you should ignore all advice, but if someone is clearly trying to talk you into giving up your dreams, you're in danger of letting their ignorance or negativity dictate your destination. Don't do it.

Here is my plan. I start by saying, "Here's what I need to do, with a deadline to get to each marker and a destination."

- 1st year
  - o Pull equity from my principal home.
  - o Find and buy a property that generates positive cash flow.
  - o Buy life insurance to protect assets (and update yearly if necessary).
  - o Create a Will and Power of Attorney
- 2nd year
  - o Pull equity from my principal home and my first rental property.
  - o Find and buy a second property that generates positive cash flow.

- 3rd year
  - Pull equity from my principal home and my two rental properties.
  - Find and buy a third property that generates positive cash flow.
  - Find and hire a property manager to manage my rental properties.
  - Start building my power team.
- 4th year
  - Pull equity from my principal home and my first, second, and third rental properties.
  - Find and buy a fourth and fifth property that generates positive cash flow.
  - Start a real estate mentoring business.
- 5th year
  - Pull equity from my principle home and my rental properties #1-5.
  - Find and buy the sixth, seventh, and eighth properties that generate positive cash flow.
  - Expand real estate mentoring business by creating a website.
- 6th year
  - Pull equity from my principle home and my rental properties #1-8.
  - Find and buy the ninth and tenth properties that generate positive cash flow.
  - Start a real estate investment group and become a public speaker in the group.
  - Start writing a book about my own experience investing in 10 rental properties.
  - Review existing life insurance and get extra coverage to protect assets if necessary.

- 7th year
  - Start co-authoring a book with one or more successful people.
  - Expand the membership of the real estate group.
  - Expand the mentoring business by offering different kinds of packages.
  - Start speaking publicly to bigger audiences.
- 8th year
  - Start writing another book to increase my credibility.
  - Become a Center of Influence.
- 9th year
  - Start writing another book with my power team to increase my credibility.
  - Become a Center of Influence of a bigger circle.
  - Start to engage in global public speaking.
- 10th year
  - Continue to pay down properties until they're all paid when I turn 55.
  - Enjoy life and continue mentoring because I love doing it.

This is a very simple plan, but you can probably see the advantage of writing it down. There is something stabilizing about predicting your own markers along the road. When your mind starts wandering and focusing on the next vacation or side road, your written plan will pop into mind. As you pass each marker, celebrate.

3. Persevere in reaching your goal.

Here are some really simple things to bear in mind when you're tempted to give up on your goal. Almost everyone faces these situations while trying to get where they want to be.

- Don't run away from a problem; deal with it, and you will grow.

- Take time to evaluate the problem and creatively find a solution.

- Don't hesitate to ask for help from other people who have more experience than you.

- Strengthen your resolve. Prepare to put in some time and work. Think often about why you want to get there, and how good you'll feel when you do.

- Develop the mental strength to persevere. Read a lot of books and listen to recordings of successful people and their wisdom.

- Get rid of self-doubt. If other people can do this, so can you. You're no better or worse than anyone else, and if you persevere, you'll find the way.

- Write down all the wins you've achieved, big and small. Keep lists of them, draw pictures of them, or put them in files, boxes, or bottles. Find the time to celebrate once in a while. When you feel discouraged, dump them out and have a little party reading about all the good things you've done.

- Don't get dragged down by the negative thinkers around you. These people are everywhere. They may be great people who sincerely believe that criticizing everything is somehow going to improve it. Just remember that being negative is like hitting your foot with a hammer before entering a race.

- Keep your mind and body healthy. I can't stress this enough.

- Keep things in perspective. Remember that you've done hard things before, and you've been successful before. You're just expanding your level of success.

- Stay true to who you are. You are your own best asset. No matter what happens, appreciate yourself. That will make it a lot easier to persevere.

- Take breaks, meditate, and sip some tea. This may be the best advice I've ever given!

- Ask the right questions. Don't think you're about to ask a dumb question. Just ask it. Do your research so you can ask more "dumb" questions, and eventually you'll be the wisest person in the room.

4. Keep investing in yourself.

There is no substitute for a good mentor. Pick someone who not only knows how to talk the talk, but someone who can (and does) walk the walk.

Your first mentor is going to be your inner voice, the impulse that guides you unerringly to your passions. Although I had a perfectly fine profession that earned good money doing work I enjoyed, the deep satisfaction I found in real estate was beyond logic.

Just as people shared their knowledge with me along the way, I help others, and the people I help will share their knowledge with the next person.

When we have our Indonesian Gatherings now, we have speakers on all aspects of real estate investing, from accountants to attorneys to mortgage advisors to insurance specialists, and so on. There is a wealth of information to glean, and finding a good mentor is like finding a vein of gold in a mine.

5. Keep it humble.

You're no better or worse than anyone else, so never hesitate to share and give your knowledge. What gives you the right to withhold your wisdom when people all around can benefit from it?

By the same token, give and teach, but do it as a humble offering from a grateful place. You'll benefit many people that way, and teaching will be a blessing to you, too. Your inner wealth is just as important as your outer wealth.

Each marker in your plan is like a street sign telling you where you are in your journey. Markers indicate that you're on the way to the joyous, free life you want to have.

In three short years, I've mentored over 50 people to financial success in real estate, and I love doing it. If you're ready to work on getting where you want to go, I'd love to help you get there.

I want to personally thank you for reading my chapter. Having a mentor is not truly an expense, but a wise investment in your future because you can leverage your mentor's experience. This is why I started mentoring.

The investment in a good mentor enables you to reap many benefits and returns beyond the mentor's fee. To thank you for reading my chapter, I'm going to offer you a complimentary one-hour mentoring session, available for a limited time at www.DownToEarthMentor.ca/Free-Gift. Or, contact me at onehourmentor@DownToEarthMentor.ca.

CHAI HARJO

Chai Harjo is the founder of Down To Earth Mentor, where he's been a real estate investor, mentor, speaker, and trainer in Toronto for over seven years, providing an honest and unbiased approach to the real estate industry.

Chai's passions are real estate and helping others create inner and outer wealth in a business they love. His area of expertise is single family, residential properties throughout Toronto and surrounding regions.

He's currently turning his successful "10-House Strategy" into a book, delivering valuable insight to aspiring investors about how the world of real estate can enhance their futures.

While his full-time career is as an IT professional, Chai's always been drawn to the real estate field and currently owns over 10 properties valued at over $5 million.

For a limited time, you can claim a free one-hour mentoring session, valued at $1,000 by visiting www.DownToEarthMentor.ca/Free-Gift or emailing onehourmentor@DownToEarthMentor.ca.

CHAPTER 18

No-More-Rent Program: Successful Implementation of Lease Options

BY HUONG LUU

Meet Jack and Janet

Jack's father died in April. His wife, Janet lost her job in May. By August, they had accumulated $35,000 in debt. This is a story about how one family was able to use a real estate strategy to get out of debt and get some extra money each month.

After a few months of living on one paycheque, and getting into more debt, Jack and Janet (J&J – not their real names) realized they needed to do something in order to get this under control. This was when I met J&J. We were at the Real Estate Wealth Expo in downtown Toronto. The music was blasting, thousands of people were there and I had a chance meeting with Janet. I was there to network and see what other consultants and investors were doing.

After they heard I had several properties and was investing in real estate full-time, we started chatting about their situation. This was when I mentioned to them, I do the rent-to-own strategy and was planning to do a few rent-to-owns in the next year. Janet was not aware of this strategy, and so we spent a couple of minutes talking about it. But as you can imagine with the loud setting there was only so much she could hear, so we exchanged details in order to touch base at a later date.

During the following weeks, Janet and I spoke over the phone about different real estate strategies, including the rent-to-own strategy. Janet expressed an interest to get to know a little bit more. So I directed her to my website (www.cashproperty.ca) where I have a few videos explaining the entire rent-to-own process which I'd like to call the "No-More-Rent" program. She was surprised such a strategy existed.

Taking the Leap

After some time assessing the feasibility of the rent-to-own strategy, J&J decided it was worth taking on. They were matched with a couple with poor credit scores looking to purchase a home in Southern Ontario. Both J&J and the future homeowner put down 10% each. This gave us a down payment of $85,000. This allowed the future homeowner to pick a home with four bedrooms, three baths, a finished basement and a two car garage. The monthly rent was $2,200 and after paying the principal and interest, J&J (the investors) would walk away with $300 cash flow each month.

As part of our calculations we used a stress test should the interest rate be double that of the current qualifying mortgage rate. At the end of the two-year term, the renters would have put down 10% along with covering all the fees. For J&J, after paying all the closing costs and admin fees, they would walk away paying off their $35,000 debt, while getting $300 each month in cash.

In order for this strategy to succeed, it is an absolute must the future homeowner's credit scores improve so they can qualify for a mortgage. I would work with them over the term to do this or they could have chosen another company to do this as well.

Open communication and transparency is also important for both parties to feel like they've succeeded and for both parties to know the risk and benefits that each side is getting for it to be a truly win-win situation. As part of the two-year timeframe, reports were provided to both the investor and to the future homeowner showing the down payment build-up to date and the amount to go.

As a consultant in real estate for portfolio growth and asset management, I find the rent-to-own strategy benefits more than just the investor, it also helps a family get into a home that they want.

9-Step Rent-to-Own Process

During one of our early meetings, we had a discussion about cash flow. What was negative and what was positive? And if there was ever a good time to carry a negative cash-flowing property. I explained to J&J that in a rent-to-own situation, there really is no reason for negative cash flow. Here is the 9-Step Rent-to-Own Process I use with all of my clients.

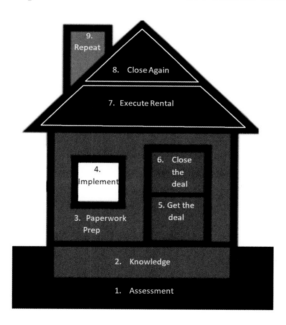

Step 1

In the case of J&J, the first thing we did was an assessment to see if investing in real estate was feasible for J&J. We looked at their risk tolerance, as all investments even in real estate have some risk. After looking at their assets, we were able to find a creative way for J&J to come up with their 10% down payment. As they were already in debt, they did not have 10% just sitting in the bank account to invest in a property.

So we came up with some creative financing to make this happen. They were able to pull funds from their RRSP and set up an RRSP mortgage, without tax penalties. As a real estate consultant, looking at the bigger financial picture allows suggestions and advice to be given as sometimes options are in the most unexpected places. If you want more information about RRSP mortgages, you can get it at www.cwt.ca.

Step 2

Step two was to look at the different types of real estate strategies that they would be comfortable with. Out of the 50 plus real estate strategies, not all of them would get to the end goal that J&J wanted, which was to be "bad debt" free. Once we determined what strategy would best fit their end goal, that was the strategy we focused on.

As part of the rent-to-own strategy, we provide both the future homeowner and the investor, a book about rent-to-own along with a binder of information. This information is vital for both parties to be successful in the program. Communication is transparent for both sides. Some of the information included in the binder is a checklist for the pre-moving in period; how to close successfully; and transitioning to your own rent-to-own property. Also, included in the binder are all the fees and the expected credit repair the future homeowner needs to do in order for the rent-to-own program to succeed.

A few things I do to help reduce the risk to the investor is ensure the family who is participating in the rent-to-own program is driven to fix their credit report and score, is capable of paying the rent on time, and has sufficient money for a down payment now and in the future. In the end, the investor does not want to have a property where they have to rent or sale. Also, by having the future homeowner pick their own home, this reduces the chances of them walking away. This is the house that fits their family's needs. We also have some requirements about the condition of the house, as well as making sure the future homeowner is aware of all the initial costs that they would have to pick up. This would include the appraisal; the home inspection; paying for the property tax and also the home insurance, not only the content insurance but also the actual home insurance. We make sure that the future homeowner has sufficient cash in the bank account to cover all these costs. We never encourage them to take money from their credit card or ask friends. Those are signs that they are not a good fit for the program.

Step 3

The third thing we did was to get their paperwork in order. This is done so that when a deal comes up that fits the criteria, we are able to act very quickly. It also ensures that we don't leave any details that would make the deal fall apart. The worst thing would be to get a deal that falls apart because we don't have the necessary paperwork or any supporting documentation. You can get a sample checklist of documents at www. cashproperty.ca/books.

Step 4

The fourth step was to implement the strategy. Sometimes this is done in parallel with step three, so we don't lose any time. With this step, we advertised and found a deal that fit the risk tolerance for J&J. This was all done with open communication through biweekly reports to J&J. Only deals that met their criteria were presented to them.

With J&J, I presented them with several rent-to-own options. They could choose to invest in a particular rent-to-own or wait until the next one. As an investor, they paid an initial registration fee to demonstrate that they were serious about participating in the program. A draft of the lease option and the tenancy agreement were provided so that they could seek independent legal advice. Any terms that they wanted to modify, of course, was open for discussion. These documents were also given to the future homeowner, as they also needed to get their own independent legal counsel.

J&J never met the future homeowner. But I did. I make a point of meeting the future homeowner, their children and all their pets. The family dynamics is one that I look for when I meet the family. I also look at their current setting to see their level of cleanliness and how well they treat their stuff. This is an indication to me of how they will treat the future home that they buy.

Step 5

The fifth step was to get a deal that made sense. Included in the step was screening the future homeowner and coming up with at least three different exit strategies. This could include changing from a rent-to-own, to buy-and-hold, flipping, or even bringing in a Joint Venture partner. In J&J's case, we looked at the worst case scenario, which is the future homeowner trashing the house. Even in this case, J&J would be ahead because the future homeowner would forfeit their down payment. J&J could turn around and either sell the property or rent it to another future homeowner.

Step 6

The next step in this strategy was to close the deal and get financing.

Getting J&J approved for a mortgage for the rent-to-own strategy was next to impossible. The regulations had recently changed such that investors are no longer able to get a mortgage from a traditional A-lender for a rent-to-own investment property. Private lenders were one of the options. As a real estate consultant, we have to resort to legal creative financing.

So here are the steps that we took to get the financing secured. It was vital that we found a lender that would allow a guarantor (in this case J&J) to be in the deal. The second thing, if possible, was to find a lender who would not put the guarantors on the mortgage. This way the investor would not have their credit report affected. The investor in this case is the guarantor. If the credit report shows a mortgage under the investor, this could prevent the investor from purchasing another property or getting access to more funds to make further investments. The other thing we do for each investment is open a corporation. The corporation is set up with a lawyer and the house purchase is made with this corporation as the buyer. The corporation is the owner of the mortgage. So although the investor(s) personally guarantees the mortgage, the mortgage does not show up on their credit report, but under the name of the corporation. Not all lenders will meet this requirement. As such, working with a mortgage agent is critical for this. And also knowing which lenders will instruct the lawyer on closing to put the mortgage and title of the property into the corporation is important to make this financially beneficial to the investor.

In J&J's case, we were able to access some of their RRSPs, and some of their home equity to fund a rent-to-own deal for them. We were also able to go to a private lender for the minimum amount so that they could still get cash flow.

Step 7

The seventh step was to have the future homeowner move in and execute the rental agreement. On the day of closing, J&J did not have to take time out of their workday to see a lawyer or to close on the deal. We took care of that for them. All the paperwork was signed electronically and sent to the lawyers prior to closing and the deposit funds were arranged with the down payment cheques made out to the lawyers prior to the closing. We went to get the keys from the lawyers and drove out to the property to meet the future homeowners. To this day, J&J have not seen the property or met the future homeowner.

On a monthly basis the future homeowner sends us an electronic transfer of the rent and top up. In turn, we send the monthly cash flow to J&J. Although this is an accounting nightmare, it works very efficiently. J&J never see the mortgage payments. All they see is the positive cash flow.

At certain milestones in the contract, we send the future homeowner special packages to keep them focused on the end goal of getting a mortgage and exercising their option to buy the property. Some of the special packages include mugs saying "*This is your home*" with a picture of the house. We also send them reminder cards showcasing their home.

Regular check-ins are also part of the process. Three and six months after closing, we did a check-in with J&J and with the future homeowner. If there had been a problem that came up during this time frame, which there wasn't, I would have stepped in and resolved the matter. Some of the issues that could come up could include late rent or unpaid bills like the property taxes, utility or insurance bills.

Steps 8 and 9

The next check-in will be at 18 months. At this time, we will initiate the process for the future homeowners to start looking into their mortgage application and get their documents ready in order to qualify for their own mortgage. Also, at this time we will start the process of getting J&J ready to release the property.

So with all the anticipated fees paid off after the day of closing, J&J can expect to make about $300 a month in positive cash flow for 2 years. In addition to that, they will make an extra $35,000 on the future closing date. In total, that is 99.2% return in 2 years (or 49.6% ROI/year).

To get details of the last two steps, visit our website at www.cashproperty. ca/books.

HUONG LUU

In an effort to help 100 families become mortgage free in 10 years, Huong created Project 100-10-10. She created the "No-More-Rent" Program to help families get into a home to grow their family. She also created a 5-Step-System to "Fire-Your-Boss" to help working professionals make every day feel like a Saturday.

Huong is a self-made millionaire through real estate and believes you can be too. Huong Luu, PEng, PMP purchased her first property while in University. Specializing in Buy & Hold, Lease Options, and financing, Huong has the ability to find options in every situation and to simplify strategies to help you be massively successful. Through her coaching, a positive mindset to balance work, finances and family are also achieved.

Looking for a speaker at your event or a mentor to guide you through your next deal? Always open to sharing ideas, Huong can be reached at huong@cashproperty.ca.

CHAPTER 19

Why Real Estate?

BY WILLIAM WONG

We are going to compare real estate to the stock market and show why real estate is the way to go if given the choice.

When I say stock market, I mean mutual funds, ETF (Exchange-Traded Fund), and individual stocks all grouped together in a category.

> *"If it wasn't hard, everyone would do it. It's the hard that makes it great."*
>
> —*Tom Hanks*

We will look at **3 key points** for why real estate is the better choice.

❖ How much you can buy.

❖ The increase in value.

❖ Access to your money.

How Much You Can Buy

Let's get started with a scenario.

Depending on what you have to work with, you can play with the numbers by adding, subtracting or just using ratios. Let's say you saved up, inherited, or won $50,000 and wanted to invest in something.

What could you do?

1. Start a business or franchise.

2. Lend it to someone and hope to get some kind of return.

3. Be one of the few to invest on your own and buy individual stocks of companies.

4. Find a financial advisor and they could set you up with some mutual funds that are available for them to recommend to you.

5. Invest it in real estate.

Most people would choose (4) simply due to the path of least resistance. All you have to do is put money in.

So how much in stocks/funds can you buy?

Take the $50,000 and divide it by how much it costs per unit or share price (ignoring commission, for simplicity). For example, at $10 per unit, you would be able to acquire 5,000 units. At the end of that day, assuming nothing changed in the market, how much would those 5,000 units be worth? Still $50,000, right?

Now let's put that same $50,000 in real estate. How much can you buy? First off, you could purchase outright a $50,000 home somewhere in the world. Generally speaking, you would have a mortgage.

Or, you could use the $50,000 as a standard 20% down payment, which is good for a $250,000 home ($50,000 divided by 0.20). At the end of the day, by investing in real estate, your initial investment is actually controlling $250,000; that is five times the initial amount of $50,000. This is what leverage is all about, unlike the stock market, which is typically a 1:1 ratio.

At this point, some savvy people may say, "You can leverage stocks, too, by buying or selling options," and, yes, that is true. But the average person will not go that route because you must be right in whichever direction you pick, otherwise you would be gambling and not investing.

Some might even say, "You can buy on margin for some leverage, too." Once again, that's true, but if the value you purchased on margin dips below a certain percentage, you would be required to bring in capital to top it back up. On the other hand, if the value of real estate goes down, you wouldn't have to top up the difference.

Let's look at a different perspective. When was the last time you saw your bank, or banks in general, advertise that they lend out money to buy stocks or mutual funds? Probably never! Can you guess why? I believe they know that the stock market is riskier than real estate; therefore, they don't want to loan you their money to put it into something risky. However, they will recommend you put your money in mutual funds, because they get to collect fees whether you make or lose money.

I mean, how often do you see ads for mortgages and rates? Probably way too frequently, right? I know a lot of mortgage brokers who are ready and willing to find money for you to buy real estate, but I've never seen a stockbroker find money for you to invest in the stock market.

How about this: Why don't financial planners recommend buying real estate? Quite simply, they don't get paid to. They can only recommend what their company has to offer. There may be some exceptions when they are fee-based advisors or consultants, since they are paid to be unbiased and actually look at what's best for you.

I am not trying to bash financial planners, bankers, or any professionals, but just look at how they earn their income; they have limited options and generally will not recommend something they won't get paid on. I know this because I used to be a financial consultant (one of my reasons for leaving).

Enough on this point. Let us explore the next one...

The Increase in Value

Building on our previous point, if you have the $50,000 in the stock market, what can you do to increase the value of it?

1. I suppose you could buy more shares of that company to inflate the price, but that would be silly. How much can one person buy to actually increase the value (unless you're a big shot like Warren Buffett)?

2. You can possibly get other people to buy into it.

3. How about hope and pray that it goes up in value? That is actually what most people do.

I'm sure we can all agree that there is little you can do to increase the value of your stock portfolio.

Now, let's look at real estate. What can you do to increase its value?

1. For starters, a fresh coat of paint could do it.

2. How about a new roof or kitchen?

3. You can possibly add a bedroom or even just some basic landscaping.

4. What about just having a tenant renting the home and creating cash flow? I bet that is worth something to investors looking for turnkey properties.

Would you agree there are many ways to increase the value of real estate? In fact, I could have a few chapters on that topic alone. While we're on the topic of increasing the value, let's compare the increased value of the stock market versus real estate.

To keep it simple, if your shares went up 10% in value, your initial investment of $50,000 will be worth $55,000, a gain of $5,000.

On the real estate side of things, the $50,000 investment that purchased a $250,000 property that went up 10% does not equal the same $55,000. The increased value is based on the property and not your initial investment.

Do the math: 10% of $250,000 is a $25,000 increase in value. The $25,000 divided by the initial $50,000 comes out to a 50% return. You may think a 10% increase in real estate value might be unrealistic in your market, but how about a mere 2%? That would give you the same return as the stock portfolio.

I hope you are seeing how leveraging real estate can compound your returns and why real estate is the better choice.

Let's briefly explore the negative side of things. If the stock value goes down 10%, your portfolio would go down to $45,000. Of course, you wouldn't be too happy, since you've lost some of your initial investment.

How about in real estate? If the $250,000 home value goes down 10% to $225,000, that's a big chunk. But wait, you still have your $50,000 though.

What's the worst that can happen in your portfolio? Well, the company you bought could technically go bankrupt and there goes your investment.

In terms of real estate, what's the worst that can happen? It burns down? Well, you've got insurance for that, and it will get rebuilt. Then, it's worth more, since it would be brand new again.

Let's look at the last point...

Access to Your Money

At some point, you would want to access the money you have invested.

How could you pull money from your stock portfolio?

1. One way is to sell it all and get the entire $55,000. When you sell, you could be subject to taxes and commissions, and what else happens? You just lost your whole portfolio.
2. You can sell a portion of your portfolio and the value will be reduced proportionately.

Looks like there are not many options for accessing your money other than selling.

How could you access your money in real estate?

1. Well, you could sell it and receive the difference after paying off the mortgage.
2. You can apply to have a secured line of credit against the property.
3. You can get a second mortgage.
4. You can refinance it and borrow up to a certain percentage of the value.

As you can see, real estate gives you more options. By taking a loan or refinancing, you keep the home intact. It doesn't affect the value of the actual home, and it's tax free.

I hope this chapter has given you insights on why real estate is a better investment choice. As a special thank you for reading this chapter, you can receive a free strategy consultation by reaching me at William@ progressivewealth.ca or www.ProgressiveWealth.ca.

"It's the oldest story in the world. One day you're seventeen and planning for someday. And then quietly and without you ever really noticing, someday is today. And that someday is yesterday. And this is your life."

— Nathan Scott

WILLIAM WONG

Born and raised in the capital of Canada, William has been through various industries from IT to sales.

He is direct and to the point, helping you find the one thing you need to focus on to achieve massive results. His goal is to educate people, change lives, and help maximize profits for businesses.

William is a problem solver at heart, an active investor with a handful of properties under his belt, including one that was literally no money down.

When he's not working on real estate-related activities, he is coaching business owners on how to be more profitable in their businesses.

As a special thank you for reading this chapter, William has agreed to offer a free strategy consultation to see what he can do for you.

Or, have a question for William? He can be reached at:

William@progressivewealth.ca

www.ProgressiveWealth.ca

CHAPTER 20

Why Passive Income Is Now Necessary to Survive Retirement

BY RINAY CHAND

> *"The key to financial freedom and great wealth is a person's ability or skill to convert earned income into passive income and/or portfolio income."*
>
> *—Robert Kiyosaki*

When you ask someone why they want more money, you will invariably get a multitude of answers. Some will say they want a bigger house or a faster car. Others may want to send their kids to college or to travel. Many may want to retire sooner, some may want to help secure the financial future for generations of family to come, and many want to generally help others in need. Regardless of the reason, when you break down all these answers to the core, the underlying desire is always the same—*freedom*.

More money equals freedom—freedom to travel, freedom to help your kids, your family, other people. Most of all, having more money allows you freedom and peace of mind.

What is Passive Income?

Most people reading this book already know what passive income is as a technical term. I want to explain what it means from a practical standpoint.

I can tell you from experience that the power of passive income is infinite. It can literally change your life, and if you are smart in the types of passive income you create, it can eventually allow you to retire faster and live financially and worry free for the rest of your life. The best part of passive income is that is it effortless. Once you establish a source, it takes little effort to maintain it. In most cases, it simply continues to pour in while you go about your life. It really does allow you to make money while you sleep.

Why Create Passive Income?

I have already stated the obvious answers to this question, but I want to hit home exactly why creating a healthy stream of passive income is much more than an option.

Today, more than ever, we are at a crossroads when it comes to our financial stability and eventual retirement. If you are lucky enough to have a pension through your employer, you know you have a reliable income source (assuming nothing happens to the pension fund), but current statistics show that almost 47 percent of Canadians aren't so lucky. This number is only growing for younger people entering the workforce.

Most Canadians are also entitled to the Canada Pension Plan (CPP), although the current payment is capped at approximately $1,100 per month. This maximum payment is also based on your earnings over the years, but does not increase even if your earnings rise dramatically.

In fact, the Canada Revenue Agency (CRA) set the 2017 maximum yearly income rate at $55,300, so even if you make more than this, you cannot contribute more to the CPP fund as a way to ensure you get more when you retire. And if you make less than $55,300, you will receive less than the capped payment of $1,100 per month.

While the CRA claims your CPP entitlement is actually only based on the last five years of your earnings, recipients quickly find out this is not entirely true. People who have been laid off or have large gaps in their earnings over the years may lose entitlement to the maximum payment.

According to the Fraser Institute, the average amount of return contributors could expect to receive in 1969 was close to 46 percent of the money they paid into the fund. In 2017, while the maximum amount you can receive is $1,114.17, according to the CRA, the average monthly stipend someone can actually expect to receive is $685.11, hardly enough to rely on, let alone retire on.

Canada also offers seniors 65 and older Old Age Security (OAS), a pension that has been around since 1952, although changes to the eligibility requirements state that if you were born after 1962, you cannot start receiving OAS until you turn 67. This change was necessary, according to the CRA because the number of seniors will almost double to 9.4 million by 2030.

OAS is based on several factors, including your annual income, your marital status, and how long you have lived in Canada. That being said, in 2017, the average amount you can receive is $578.53 with a cap on your individual income of $119,615. How many people do you know who can survive on this?

The reality is that more and more seniors will fall into poverty over the next few decades. You may be able to survive with a combination of government sponsored pensions, but I think most of us didn't work our entire lives simply to *survive* when we retire. I know I want much more.

As such, having a source of passive income is no longer a luxury—it is a necessity. In order to survive retirement, you need to be proactive, especially if you want to be able to help other people, be it family or otherwise. As avid flyers will attest, you must always secure your own oxygen mask first before you can help someone else. Planning your retirement is no different.

While each of us will have our own reasons for why we want to ensure we have a secure source of extra income, here are a few general reasons that will apply to everyone.

4 Reasons Why You Need to Create Passive Income—NOW

1. **Attain Freedom:**

    I mentioned freedom above, but it is so vital to our general wellbeing that it is worth mentioning again. Freedom comes in a variety of forms and can be different for each of us. While passive income creates peace of mind in the form of financial freedom, there are so many other ways it can bring you a sense of independence. For instance, when you have a secure source of income, you also have more time to do the things you planned to do when you retired. No longer shackled to having to make money through a paycheque, working 9-5, life suddenly becomes wide open.

Maybe you want to travel. Maybe you want to spend time with your family. If helping others is your dream, passive income can open the door. Whatever your retirement dreams, having passive income allows you the freedom to do so. Nelson Mandela put it best when he said, "Money won't create success, freedom to make it will."

2. Grow Financially:

You've likely heard the saying, "money begets money." When you have extra money—money that isn't all going to pay bills and keep you going month-to-month—you can use that money to invest in other money-generating options.

For instance, once you have a rental property that is generating stable income, you can use that property to buy another one. Those two properties can then help you invest in other opportunities or buy more properties. Passive income allows you to take advantage of investment opportunities you wouldn't otherwise be able to even look at. As your financial portfolio grows, so does your ability to create even more passive income. If you are smart and do your research, you will always have a source of income at the ready. And it all starts with just creating just one source of passive income.

3. Attain Stress Relief:

We all live with stress in this fast-paced world, but knowing you have a secure, ongoing source of income can eliminate one of the biggest stressors most people endure. More and more, science shows that stress can cause a slew of physical, emotional, and spiritual issues. In fact, according to studies, up to an amazing 90 percent of all visits to physicians are for stress-related complaints.

If you have ever been stressed over money, you know exactly how much it affects every part of your life.

When we are stressed, we can become depressed, angry, apathetic, and physically ill. The kicker is that the more stressed we become, the less productive we are and this, of course, can affect our ability to show up to work and make the money we need. The only way to break the cycle is to find a way to create secure income that works for us even when we can't, and that is exactly what passive income does.

4. **Pursue Your Dreams:**

Most of us have dreams of what we want to do when we retire. They are what keeps us going when the daily rat race becomes a chore. Simply thinking about all the things you'll do when you're finally able to leave the daily grind is a powerful motivator.

But what happens when you are nearing retirement and you don't have the money put away that you thought you would? What if you want to retire earlier?

Living paycheque to paycheque is certainly not going to allow you to retire in the lifestyle you dreamed about. In fact, for some people, retirement may seem like a pipe dream or even a nightmare if they don't have the resources they need. Well, once again, passive income can assure you are set when you decide to retire. And if you start creating passive income today, you may even be able to retire earlier than you planned. How would knowing you could retire anytime you want change your life? What are your dreams? What if you could start living them sooner? Would you? The beauty of passive income is that it gives you that choice.

So, why are more people not generating passive income? The short answer is that they don't know how, or they have a skewed sense that you have to have a lot of money to create money. While having money can certainly help you create passive income faster, there are countless ways you can start creating passive income today, even if you don't have a lot of extra disposable income. Here are a few steps to get you started.

4 Steps to Creating Passive Income

Part of the reason the majority of people don't even attempt to create a steady stream of passive income is a lack of extra income. For example, while investing in an income-generating property obviously takes some money, it doesn't have to be your money.

One of the biggest mistakes you can make is "waiting" until you have enough money to invest before you consider looking into a source of passive income. Time and opportunities will pass you by when there are other viable options. So, with that in mind, here are 4 steps you can take today to start generating passive income.

1. **Find a Good Mentor**

   One of the best ways to learn how to do something is to simply imitate the behaviour of someone who has already done what you want to do. A good mentor can help you in a variety of ways. Maybe you need someone to help keep you motivated or teach you how to best invest your money for a good source of passive income. A mentor can be anyone you admire and respect. If they have already accomplished the goal you want to reach, they will also know the pitfalls you should avoid. This can save you both time and money. Having someone who can guide you with your best interests in mind is invaluable.

2. **Forced Savings**

   According to a 2016 survey by the Canadian Payroll Association (CPA), almost 1 in 4 people (24 percent) don't think they would be able to scrounge up even $2,000 if they were faced with an emergency in the next month. In fact, nearly half of all Canadians are currently living paycheque to paycheque, making any thoughts of retirement by the age of 65 a fantasy.

   The problem is not that people can't put the money away; it's when they have a paycheque in hand, it is much harder to justify putting it into a savings account when you think about all the things that money can buy you in the moment. So, the solution is to force yourself to put a specified amount away, be it 5 or even 2 percent to start.

The theory is that what you don't see, you don't miss. There are a number of ways to do this. In some cases, your employer may have a program in place. You can also set something up with your banking institution where they can automatically transfer a portion of your paycheque into another account. If this is the route you choose, it is a good idea to have the money placed in an account that makes it hard for you to withdraw money immediately, thus lowering any temptation to dip into that account.

3. Put Some Extra Money You Get into Your Savings

Treat any extra money you receive, such as your income tax return, GST payments, or work bonuses, for example, as savings. If you can automatically put this money away, it will add up in no time. Any money you get beyond your regular paycheque is an opportunity to save. Add this money to your forced savings account, and you'll have the money you need to start generating some great streams of passive income.

4. Leverage Other People's Money

If you don't have the capital to invest yourself, there are plenty of people who are looking to invest with someone who is willing to do the work. Investing in an income property is not only a wonderful way to secure a steady stream of passive income, but it also builds equity to invest in more real estate.

Some joint venture partners may want to split the risk 50/50 or even 60/40. The money you save through your forced savings accounts and your bonuses and tax returns may be just enough to attract an investment partner and get you started with your first investment property.

You may even be able to find someone who is willing to put up all the money in return for a large payout if you are willing to do all work, such as renovating a fixer-upper. The point is that a lack of initial investment money should never deter you.

Whatever way you choose to create a source of passive income is up to you. The important thing is that you start doing it now. We live in a time when we simply can't rely on pension cheques or government benefits. And even if these sources come through, they do not guarantee you will be able to live the lifestyle you dreamed about.

Retirement is supposed to be the reward for all your years of hard work. It should be a time when you can do whatever you want, go wherever you want, or simply do nothing and relax in the home you built for you and your family if that is what you want. The point is that whatever you choose to do, it should be a choice you can make without having to question if you have the resources to make it. Passive income can give you that freedom.

RINAY CHAND

Rinay Chand has a passion for helping as many people as possible. He knows that God has put us here for a reason—to help Mankind and leave behind a legacy to be cherished forever!

In 1995, Rinay immigrated to Toronto from the Fiji Islands & began his professional life as a Dental Assistant. He quickly realized this wasn't for him since most people associate dentistry with pain and he wanted to bring happiness to people.

When his parents bought their first dream home in Canada, they insisted that his name should also appear on the title to the property. So, at 19, Rinay got his first taste of owning real estate.

In 2005, he jumped into the real estate industry. Rinay began to attend numerous courses on positive thinking, personal growth development, real estate investments and financial freedom. He also began to network with the Robert G. Allen Group and now Rinay is the co-founder of Elite Training Pros, a company designed to educate and help real estate investors achieve their financial goals.

You can reach Rinay Chand at:

RINAY@ELITETRAININGPROS.COM

WWW.ELITETRAININGPROS.COM

CHAPTER 21

How to Get Started Investing In Real Estate

BY DENNIS HENSON

Have you ever tried to solve the Rubik's Cube? The Cube looks easy, but it's not. All you have to do to solve the Cube is begin twisting the sections around until the colors are the same on all sides. However, you will soon realize this is not as easy as it seems. In fact, it is extremely difficult, and I have never been able to solve the Cube myself.

Personally, I don't have the patience to work on a puzzle for two or three days. I've tried solving the Cube using the instructions and made a little progress, but even with the instructions it's still extremely challenging.

What has the Cube got to do with investing in real estate? Well, real estate investing and trying to solve the Cube are very similar. Both are equally difficult to master, even with instructions.

There are various ways to invest money, and I have listed a few examples below that allow you to receive a return on your investment.

Bank CD's

Stock Market

Mutual Funds

Bonds

Stock Certificates

Bank Certificates

Over The Counter Investments

Then, there is investing in Real Estate.

If you were to go to a bank to invest $10,000 in a Certificate of Deposit (CD), how long would that take? Just a few minutes! You simply fill out the paperwork, they take your money, and your CD starts making money for you. To buy stock, you sign up for a Brokerage Account and whenever your account is activated or funded, you can begin trading on the internet. You can buy whatever you want in just a matter of seconds with the click of your computer mouse.

Real estate investing is not as simple as the other types of investing I mentioned above; plus, there can be some risk.

Your bank investments might earn you 5% if you have a good year. If you have a great year in stocks, you might make 10%. Last year, with my mutual funds, I made 20%, but that doesn't happen every year. A successful year in real estate could earn 100% to 500% or more. There is really no limit to your earnings, if you know what you're doing.

Types of Real Estate:

Raw Land

Commercial

Hotels

Apartments

Duplexes and Fourplexes

Single Family Homes

To Get Started In Real Estate Investing,

You Must First Choose the Right Path

I do not recommend starting out with commercial real estate because it is very complex, and you're talking about investing a larger sum of money. Investing in commercial real estate takes a lot of skill and knowledge. Normally, being a new investor, you might not have the skills needed to become successful if you want to invest in commercial real estate.

Other types of real estate include raw land, hotels, apartment buildings, duplexes, fourplexes, and single family homes. Out of all these—single family homes have the highest supply and demand. When starting out, it is easier to begin with simple – then, move up.

There are a few things you're going to need before you get started investing in real estate in order to actually work this business. You're going to need your time, energy, motivation, knowledge, car, cell phone, and office supplies.

Things You Will Need

- Time
- Energy
- Motivation
- Knowledge
- Car
- Phone
- Place to work
- Computer
- Cellphone
- Maps
- Access To Money
- Vaulting System
- A Good Team

Carleton Sheets, a well-known real estate investor and national speaker, speaks of a blind woman who is a real estate investor. She does not have a car, nor can she drive. She reads the classifieds in Braille, and buys real estate property over the telephone. She has a team that completes her contracts, and she has been very successful with her investing.

For today's investing, you need a computer and a cell phone. My cell phone has an app that allows me to record anything. If I am in my car driving around and I see a house where all the bushes and grass are overgrown and the home looks abandoned, I can easily record my thoughts on my cell phone, and send out a letter to the homeowner later that day. When I see a sign that reads "must sell," I'll stop and take a picture and call the number when I get home to find out if they are really motivated sellers.

"Evaluate My Deals" Tells You What To Offer"

The comps on a property will allow you to understand what the properties are worth all fixed up, or the ARV (After Repair Value). If you try to invest in a property without knowing the ARV, you're going to lose your shirt, so that's a critical element. Next, there is a fantastic software program called "www.evaluatemydeals.com," which is an investing tool with a format similar to Turbo Tax. Evaluate My Deals asks you for all the pertinent information. You simply fill in the blanks, and it gives you a summary report.

"Evaluate My Deals" also tells you exactly what you should bid on a property and allows you to print out a report in a format you can take to your banker or mortgage company. Read more about "Evaluate My Deals" on my website, at www.dennisjhenson.com.

Put Together a Team

- **Mentor**
- **A Real Estate Attorney**
- **A CPA or an Accountant**
- **One or More Realtors**
- **Bankers, Mortgage Brokers, Investors**
- **A Title Company**
- **An Insurance Agent**
- **Realtors**

Every Real Estate Investor Should Put Together a Great Team of Professionals

The most important team member is your coach or mentor. Most professional sports stars, like Tiger Woods, have coaches. Whether you are a new investor or have experience with investing, you should hire the services of a coach with a proven track record that will keep you moving towards your goals.

The second most important team member is a real estate attorney, someone to keep you out of trouble, help you set up your business, and answer your legal questions.

The first attorney I had was not a real estate attorney and it created many problems for me because he couldn't answer my real estate questions. It is important to find a real estate attorney who knows the laws in your state. Also, it would be helpful to find an attorney who owns a title company. You should work out a deal where they answer your legal questions, and in exchange, you will bring all of your business to their title company.

The third most important team member is an accountant to help with taxes and your company structure.

Realtors are critical members of your team. You'll need at least one realtor that will help you even if they will not profit from it. You will also need several other realtors that are always looking for deals for you because they know you're serious about buying. You cannot have too many realtors working for you because someone else is paying them and that is a great situation for you.

In order to help you become more successful, you need access to money. Form relationships with bankers, mortgage brokers, friends, and other investors.

Find a title company that you enjoy working with. All title companies will work with you, but you need a close relationship where you can request timely closings or have some other business handled quickly.

A super team will have an outstanding insurance agent ready to handle all your needs.

You want your properties in the best condition, ready to rent or sell at all times, and finding the right people to help you with your properties is very important.

That is just the tip of the iceberg for your team members, but all the above members are critical. If you don't have any of these people I mentioned, you need to find them as soon as possible. Create a list of team members and contact numbers.

Let's Start Investing

- **Pick an Area**
  - **Choose Some Zip Codes**
  - **Mark a Section of a Map**
- **Set Criteria**
  - **Number of Bedrooms, Bathrooms & Parking**
  - **Square Footage, Age & Price Range**
  - **Extras**
  - **Pools, Spas, Etc.**

Teaching you how to invest in real estate is a lot like trying to teach you how to swim. You have to get in the water to learn how to swim. I can give you all kinds of advice about swimming, but until you actually get in the water and try it, you're not going to learn. You will end up with a lot of knowledge and theory, and very little practical experience.

If you really want to get started in real estate investing, you've got to make offers. Let me repeat myself. If you really want to get started in real estate investing, you have got to make offers. Here's how to get started: pick an area that isn't too large if you're just beginning. I purchased a house that is far from where I live, and another house one block away. I'm going to make about the same profit on both properties, but if I had it to do over again, I would buy two houses a block from my house. The reason I like to have my investment properties close by is when something goes wrong, I do not have very far to go to check on the properties.

You should pick an area in a nice neighborhood with well-kept homes. Take a map and circle your area. Soon, you will be driving around in that neighborhood recording your thoughts about the houses you see that might have possibilities, and then you can contact the owner and start making offers.

It is important to know what kind of properties you want to buy.

How many bedrooms, bathrooms, what size garage?

Range of square footage?

Knowing your criteria will save you a lot of time and money.

After you know the "what" and "where" of your criteria—you need to know the "how"—how are you going to find these houses? There are a lot of ways to do this. Some examples are: Contact "For Sale by Owners," run ads in papers, mail to foreclosure lists, look for empty homes, find real estate owned by banks (REO), check out Housing & Urban Development (HUD), Veteran's Administration (VA), property auctions, and do probate research at the courthouse. Make friends with bankers and have them call you to let you know when they have foreclosed and taken back a property.

You can work any one of these markets exclusively, and they will produce great deals for you, but you need to fine tune your skills.

Decide on Strategy

- **Contact "For Sale by Owner"**
- **Ads in Papers (Theirs and Yours)**
- **Foreclosures**
- **Empty Homes**
- **Real Estate Owned by Banks (REO)**
- **Housing & Urban Development (HUD)**
- **Veteran's Administration (VA)**
- **Property Auctions**
- **Probate**

You can work HUD, VA, or other property auctions. I once believed you couldn't make any money working public auctions, but one day, there was an auction near my house and I decided to go—hardly anyone showed up because it was raining. It was a $200,000 house that sold for $109,000. It was then I realized that you can actually make money on auctions. If I had been prepared, I would have bid on that particular house. You need to be prepared in advance and have the funds available if you are going to make bids.

You should try several different types of investing to see what fits you best. Many of the homes I purchase are HUD homes—I have a system in place now where my assistant and realtor do most of the work. All I have to do is decide what to bid on and how much I should offer. I choose the properties and my assistant prepares the documents. I decide what to bid and have the realtor complete the bidding process. I am able to purchase one to two HUD houses each month by using this system.

Research

- **Locate Promising Properties**
- **Make Owner Contacts**
  - **Ask "WHAT" Questions to Find:**
    - ➤ **Determined, Motivated Sellers**
    - ➤ **Properties With Possibilities**
- **Do Research**
  - **Determine After Repair Value (ARV)**
  - **Visit to Check for Needed Repairs**

You should decide on the best strategy that is right for you, and then master it. If you want to try something else, do your due diligence first, but only after you have conquered the first strategy.

Remember the "W H A T" Questions

To master speaking with home owners and realtors who want to sell their property, you should call and actually speak to at least three people every day. To do this, you need to locate ten to twelve properties that meet your criteria and contact them. Out of ten calls you will likely reach about three. As you are making contact with the potential sellers, you should ask them the "W H A T" questions.

What are "WHAT" questions?

W - *What is it worth?*

H - *How much do you owe?*

A - *Asking price?*

T - *Tell me why are you selling?*

When you make or receive a call on a particular property, the "WHAT" acronym will help you with your communication. ***Remember—you are only trying to determine if you want to go see the home.***

When you ask a seller what the house is worth, they'll answer you immediately. When you ask the seller what they owe, they may tell you it's none of your business. If the person on the phone will not tell you the balance of their mortgage, they probably are not a motivated seller.

Actually, they have saved you valuable time. However, do not write them off just yet. Keep their number, and remember to call them back in two or three months. Time has a way of motivating people to become more motivated.

On my website, www.dennisjhenson.com, there is an excellent form for screening prospects. I recommend you get this form and use it when you make calls. It will help you determine whether the seller is motivated and if the property has potential.

After you have found a couple of properties, go see them and run comps to find After Repair Value (ARV).

During your visit to the home, have the seller show you around. This will give you time to complete the repair form found in Evaluate My Deals. Be sure to communicate with the seller how much it will cost to bring their property up to the ARV.

Make offers that, if accepted, will insure you a good profit.

Please pay close attention to what I am about to tell you because here is where you will start making money. The key to successful real estate investing is *making offers*.

If you make offers that, if accepted, will insure you a good profit, how could you lose?

A friend of mine once told me she was trying to buy a home worth about $90,000 but the sellers were asking $100,000. I told her to offer them $70,000. There was silence on the phone. Then, she said the seller would be insulted by that offer. I told her that if that is the case, I must insult 30 – 40 people every week.

If you're going to become a successful real estate investor, you will offer what a home is worth "to you." And you will have to do so with a straight face. Because if you offer more—you lose.

At first, the seller may be shocked—but they may really need to sell the property. They could be sick and just stopped caring. They may be getting a divorce and never want to see the house again. They may have inherited the property and it has been nothing but a big headache. Maybe they have moved and are paying two mortgage payments. Or, they just want out. When these things occur—or any number of other things—sellers become motivated to sell and if you make an offer to purchase—they will sell you the house at your price.

This is why HomeVestors is able to buy hundreds of thousands of houses every month. They make lots of offers because people have problems.

Another way to make offers is auctions like HUD, commercial, or bank auctions. Auctions make making offers easy—you just place your bid and wait for the results.

Make Deals

- **Make Lots of Offers**
  - **This is a Key to Success!**
  - **Make offers that—if accepted—will insure you receive a good profit from your investment**

- **Negotiate With the Sellers**
  - **Price**
  - **Terms**
- **Get Signed Contracts**
  - *"Verbal offers are not worth the paper they are not written on."* **Carleton Sheets**

If you make a lot of offers, sooner or later one of them will be accepted.

After you have invested for a while and make your name known as a real estate investor people will begin calling you instead of you calling them. Their calls might go something like this: "I'm going to be foreclosed on within a few days, and the bank will take my house. Can you help me?" Or they might say "I really need to get out from under the payments for my home and heard that you might be interested in buying it." Additionally, you could offer $1,000 as an incentive to help them with their moving expenses, and many times they will accept.

Part of what you should learn is how to become a negotiator, because the better you get at negotiating with sellers, the more money you'll make. You need to be able to talk the talk and walk the walk with the sellers to make deals that work. Another thing you should learn is how to locate these motivated sellers. The more motivated they are, the easier it is to work out a profitable deal.

Once you make an agreement with someone, you should get it all down on paper and get a signed contract as soon as possible. If someone agrees to sell you a house at a really good price, don't leave it up in the air. Get them to sign a contract so they feel committed to you. If you delay—someone else might come along and offer them another $500 and the sale will go with them. Get a signed contract at the time you agree on a deal—so the seller will feel committed to you.

Before you are ready to close, have the title company give you a copy of the closing papers because almost 100% of the time, there will be mistakes.

There will be mistakes.........

While you are searching for homes to purchase, or while you are finding homes you want to make offers on, you should also be looking to find the money needed to buy the properties. To do this, you will need to start making contacts with people and institutions that have lots of money. Finding the money is equally as important as finding the deal. If you do not develop the skill of finding money, you will soon find your efforts may be wasted. The skill of finding money is a major key to your success as a real estate investor.

Prepare

- **Get money together**
  - **For the down payment**
  - **For closing costs**
- **Prepare for and go to closings**
  - **Have title company prepare documents**
  - **Inspect closing documents for errors**
- **Take ownership**
  - **Do fixup**
  - **Start the marketing process**
    - **To rent**
    - **To sell**

You're going to need money for a down payment and closing costs. Many people don't realize that when they buy a $100,000 house, it's not going to cost them $100,000. It is going to cost $105,000 to $107,000 due to additional costs for the title and mortgage companies. The title company will prepare the paperwork, close the purchase, and record the documents. Choose a good title company, and give them the contract immediately, so they can begin to prepare the closing documents.

Remember, the title company will do all the work for you—*but right before you get ready to close, have the title company give you the closing documents so you can go over them and uncover any mistakes. About 100% of the time there will be mistakes and about 95% of the time those mistakes are not in your favor.*

Make sure you look for any mistakes in the closing documents because every time you find a mistake, you've put money in your pocket.

The IRS is going to Eat Your Lunch if You Buy a House and Sell it Before a Year.

You've bought the property, gone to closing, and the property is yours. Now what!? Well, this is when your work really begins because you own an empty house and the longer it sits there, the more it's going to cost you. The number one cost in the real estate investing business is "holding." Before you purchase a house you should have a plan in mind. Don't just buy a home and decide what to do with it later. Some options include: rent it, "rent to own" it, retail sell it or wholesale it. Always have a plan in mind before you purchase a home.

Some people think investing is buying a house, fixing it up and selling it and making $20,000. That is not investing. Investing is when you go to the bank and put money in a CD and keep it for five years.

If you want to invest in real estate you've got to put your money in and let it grow—and it grows by renting it out or selling it to someone over a long term by helping them improve their credit and selling it to them after a year.

Why do I say after a year? Because—*the IRS is going to eat your lunch if you buy a house and sell it before a year. They're going to take a big chunk of your profit.* If you hold it a year and a day, then you're what the IRS wants you to be, a "long term investor," and your tax rate takes a big drop.

Now—what if you are cruising along, renting your houses and one year, you decide you need to buy and sell several houses? The IRS could decide that you're not an investor anymore, but now you are a dealer—they're not going to give you any of the investor's tax breaks. My point is that it is very important that you enlist the services of a good accountant and attorney for your team. Your team will help you avoid many of the pitfalls experienced by most new investors.

Success is Like Starting a Fire

- **Starting a fire requires**
  - **Fuel**
  - **Oxygen**
  - **Ignition**
- **Investing Success Requires**
  - **Fuel = Good Deals**
  - **Oxygen = Money**
  - **Ignition = Your Energy**

Now, we've come through the entire process. Let me give you a little formula to take with you. Getting started investing in real estate is like starting a fire. You have to have three things to start a fire—fuel, oxygen and ignition. To get started investing in real estate you need fuel (good deals), oxygen (money), and ignition (your energy). You must have all three or the fire will never burn.

"You Are Going To Become What You Think About."

Go out and look for deals and MAKE OFFERS, MAKE OFFERS, MAKE OFFERS.

Also, finding money is very important. You can find people with money who will be happy to work deals with you if you look for them, but you must work hard on finding money the same as you did finding the deals.

Remember these three things: ***Good Deals, Money and Your Energy***

Now, get busy and go out and find the deals and the money and make it work.

Also, never forget that continuing education is very important to your success in this business. You need to be consistently listening to different CD's and programs whenever you are driving to make good use of your time. Keep bombarding your brain with real estate and you'll do fine. Read something every day. Make these things a habit, but if you want to supercharge your success in this business, the easiest way to learn is by employing an experienced real estate mentor.

There are two ways to acquire knowledge and those are (1) learning from your own mistakes or (2) learning from others' mistakes. To learn more about how to find and what to look for in a mentor—visit www.dennisjhenson.com.

Don't give up, keep on moving forward and learn all you can.

You have to think of this as an entirely new job. You need to work on this at least eight hours a day just like you would any other job and, if you don't, you'll probably never make it as a big real estate investor. If you just want to invest $100,000 of your own money you can use these techniques and go out and buy one or two houses and over the years the property values will grow and you will make money, more than you could in any other way.

You're going to become what you think about, so if you think about being at home and watching TV—that's where you will find yourself. If you're going to become a real estate investor, you've got to think about real estate investing. You've got to think about it all the time. If you focus your mind on real estate investing success and hold on to that thought—everything will begin to fall into place. One day in the not too distant future, you will arrive at the destination you desire.

For more information and educational materials go to www.dennisjhenson.com.

DENNIS HENSON

Dennis Henson is the President of Vanguard Marketing and Investments, Inc. and the AREA (Arlington Real Estate Association of Investors.) He is the inventor of "EvalutateMyDeals.com," the author of Becoming Wealthy in Real Estate. *An Investor's Guide to Riches*, and other books on real estate investing.

An expert at controlling property for profit without taking title with over 45 years investing experience, Dennis specializes in single family real estate. Owner Finance, Probate, Private Money, Rent to Own, Land Contracts, Foreclosures, Land Trusts, and learning how to design Creative Financing are a few subjects he offers. He stays on the cutting edge by actively seeking out and teaching the latest innovated real estate ideas, and has guided thousands of new and experienced investors on how to take their business to the next level. Examples of his training can be seen at http://dennisjhenson.com.

CHAPTER 22

Real Life Report Card

BY VICTOR M. QUACH

What is Credit? What is a Credit Score?

According to Investopedia, *credit* is a contractual agreement in which a borrower receives something of value (such as money) and agrees to repay the lender at some date in the future, generally with interest. Financial institutions are not in the business to teach you about the power of credit. They are in business to make money selling their products and services.

The Banks make their money by charging interest on the loans or lines of credit you borrow. It is your responsibility to understand your agreements and how to manage what you borrow. In this chapter, I will teach you the basics of how to leverage the credit system to grow your wealth.

We live in a credit-driven world, and without highly effective credit, it is difficult to take advantage of wealth-building opportunities when they present themselves to you.

> *"Here is the rule about borrowing money: Borrow money only when you can use those funds to make more money."*
>
> *—Victor M. Quach*

A common line of thinking is that we should save money until we can afford to pay for a house. While this may work, it can sometimes take a long time to save up enough money. Why not use a proven system to get into the real estate market earlier?

Utilizing real estate is an investment vehicle that more than 85% of millionaires use to grow their wealth. Our goal is to have a great financial report card that will make it easier for banks to lend you large amounts of money that you can use to build your own fortune through investments.

A *credit report* is your financial report card. Your *credit score* essentially is a grade on your financial report card. It summarizes how well you have met your financial responsibilities to lenders and managed the money you borrowed through means such as credit cards, lines of credit, and loans.

A higher score typically shows that you are more likely to pay your loans on time, making it easier for you to receive loan approvals and lower interest rates.

Some Important Truths and Myths About Credit:

Credit truths:

- You are allowed one free credit report per year from each credit bureau.
- The credit system is a forgiving one - no matter how bad your credit score, you can always repair and rebuild your credit to get the rewards you are looking for.
- Over 90% of declined credit applications in North America are due to an error in the credit report.
- Having a high credit score does not guarantee your approval.
- By leveraging the credit system, you can build wealth.

Credit myths:

- If you request your credit report too often, your credit score will drop.
- The less credit you have, the higher your score.
- You should only have 1 or 2 credit cards.
- Cancelling your old credit cards will improve your credit.
- Banks will not give you credit if you file for bankruptcy.
- By paying off late payment accounts, your credit will increase.

- You need to carry a balance to have a good credit score.
- Never using your card will improve your credit score.
- Having a high credit score will guarantee your approval.

Where Can You Obtain Your Credit Report?

You can obtain your credit report from either of the two main credit bureaus in Canada: *Equifax Canada Inc.* and *Trans Union of Canada*.

Different banks or credit companies report to either of these credit bureaus, so it is very important to make sure the credit reports from both bureaus are accurate. This ensures that your credit score is as high as possible.

I had a personal experience where my credit report from Equifax was accurate and clear, but my report from Trans Union had an error showing a balance on my student loans that I had paid off seven years prior.

This one error caused major delays in mortgage approval and unnecessary headaches! This is why it is important to check your credit report at least once a year - to prevent delays in obtaining credit to use towards building your wealth.

Tip: I recommend you review your credit report at least once a year; it's free anyway!

To get the link to your free credit report, email me at strongheartproperty@ gmail.com.

Components of a Credit Report

There are five main categories in a credit report:

1. Identification information
2. Employment information
3. Credit information
4. Public record information
5. Inquiries

You need to make sure the information in all five categories is accurate. Discrepancies must be corrected as soon as possible. This includes "questionable" items such as credit cards or accounts that you don't recall opening, or large debts that show an inaccurate balance.

Why is it Important to Have an Accurate Credit Report?

You may be asking yourself, "Why is it so important to check my credit report right away, and why is it so urgent to correct any errors on it?" The content of your credit report is likely the **most** important factor in determining if lenders will do business with you. It is more important than your annual salary or your net worth!

Some of the advantages of having a good credit score include:

1. Lower interest rates
2. Better terms on loans and mortgages
3. Access to business loans and major credit cards
4. Access to up to $300,000 in unsecured credit to build your wealth

The credit bureau acts only as a record keeper. It is your responsibility to confirm the accuracy of the information in your credit report. To do so, you, as a consumer, have the following rights:

- To know who has inquired into your credit file.
- To obtain a free credit report yearly from the credit bureau.
- To have missing data added to your file.
- To have unfavorable credit information, such as bankruptcy, removed from your file after seven years.
- To protect the privacy of the information in your file.
- To receive an explanation of your report without being charged a fee.
- To know exactly why you were refused credit. You must contact the institution refusing credit as soon as possible to find out the reason.

Repairing Your Credit Report:

At least 80% of North Americans will have a minimum of one error on their report. Having an error that lowers your credit score can have a profound impact on your ability to obtain low interest loans or credit cards. You do not want any unnecessary obstacles holding you back from building your fortune!

Here are some common errors on credit reports that must be corrected:

1. *Duplicates*: Accounts listed more than once on your credit report can impact your credit negatively and should be removed as soon as possible.

2. *Personal information*: You could be a victim of identity theft or involved in a case where your identity was inadvertently merged with somebody else. It is very important to correct this right away, especially if the other person has bad credit! The last thing you want is to be connected to fraudulent activities such as someone using your personal information to obtain multiple credit cards.

3. *Incorrect Credit Limit*: If the credit limit shown is less than what it should be, it may be more difficult for you to obtain lower interest rates. This leads to unnecessarily high monthly payments on major purchases such as a home or car.

4. *Incorrect account status*: If you have an account that is 60 days past due date, it should be labeled an R2. If labeled R8, this needs to be corrected immediately. (The different ratings are discussed in the workshop that I offer)

5. *Bankruptcy error*: Inaccuracy on a bankruptcy can make it very difficult to re-establish credit worthiness

Tip: If an account with outstanding debt is sent to a collection agency, you should seek help from a Licensed Insolvency Trustee to help arrange a consumer proposal instead of filing for personal bankruptcy. Personal bankruptcy remains on your file for seven years from the date of last activity. A consumer proposal, when paid, will be removed three years from the date paid. Having a consumer proposal rather than personal bankruptcy allows unfavourable information from your report to be removed much earlier.

If you find an error on your credit report, you must immediately file a written dispute by filling out a dispute form and submitting it to the credit bureau via mail or fax.

How Is Your Credit Score Measured?

Your credit score is determined by 5 factors, weighted differently:

1. *Payment history (35%)*: Lenders want to know that you pay your bills on time and according to the credit agreements. For example, late payments (over 30 days) will lower your score.

2. *Amounts owed (30%):* These are balances you are carrying on your accounts and the types of accounts these are.

   Tip: Never borrow 100% of the credit available. Just use up to ⅔ of your limit. An easy action I always have my students do is to call every credit card they own and ask if they are *pre-approved* for any credit limit increase. The key word here is *pre-approved* - this means the bank will not run a credit check, which will lower your credit score for a short period of time. For example, if your credit card has a limit of $1,000 and you spend $400, this is already more than ⅔ of utilization. By increasing the limit to $2,000, your utilization will be below ⅔, therefore increasing your likelihood of having a higher credit score.

3. *Length of credit history (15%)*: The longer you have had an account open for, the better it will be for your credit score.

   Tip: Do not ever close old accounts unless you have no other choice!

4. *Types of credit used (10%)*: Credit bureaus look at the number of different types of accounts you hold; credit cards, retail accounts, installment loans, mortgage, etc.

5. *New credit (10%):* This includes the number of recently opened accounts and the number of recent credit inquiries.

Taking Action:

Now that you have profiled yourself and have a great financial report card, it is time to go and apply for credit. This part is very simple! Your first step is to make an appointment with every single bank and state that you would like to do business with. The banker you meet with will likely ask for personal information, employment, and reason for applying for credit. Be confident with your responses! Because you have a great financial report card, there is no reason banks will not want to lend you money! This is why I keep stressing how important having a good credit report is!

Within two weeks of visiting banks and applying for new credit, my spouse and I were given access to more than $150,000 in new credit. With this solid financial resource, we soon strategically purchased our first house. Seeing how successful and easy this system was, we helped several other students to apply the same concept. One of my students was able to obtain $290,000 in credit. She then taught her spouse this system and he was able to get another $160,000 in new credit. With close to $450,000 in new credit, they now have enough money to invest in any almost financial endeavors they want. Shortly after amassing this wealth, they purchased their first home using borrowed money for the down payment.

Tip: Each individual (even in couples) should apply independently for credit. Unless in dire situations, never co-sign for another person's loan or line of credit - you will also be held responsible if they do not pay it back and this will negatively affect your credit score.

I have only given you a general picture at this point. For more details on how to take action, sign up for one of my workshops or email me at strongheartproperty@gmail.com to arrange a one-on-one session.

What Do You Do with All This Credit?

Now that you have amassed all this credit, it is important that you use it responsibly. Here is the rule about borrowing money: *Borrow money only when you can use those funds to make more money.* You should only use borrowed money (credit) to invest in assets that increase in value, referred to as appreciating assets. Income-producing assets show positive cash flow, meaning you will still have money left after making your loan payments and expenses each month. Never use borrowed money to purchase consumer goods such as clothing, jewelry, or new cars, since these items do not increase in value over time. A great example of an appreciating asset is real estate! Now that you have the power of credit and the knowledge of how to leverage it, let's talk about purchasing your first home.

How Much Should You Put for a Down Payment?

You may already know that as a first-time home buyer, you have the option of putting as little as 5% as the down payment towards a home. Doing so will require that you pay the Canada Mortgage and Housing Corporation (CMHC) fee. Most lenders/banks will recommend you put 20% as a down payment, supposedly to avoid the CMHC fee. It is true that with a 20% down payment, you will save the CMHC fee, but as sophisticated investors, our goal is to keep the most cash flow possible to use towards acquiring more investments. Banks loves having a 20% down payment from you because this gives them more money to lend to someone else at a much higher interest rate.

Tip: The Home Buyers Plan (HBP) allows you to withdraw up to $25,000 from your RRSP tax-free to put towards a down payment on a home. More information about this can be found at http://www.cra-arc.gc.ca/hbp/.

I teach all my students to put as little as possible towards the down payment. In my workshop, you will learn more about the breakdown of the CMHC and why it is worthwhile to pay this fee! By keeping more money in your pockets, you will have more to invest in a second and third property.

I recently met a couple who worked hard for many years to save up enough money for a house. They were ready to put a 20% down payment to avoid the CMHC fee. After learning about how to leverage the credit system, they are now able to use this same amount of money towards purchasing two properties instead of just one!

Getting accurate facts from experts in the field will help you grow your wealth much quicker. Successful people only make quick decisions once they have all the facts, and not just opinion. Armed with a great credit report, you are now ready to jump into wealth-building opportunities, such as real estate, when they present themselves to you. With the knowledge from this chapter about the credit system and how to use it effectively, you are now another step closer to building your fortune through real estate and smart investments!

Please feel free to reach out to me at strongheartproperty@gmail.com for a free 30-minute mentoring session or to find out about the next free information seminar.

VICTOR M. QUACH

Victor M. Quach is a certified Think and Grow Rich instructor, eye doctor, author, real estate investor, and wealth coach.

Much of Victor`s success is attributed to having great mentors, a growth mindset, and constantly masterminding with his wife Jennifer. He is a practicing optometrist and owner of several successful optometry clinics. In addition to eye care, he is passionate about finance and investments and wishes to help others build long term wealth through the power of real estate and other investment vehicles.

As an instructor for Think and Grow Rich, he teaches the success principles of Napoleon Hill to his students and inspires them to succeed. His focus is on transforming people's lives and helping them achieve financial and personal independence.

You can reach him at strongheartproperty@gmail.com for a free 30-minute mentoring session or to find out about the next free information seminar.

CHAPTER 23

How to Create a Multimillion Dollar Portfolio with ZERO Capital

BY NAM RATNA

Let me start by saying that growing a multimillion-dollar portfolio and creating the life you dream of is not easy. However, it's not impossible, no matter how many people tell you it is, including your family. They're wrong.

My journey started with many naysayers, especially since I decided not to practice medicine and started a real estate investment company instead. Knowing that others had accomplished wonders and created their dreams using real estate inspired me to ignore the naysayers and take action.

No matter what everyone was saying, I could not deny history. The vast majority of financially free individuals built their foundation in real estate. My business partners and I founded Go Get It Real Estate based on the realization that real estate was the best vehicle to build passive income and intergenerational wealth, which is our "Why."

The strategy we use and encourage others to start with is ***Buy, Fix, Refinance, and Rent (BFRR)***. This strategy is one of the best and quickest ways to *grow a multimillion-dollar rental portfolio with zero use of your own money.*

There are two main advantages to this strategy.

1. It allows you to reuse the same capital to continuously build your portfolio. (How, you say? We'll explain.)

2. While you're building intergenerational wealth and equity, you're also building a cash-flowing business. My company's business model requires a minimum of $250 profit per month after the property has been repaired, refinanced, and all expenses paid. We use single family homes only.

Where to Buy

Winnipeg is our home, and we love it! It's a stable market, and price points are low relative to other cities. If you're a beginner, I would suggest investing in markets with the same type of environment. I would also encourage you to purchase properties in areas that predominantly house working families, individuals, immigrants, and students. These communities should also have many schools, grocery stores, and access to public transit.

What to Buy and How to Finance

Using the BFRR strategy, you should purchase single family properties (bungalow, 1.5, or 2 stories, preferably 1945 or newer) at 60 cents on the dollar or less. Look for the ugly homes in good neighbourhoods. This strategy can be implemented in multiunit properties as well.

How do you find discounted properties? Once you determine the right community, start marketing. To find the right type of property, you must have a variety of marketing campaigns firing on all cylinders, and you must sharpen your negotiation skills!! It's crucial to consistently track, measure, and adjust your marketing, such as direct mail, door knocking, postcards, networking, cold calls, and bandit signs (inexpensive yard signs).

How exactly does BFRR work? Your purchase price depends on repair costs, holding costs (financing, closing fees, utilities, and property tax), a joint venture (JV) fees, after-repair value (ARV), appraisal costs, and your desired profit. It's good to have financing preapproved before you make your offer.

I might work with an investor who will either lend me money to buy and repair the house or who is prequalified to buy. If so, I'll negotiate a JV fee. I might offer 8-12% interest on the loan, or I might simply offer 50% of my profits upon the sale of the house.

Other times, I'll prequalify or pay cash without an additional investor. It all depends on the individual property, which is where experience, teamwork, and organizational systems are key.

Either way, I find the property, run the numbers, negotiate, and put in an offer to buy at a discounted price. After all the repairs are made (usually within 3-6 months), I've forced the house to appreciate, so I need to get a fresh appraisal to document the ARV. With the appraisal in hand, I can now go to the bank and refinance the house with a much larger mortgage, allowing us to pay the installments and get back the capital we put in.

I then rent the property, my tenant starts paying the mortgage off for me, I get an adequate cash flow each month, and still have capital back for the next property.

For people new to the industry, I recommend doing your own property management until you've got 30-40 deals under your belt. That's because you need to know how to manage property before you know what to expect from a property manager.

Can you see why the BFRR strategy works so well?

Many investors run into problems growing their portfolios because their capital gets stuck in the first couple of rentals. Doing this correctly gets all the capital back plus interest when you refinance.

Raising Capital

To purchase properties with zero of your money, you must raise capital. If you find the right discount and constantly network to build a list of investors, you'll get financing. A good tip to creating immediate credibility with potential investors is to partner with an active, successful mentor.

Your investor will see that you're being mentored by someone with a proven, documented track record.

To purchase, you can use a private investor or your own capital (including personal lines of credit, equity credit lines, or RRSP's) for the entire price (usually quicker) or the down payment plus renovation budget, holding costs, and closing costs.

You, your business partner, or your JV partner must be preapproved through a credit union, mortgage broker, or traditional bank so you can refinance the property after the property is repaired.

An Example in Winnipeg

One of our marketing strategies is to keep track of all MLS properties below $250,000 in Winnipeg. Go Get It Real Estate works with appraisers approved by the bank. As professional investors, we anticipate the refinance value of a property by researching comparables.

One property popped up at $120,000 which was below market value. Three comparables justified an ARV of $200,000 telling us it could be sold quickly. We knew the seller was motivated (it was an estate sale), and that it would sell quickly, so we prepared an offer and saw it within an hour of listing (motivated by our "Why," our mentor, and our great realtor).

We knew how much the costs would be for the extensive repairs, and we made an offer in 15 minutes. The offer was unconditional with a quick possession date and a one-hour deadline to accept. That strategy got us the property for only $100,000.

We financed the initial purchase and repairs ($100,000 plus $40,000) using a private investor we met at a networking event. No mortgage meant that we didn't incur most holding costs.

Within 250 days, the property was reappraised at a value of $200,000 by Kevin Olfert from Olfert Appraisals, and we refinanced at a local credit union. That covered property taxes and utilities, and the investor received his principal back, plus his JV fee of $12,458 (a $50 per day return on his investment). I retained ownership of the house, and found a wonderful professional couple to sign a one-year lease for $1,450 monthly and all utilities.

The instant equity in the property was $40,000 upon closing, used for 20% down on the $200,000 mortgage.

The cash flow is $270 x 12 months, or $3,240 annually. Zero capital was tied up. Infinite return!!

Repairs and Renovations

Purchasing at 60 cents on the dollar allows you to renovate the property to a quality standard, manage to hold costs, and provide solid returns for your capital partners and yourself. Most importantly, on the refinance, you'll receive the initial capital back to rinse and repeat the steps.

It's crucial to provide a quality product for potential tenants, as that sets the tone for the type of tenant you attract. Your repair costs should be determined during the purchase process. This is a rental, so make sure all mechanical, including electrical, plumbing, furnace, and the roof, are updated and in good working order.

It's best to purchase homes with a solid foundation, meaning no basement issues, cracks in the walls, etc., and with as many updates as possible such as electrical, plumbing, and roof. You're mainly looking for properties that need only cosmetic work that will appreciate the house, especially if you're a beginner. This includes paint, kitchen, bathrooms, and flooring.

To get the best value, focus on kitchens and bathrooms. Make sure they're functional, nicely renovated, and current on design trends. Our goal is to earn $2.00 in property value for every $1.00 we spend.

You don't typically want to spend more than $30,000 in repairs and renovations. In our example, we put in $40,000 worth of repairs due to some unanticipated foundation repair. However, purchasing at 50 cents on the dollar gave us wiggle room.

Building a Team

To grow your portfolio efficiently, it's crucial to have a detailed scope of work, a trusted and skilled contractor, and a terrific team.

When I'm looking for contractors and advisors, I look for character and core values first. Will they respect the time frames, be honest about problems and observations, and maintain good mannerisms, relationships, and integrity? I might even meet them for coffee.

Once they've passed the first hurdle, I'll verify their skills and history. Also, are they licensed? Do they have liability insurance and references?

Go visit the property where they last worked, and look at it. Ask the people there how they were treated. Ask if the contractor gave written invoices.

Don't cut corners on your team. Get professionals, not amateurs. A pro will be on time, work at a good pace, be professional, and do quality work. An amateur will do a poor job and get it done late. You'll also need to get a wholesale price if you can give the contractor regular work.

Refinancing

To ensure that you get all the initial capital back, you need to estimate your ARV by reviewing comparables before making an offer on the property. This way, you won't be surprised by the value the appraiser gives you. If your projected value and your appraiser's value don't align, use the comparables you reviewed to refute the appraisal report. We've rebutted appraisals successfully 100% of the time (2/2) using this technique.

Once a value is agreed upon, the appraiser will send the report to your bank of choice. It usually takes 1-3 days to receive the new mortgage, normally 75% - 80% of the new appraised value.

That essentially gives you tax-free instant equity. The mortgage will pay off your initial, smaller mortgage, pay your JV fees, and give you some profit for yourself, as planned.

The most important point is that you now own a rental property and got all the initial capital returned to you for further use. It feels like you bought the property for free!

Best of all, your tenant is paying down your mortgage.

Property Management, Maintenance, and Leasing

You need cash flow for your portfolio to be sustainable, flourish over years, and provide long-term equity and intergenerational wealth! But, that involves property management, maintenance, and leasing.

Most people dread this part and use it as an excuse to avoid the real estate game. However, if you treat your portfolio like a business, which it is, you'll have success.

You must develop systems and processes for every inch of your business. It's all about systems! An entire book could be written on this topic alone.

Let's hit the main point: leasing.

Make sure you set up a thorough qualification process that includes ID, references, credit checks, and criminal record checks at your discretion. Talk to the prospect's boss at work, if possible, to see what kind of employee she is and if she's in danger of getting fired.

Go to the previous landlord (don't just call). As the landlord speaks about the tenant, check the body language and the state of the property.

When you provide a quality product and a thorough qualification process, you'll attract the right types of tenants. When you meet potential tenants and observe their mannerisms, hygiene, and even the state of their car, you'll have an idea of how they might treat your property.

To ensure you have a proper lease, touch base with a mentor who is doing this successfully. Make additions to the rental requirements and forms as you see fit, and make sure you confirm your additions with the local Residential Tenancy Branch.

Have systems ready for everything: move-ins, move-outs, evictions, late payments, repairs, and periodic inspections. Anything you can think of, have a system for it.

Technology has made collecting rent a lot easier by using electronic transfers. If your tenant is on social or other assistance, make sure the rent cheque goes directly to you.

At the end of the month, you should be able to pay the mortgage, property tax, insurance, and a reserve of 3% for vacancy and 4% for maintenance. Your cash flow should be at least $250. (Remember, our rentals are completely renovated.) This number can vary depending your risk tolerance, other income, and overall financial situation.

You Can Do It - Follow My Example

Using the above strategy, you can grow a multimillion-dollar portfolio at the pace you desire. Whether two, three, four, or ten properties a year, or even multiunit buildings, the BFRR model will allow you to achieve your goal. The time lines, cash flows, and net worth will be variable, but the system remains the same.

To avoid costly mistakes, save time, and have a lot more fun, find a mentor who does this often and well.

For example, my business partners and I at Go Get It Real Estate have built an equity portfolio of $850,000 in 1.5 years, which will grow into more than $1,500,000 in 5 years. More importantly, the BFRR pulled the three of us out of the Rat Race!!

If we can do it, so can you!

What do you want to do?

If you want to acquire $1 million or more in equity within 10 years or less, connect with a professional like me. Educate yourself and take action!

I love helping others, and I'm really good at it. To provide you with extra value today, I created two free gifts for you: a thorough breakdown of the case study above and a complimentary property repair sheet (worth $90).

You can access both of them and apply for a free, 30-minute strategy session here: www.gogetitrealestate.com/freegifts.

I can only offer the free strategy session for a limited time, so reach out quickly!

Last-Minute Keys to Powerful Success in Real Estate

1. Connect with an active, proven investor and mentor like me.
2. Take action and learn.
3. Build a committed power team.
4. Do the hard self-development work getting started, because the reward is infinite return (and it gets much easier).
5. Take advantage of my free gifts.

Reach me at 1 (204) 997-3662, email nam@gogetitrealestate.com, or visit www.gogetitrealestate.com to build your portfolio.

Nam Ratna

Co-Founder, Go Get It Real Estate

"Where Dreams are Big, but Taking Action Is Bigger!"

NAM RATNA

Author and co-founder of Go Get It Real Estate, Nam's a colossally successful real estate investor working in Winnipeg, Manitoba with co-founders and business partners Saran Ratna and Tayler Fehr.

Go Get It Real Estate specializes in securing and renovating discounted properties. Nam's developed creative ways to buy, fix, refinance, and rent properties while tying up zero of his own capital. In four years, he's acquired over $3 million in properties with an equity of $850,000.

Nam's "Why" is control over his time, which is why passive income is essential. He enjoys spending time with his 2-year-old daughter, 5-year-old stepson, and their (big) family, while enjoying all the goodness this world offers.

For Nam's valuable rental repair cheat sheet and detailed case study, and to apply for a free, 30-minute strategy session, go to www.gogetitrealestate.com/freegifts. You can also reach him at nam@gogetitrealestate.com, www.gogetitrealestate.com, or call 1 (204) 997-3662.

CHAPTER 24

If a Single Mom Can Invest in Real Estate, So Can You!

BY TAMMY SMIT, RN

Have you ever wondered how to get started in real estate? Does fear stop you? If a single mother like me can profitably invest in real estate, so can you.

You can do exactly what I did to make significant money in real estate, even if you're just getting started or don't have wads of cash. And I want to show you how.

When I got started, all I ever knew about real estate was from late-night TV infomercials. I couldn't even afford to buy one of those too-good-to-be-true packages. So, I gave up an unhealthy habit, and the money I saved makes me money every month now.

I fumbled through my first property out of sheer necessity, but it made me money anyway. Now, I own six homes, participate in joint ventures and new construction, and make an annual income above and beyond my salary as a nurse while I sleep!

My purpose in this book is to show you what I did so you can move forward in real estate, no matter where you are. You can start today, even if you don't have good credit, lots of money, or any experience.

HOW I KICKED A BAD HABIT FOR MY FIRST PROPERTY

I was stagnant in my goals to earn passive income and get rid of my J-O-B (Just Over Broke). Although I thought of real estate investing every day, I used every excuse imaginable to stay right where I was: not enough money, not enough time, no information. (Do any of these excuses sound familiar?)

I needed a bright idea, but I realized that:

Excuses can either overwhelm your decisions or decisions can overwhelm your excuses.

—Tammy Smit

Sounds profound in theory, but where would I get a great idea?

It came at 5:30 some dark morning on the way to work, sitting in the Starbucks drive-through, waiting for my delicious cup of heavily-caffeinated espresso.

Oh, the things I would do to make it to Starbucks to part with $5.50 each morning! I had to drive out of my way daily to get to a Starbucks, whether a workday or a day off. I wanted my Starbucks coffee so badly that my time, efforts, and impending poverty didn't matter.

It didn't take me long to figure out that I had an expensive coffee addiction. Then it hit me: What if I could transfer my coffee addiction to real estate?

Little by little, I weaned myself from my heavy dose of caffeine and created an addiction to success in its place. The money that I didn't spend on coffee went into my new "real estate fund" in a glass mason jar, which grew by $5.50 a day.

Yes, it seemed tiny compared to the amount I would need to purchase real estate. But in thirty days, I saved $165.00, which meant I could save $2,000.50 a year! I used it as an excuse to feel good about getting started. (Besides, the $5.50 didn't even account for the time and gas money I spent finding the closest coffee houses.)

Although excuses played over and over in my mind, I was focused, motivated, and even excited. How could I get more money? What sacrifices could I make to start saving some? I kept going.

I didn't know what to do next, so I simply started going through the Multiple Listing Service (MLS) on the Internet at www.realtor.com. I only searched properties under $100,000 in my own small town. At that time, $100,000 seemed like $10 million to me.

Fortunately, I ran across a single-wide manufactured (mobile) home with some land, a fenced-in yard, a cement driveway, and a big tree in the front yard. The cost was $21,000. I was in immediately.

I knew that this property could generate monthly passive income.

How did I know the rent I could get? Or how to estimate the vacancy rate? Here is the financial breakdown of my first property:

Annual Income and Expenses - Property #1

Expected Income		
Gross rent ($525 x 12 months)		$6,300.00
Vacancy rate (5% x $6,300.00)		($315.00)
Gross Operating Income		$5,985.00
Mortgage	$2,172.00	
Property Tax	$311.19	
Insurance	$600.00	
Repairs and Maintenance	$200.00	
Total Expenses		($3,283.19)
Net Annual Cash Flow		$3,016.81

Oh, and please don't forget that I also saved $2,000.00 a year by not drinking my coffee in the times when I had no vacancies! The net cash flow plus the savings from breaking a habit were: $3,016.81 + $2,000.50 = **$5,017.31 annually.**

That's like an extra month's salary every year!

Now, manufactured homes do not build equity like a standard brick and mortar home, so this is not the strategy that I currently recommend. However, the cash flow was over $3,000.00 per year and could certainly be put into investing in an equity-building property.

With a little time and effort, combined with the decision to move forward, I had just kick-started the dream of dumping my J-O-B. I had over $5,000.00 in the bank after only one year, and I was on my way. It was time to invest in equity-building properties.

Do you see how easy and profitable this can be?

HOW MY OWN HOME MADE ME AN ACCIDENTAL INVESTOR

After a divorce, life became chaotic. I didn't realize at the time that the negatives would someday turn into positives.

I was trying to find a new place to live with two small children, ages four and eight. I had not rented an apartment by myself in over 15 years, and although I had lived in a home with my husband, I certainly did not know anything about buying a home for myself.

> *"Do what you can, with what you have,*
> *where you are."*
>
> —*Theodore Roosevelt.*

It felt daunting and seemed like something only other people do. But, I struggled to look for a home so we could start rebuilding our lives.

How Did I Find the First Home of My Own?

I had no idea how to find a home, so again, I checked www.realtor.com. I entered my search criteria — in my general area, less than $100,000 and close to a school. I use these same criteria today for investment properties.

After much searching, I finally ran across a 1,200-sq. foot brick home with three bedrooms and two baths. It was only four years old. I couldn't believe that the price was $78,000 and wondered if the back of the house was missing or something.

I immediately called a realtor, and we were at the home within hours. It was in a different town, but there was nothing wrong with it, and even the carpet was clean. I couldn't believe my luck. I instantly put in an offer and drained my bank account for the earnest money.

Now, I had to find out how to put in a down payment.

My amazing realtor let me know about FHA (Federal Housing Administration) loans that let first-time homebuyers put down as little as 3% of the purchase price. I was a technically a first-time homebuyer.

My happy thought, "Another stroke of good luck," soon turned to stress and anxiety. Although 3% is not a lot of money to some, it was a lot to me. I now had 45 days in which to come up with $2,250.00.

Thankfully, there was a great shortage of nurses during this time, which allowed me to work as much as I could to come up with the down payment. On closing day, I made the down payment in full, and we moved into our new "lucky" home.

Our new home was great for the first year, but my children and I missed our small town and the school they had gone to. As we decided to move, we were about to find out just how lucky our first home was going to be.

After putting up our new little home for sale, the competition got rough in our cul-de-sac. A lot of properties were going up for sale. The new school year was approaching, and I was running out of time. I decided I would use my little home as a rental property, allowing us to move without worrying about the mortgage payment.

Here is the financial breakdown of our "accidental" rental property:

Annual Income and Expenses - Second Property

Expected Income		
Gross rent ($1,100.00 x 12 months)		$13,200.00
Vacancy rate (5% x $13,200.00)		($660.00)
Gross Operating Income		$12,540.00
Mortgage, property tax, and insurance	$9,384.00	
Repairs and Maintenance	$1,000.00	
Total Expenses		($10,384.00)
Net Annual Cash Flow		$2,156.00
Net Monthly Cash Flow		$179.67

I kept this home as an investment property for 10 years.

10 years x $2,156.00 = $21,560.00 **passive income**. That's equivalent to having a second full-time income without working.

In addition to the $21,560.00 income over 10 years, I sold the home for a profit close to $40,000.

I made over $60,000.00 as an accidental investor!!!

Wow! As you can imagine, I started feeling great about real estate as an opportunity, even for someone like me who had no experience or knowledge about it. I reinvested that $60,000.00 into equity and cash-flowing real estate.

5 EASY STEPS TO GETTING STARTED IN REAL ESTATE

Now, let me share with you **five easy steps** to get started in real estate investing no matter what your previous skill, knowledge, or experience.

Everyone's finances and education are different, but that makes absolutely no difference in the investing world. It's a level playing ground. When I reflect back, my good luck is still possible to replicate today.

*"The journey of a thousand miles begins
with a single step."*

—Lao Tzu

Luck comes from focus, diligence, and taking the first step. It comes to you because you take the steps, not because you're dreaming about taking them.

Do the thing that you fear, and fear will leave you.

Remember my $5.50 daily savings fund when I had nothing else to invest? My exact path wasn't clear, but I had the intention, and I took the first step. The way to success doesn't have to be obvious. Just take the first step (even if it's tiny).

Let's get you on your path, now, so you can create the dream you've been keeping in your head all this time….

Step 1: Decide to get started.

The only factors that differentiate me from millions of others is that I got excited and took the first steps.

Step 2: Focus on finding money to get started:

- Give up an unhealthy habit.
- Ask for loans at local banks, not mega ones.
- Set aside a portion of your savings account (and if you don't have one, start one now).
- Capitalize on your home equity through Home Equity Lines of Credit (HELOC).
- Get private investor funding.
- Join an investment club.
- Partner with friends or relatives.
- Work an extra job.
- Borrow against a retirement account (ask me how).

Step 3: Look for a property:

- Try MLS
- Ask realtors for pocket listings (properties available BEFORE they hit the market).
- Learn to use Craigslist without getting scammed.
- Scour newspaper classifieds.
- Search estate sales (www.estatesales.net, etc.).
- Drive neighborhoods For Sale by Owner (FSBO).
- Have everyone look for vacant properties for you.
- Help families offload inherited properties (probate sales).
- Provide divorcees peace of mind by providing a stress-free selling process.
- Explore government tax sales (www.bid4assets.com, etc.).
- Connect with other investors through local meetings.
- Check the foreclosure sites.
- Connect with wholesalers.
- Get help from your coach or mentor.

Step 4: Determine if the property is a good choice for you:

- Get a mentor to help save time, effort, money, and legal problems.
- Get a good team in place: realtor, repairmen, legal beagles, property managers.
- Check on repairs and cost.
- Determine if you'll do the repairs or hire someone else to do it.
- Will you rent the property or flip it?
- Do all the numbers add up to profit?

Step 5: Do it!

It's your turn to get going. Write down what you'll do to complete each of the 5 steps above. If you take a small bite out of each item, it will seem effortless.

It may seem overwhelming, but taking small, doable steps takes the fear and overwhelm out of the decision to move forward. Trust your gut and double-check everything. Get someone who has done what you want to do and follow their direction.

HOW YOU CAN PROFIT, TOO

I only covered two tried, tested, and proven ways to getting you started in real estate investing.

Another idea is bypassing all the work and becoming a passive investor in a joint venture. Someone else finds the deals, provides a portion of the funds, and does all the work while you simply contribute a designated amount of funding and split the profits. This is a great way to leverage your investments and create massive wealth quickly.

There are many other ways, but I can't tell you everything right here.

If you are new to investing, want to learn as you go, or want to exponentially build your real estate success, then I may be the person for you to connect with.

I actively look for people who want to partner with a successful real estate investor like me. I build great teams, and I'm also one of the nicest people you can find to work with. I'm not able to help everyone and I do actually select my partners. But once we click, there's nothing stopping us.

GET STARTED WITH FREE GIFTS!!

Because you're taking your precious time to read my book, and because I love to help people get started, I'd like to offer you a special gift that will help you regardless of your experience or investment knowledge. Please go here to claim your no-obligation free gift:

www.7WaysNoMoneyDownRealEstate.com

Or, feel free to contact me at 1-817-991-2709 or info@123OwnerFinance. com.

I'd love to be the one to show you how great it is to find peace of mind and the freedom you deserve.

Regardless of what path you decide to take, be good to yourself. Get started today, and don't be a slave to a J-O-B. Let your money work for you!

Remember; figure out what you really want, educate yourself, connect with the right people who can lift you up, find a competent mentor, and above all, take action. Without taking action, no dream comes true.

I want to thank you for investing in this book and believing in your dreams.

TAMMY SMIT

Tammy Smit is a mother, full-time Certified Registered Nurse Anesthetist (CRNA), entrepreneur, highly successful part-time real estate investor, author, and public speaker.

Tammy's dreams of financial freedom and more family time fueled her drive to create passive income through her businesses and investments.

Early in Tammy's investment career, she realized the importance of getting a mentor. Her results became astonishing. She partnered with a co-worker and used advanced wealth-building strategies to do over $1.2 million in real estate transactions in the first year, including rentals and fix-and-flips.

She developed a passion for connecting real estate investors like herself with the perfect real estate venture capitalists, using valuable properties that ensure investment security. She now helps others become highly successful real estate investors.

To learn how to create massive wealth by benefitting from Tammy's passion, skill, and experience, call her at 1-817-991-2709 or email her at info@123OwnerFinance.com.

CHAPTER 25

The Right Mentor is the Key to Millions

BY SHAHZAD AHMED

There is nothing more satisfying in this world than watching as a tiny being triumphantly takes their first step.

For both the child and parent, the undeniable joy and self-confidence a child gains from this moment is priceless and something he or she will carry with them for the rest of their life. As a parent, you never feel that your child failed, even though they repeatedly stumbled before finally mastering the feat. You simply guide and encourage them.

As we grow and become more independent, however, somewhere along the way we learn that trying and failing is a "bad thing." We lose the unbridled enthusiasm and even the motivation we had as that young child, instead of using the many falls as the ultimate springboard to walk.

Unfortunately, when it comes to business, and especially entrepreneurship, this ingrained thought pattern can quickly turn into the fear of failing, and as such, rule our lives. We forget that "failing" is natural and even necessary for success, which causes fear and even paralysis, knocking out the first major component of success – the courage to keep trying.

Even more unfortunate is that many people also feel that asking for or needing a little help is a sign of weakness, which knocks out the second major component of success, mentorship.

But the truth is, no great success is ever achieved without failure. In fact, some of the most wildly successful people in the world have done their share of failing before ever achieving their dreams.

"Only those who dare to fail greatly can ever achieve greatly."

—Robert F. Kennedy

Looking back, it's hard to imagine where our world would be without the failures of great innovators and their ability to use their setbacks to catapult their visions. Had Edison decided to throw in the towel after his 100th failure to develop the light bulb, who knows where we would be? It took him 10,000 failed attempts before he finally made the bulb that is now the cornerstone of our modern lights! In fact, he never saw these as failures. He saw them as 9,999 ways not to make a light bulb.

Had Orville and Wilbur Wright decided to give up after their many years of repeated and sometimes very painful failures, who knows if we would be where we are today in aviation? When it comes to business, almost every highly successful entrepreneur has had their share of failures. Only in failure can we gain a good prospective of success.

Winston Churchill, an outstanding commander who successfully led the British through WWII, as well as a Nobel Prize winner, clearly understood that.

"Success is not final, failure is not fatal: it is the courage to continue that counts."

—Winston Churchill

The second component of great success is being able to ask for help.

You would never dream of taking up the piano without instruction or hoping to hit a "hole in one" in golf without a little help from an expert. In fact, to be truly successful in anything, we need the guidance and mentorship of others. The most successful people in the world understand this.

Bill Gates, founder of Microsoft and a Harvard dropout, accredits his success in part to the mentorship he received from businessman and investor Warren Buffet. And, the decidedly successful Virgin Group founder, Richard Branson, states, *"If you ask any successful businessperson, they will always have had a great mentor at some point along the road."*

Branson turned to British airline entrepreneur Sir Freddie Laker when he was struggling to get Virgin Atlantic off the ground.

Even Mark Zuckerberg, co-founder and CEO of Facebook, who made $1.6 billion in a single day and skyrocketed his net worth to $33.3 billion, acknowledges that his mentor, Apple founder Steve Jobs, was key to his meteoric rise to being one of the richest men in America. They all learned what works from their mentors. Their mentors paved the way through their failures and eventual successes.

Finding the Right Mentor

The first step to finding a mentor is actually believing that you need one.

Often, we allow our egos to dictate when we actually need common sense. While doing it alone may seem honourable or even courageous at the time, more times than not it proves to be unnecessarily reckless.

I am the perfect example of someone who finally realized they needed to find a mentor. I had all the ambition in the world. I wanted to succeed, worked endless hours, and put thousands of dollars into different businesses over the years, each time hoping I had finally found the key to success.

It took me $153,000 and seven failed businesses before I realized I needed help.

When I finally took that step, everything changed. I went from struggling to unlimited success. Everything finally clicked, and I found myself featured in Canada's biggest real estate magazine for three years in a row, sharing stages with the biggest names in the industry, such as Robert G. Allen, Brian Tracy, and Jack Canfield. I became the author of three bestsellers, including one international bestseller, all because I reached out and looked to someone who knew what they were doing and taught me to do the same thing.

I now have several mentors in different parts of the world, but I would like to acknowledge and recognize my first official mentor, who influenced me in so many ways. His guidance, help, and support has led me to the level of success I have achieved today. He is a brilliant speaker, a #1 bestselling author, and an excellent mentor. I respect him as a mentor from the bottom of my heart. His name is Sunil Tulsiani.

Once you make the decision to work with a mentor, finding the right one is key. There are countless people these days who call themselves mentors or life coaches. And who knows, they may very well be able to help some people. But, to be a truly successful mentor, you must have lived what you teach. At least, that is my philosophy.

It doesn't matter what field you are in—sports, arts, real estate, finance, business, or anything at all—unless a mentor can relate to you on a very basic and personal level, one that stems from having already done what you are attempting to do, they won't be able to genuinely guide you around and through the pitfalls that inevitably lie ahead.

You can't expect someone who has never skated before to turn you into an Olympic figure skater. The thought is absurd. In the same vein, you shouldn't expect someone who has never failed in business and crawled their way back to success to be able to teach you how to be successful yourself.

> *"Unless a mentor can relate to you on a very basic and personal level, one that stems from having already done what you are attempting to do, they won't be able to genuinely guide you around and through the pitfalls that inevitably lie ahead."*
>
> *—Shahzad Ahmed*

Your Attitude is Also Key

I am a true believer in "what you think about, you bring about." What I mean by that is that you can't expect to be successful if you don't believe you can. We all know people who are consistently negative. It is not only frustrating to listen to them, but it is also draining for everyone around them. In my experience, there are four types of people:

Blamers—People who never take personal responsibility for anything that is wrong in their lives.

Skeptics—People who have doubts about many things.

272

Know-it-Alls—People who think they know everything there is to know about everything.

Action Takers—People who are proactive, understand they are in control of their own lives, and take action to make things happen.

I would never disparage anyone for how they choose to live their lives, but I do choose who I want to mentor. I pride myself on being able to help people in a variety of areas, but I also know my limits. My years of experience have shown me that I cannot work with people who blame others for their misgivings or those who think they "know it all." I simply don't feel they are in a place to accept my mentoring. After all, if they actually "knew it all," they would have done it.

On the other hand, I encourage people to have some scepticism. It is actually healthy and can be a real asset in business, as long as you are also open to hearing other people's points of view and accepting sound advice.

I also love working with action takers. While these types of people are typically eager and ready to do the hard work necessary to succeed, as a mentor I can teach them that not all action is essentially good action. I can also teach them when to move and when to stand still, something action takers often overlook.

You obviously play a crucial role in whether or not you succeed, even with mentorship, so adopting an attitude of already being successful is vital. At the very least, you need an attitude that is open to success. You'd be surprised at how many people I have spoken to in my 10+ years in business that say they want to be successful, but when it comes down to it, they find there is something holding them back. As a mentor, I can help my mentees find their way if they're open to moving past this resistance.

Characteristics of a Good Mentor

This brings me to the other key to finding a compatible mentor—trust.

When you start to work with a mentor or coach, you must dig deep at times, which means you often have to share personal information, be it financial, emotional, or otherwise. If you don't feel like you can trust your mentor or vice versa, it is simply not going to work. I believe a good coach has to be willing to always put your best interests first.

One of the most telling characteristics of a good mentor is whether they have already successfully done what you are trying to do.

Let's say, for example, that you want to make a million dollars. You will need to find a mentor who has done this, so they can show you exactly what works and how you can also make that one million dollars. But, even if you were successful with your first mentor and made a million dollars, if your next goal is to make $10 million and your current mentor has not been able to make $10 million, they are probably not the right mentor for this particular goal.

It has nothing to do with how good that mentor is (they were obviously good at helping you make your first million). They just don't have the real-life experience you will need to get you to your next goal.

The same holds true in real estate. As a mentor, I will never tell my mentee to purchase an investment property in a particular area if I have not also either bought there myself and made money or done my due diligence. I ask myself, would I advise my mother, my sister, my family to buy this property? If the answer is no, then I am not going to advise you to do so. I believe this is what a true mentor does. So, when looking for your mentor, you need to make sure they are truly looking out for you. All too often, I see "cubicle coaches," as I like to call them—coaches that are not "boots on the ground," in the trenches, so to speak, but simply advising others from a scripted list, having no idea if what they are suggesting will actually work.

When choosing your mentor, make sure you ask them questions about why they feel they are a good fit for your particular situation. Everyone has different goals, so it's never a "one mentor fits all" situation. Don't be afraid to ask them if they have ever failed in business. Remember, failing is not a negative. A mentor who has failed and turned that failure into a positive, is that much wiser and stronger for it, because they can also tell you what NOT to do. The important thing is that they forged on and eventually succeeded, and that is the value they can bring to you.

You will also want to make sure your mentor has successfully helped others achieve their goals. It doesn't matter how many people a mentor has worked with if only a few of his or her mentees have ever reached their goals. Mentoring is definitely a situation when quality is more important than quantity.

Like that parent watching their baby walk for the first time, your mentor knows you can do it and understands the falls along the way. Choose one who's achieved what you want to achieve and who has your best interests at heart.

SHAHZAD AHMED

Shahzad Ahmed is well-known for being Canada's leading real estate expert, Elite wealth coach, international bestselling author, and a world-class speaker and trainer. Shahzad has written books and shared stages with Sunil Tulsiani, Robert Allen, Brian Tracy, Jack Canfield and many others in different countries of the world.

Shahzad is one of the most sought after real estate coaches in Canada and has been featured as an expert in Canada's top real estate magazine in 2015, 2016 and 2017.

Shahzad has trained thousands and helped hundreds of individuals and families in creating passive income. He is directly responsible for hundreds of success stories, many come from his students who he personally mentored.

Shahzad wants to empower those who are willing to change their lives with his strong leadership, persuasive messages, and exceptional education. His mission is to touch the lives of millions of people around the world and leave a positive impact on them. He is the President of Elite Training Pros.

CHAPTER 26

7+ Proven Marketing tools to build and grow your business

BY RANDI GOODMAN

Creating wealth through lead generation is one of the most important pieces of an entrepreneur's business. I am Randi Goodman, mom of four gorgeous young men, a three-time #1 international best-selling author, international speaker, digital marketer and CEO of multiple conferences and workshops such as the Toronto Women's Expo, Empowering Women to Succeed, Action Think Tank Academy and Business Wealth Summits. To date, I have made 40 authors into #1 international best sellers.

Through trial and error, and plenty of failures, I have built an incredible team around me. I have an unbelievable business partner and we are going gung ho forward! If I can do it in my forties, after a separation, you can do it too!

Through my experiences, I have found what works and what doesn't work. I will share with you some tools and resources that work for me.

What are you doing right now to attract new business? There are numerous tools you can use to generate more business, things you can implement that can have an immediate effect on your business.

We will review seven of them here.

1st Tool: Website vs. Landing Pages

A website is a collective of pages that contain specifics about your business and services. Pages will include information about you, your company, products, services, events, resources, terms and conditions, privacy, contact info, blog, podcast etc.; people can get easily distracted on your website.

A landing page is a distinct page on your website; it is used to capture contact information and to focus on one specific product, service or event. It doesn't mention other products, services, or programs you are offering. There is no need for excessively long landing pages; only the relevant information and no other distractions. You can also use a landing page for contests or to promote an event.

Creating landing pages or squeeze pages are an art if you wish to have the right client or click conversions. You can create them yourself or hire someone to do it for you.

Where do I find programs or software to create landing pages?

Here are a few suggestions:

Leadpages

Starting at $37/month

http://link.leadpages.net/aff_c?offer_id=6&aff_id=15374

Clickfunnels http://goo.gl/1f99n2

Starting at $37/month

WordPress landing page plugins

    a.   Thrive Content Builder + Landing Pages, starting at $59

    b.   OptimizePress 2.0, starting at $97

    c.   WordPress Landing Pages, integration with email starts at $25

    d.   Themeforest themes for Wordpress

http://themeforest.net/?ref=randig71

2ⁿᵈ Tool: Opt-ins

What is an opt-in? An opt-in is when someone gives you their email address. Typically, you are giving them something of value in return, like a download or access to something that is free. Consider it an ethical bribe.

Why do you want to have an opt in? You want to build a community of people who opt-in to receive communications on new products or services, events, resources and shared updates. We achieve this by collecting their email addresses through opt-ins, events and anywhere else we can obtain them organically.

Where do these emails go? They are collected in an email program such as Infusionsoft, Constant Contact, MailChimp and others. You can choose from simple to more complex programs. It all depends on your needs and application. Building an online community requires the use of an email marketing program if you want to communicate regularly with your audience. For example, if you were a Realtor, and there are over 30 thousand agents in your area, how would you set yourself apart? If you are not front and center in someone's mind, they will not think of you! That is why it is extremely important that you have regularly scheduled communications with your community; you will be the first one that comes to mind when there is a need. Communicating helpful information and resources to your base may inspire them to share your link with their network, which in turn will help you build your mailing list.

To garner as many opt-ins as possible, make it simple; request a minimal amount of information. More times than not, they will give you their email address. If you begin requesting last names or phone numbers they are less likely to opt in to the mailing list. You may lose sign-ups when asking for too much information or a phone number.

3ʳᵈ Tool: Giveaways

Very few of us want to give away anything for free. Why would you expect someone to give you their email address for nothing in return? By offering a giveaway that is of value to them, chances are they will give you their email address. You can give away all sorts of things that would be of value to people:

- Educational paper
- Discount
- Free trial class
- Free webinar
- Audio series
- Video series
- Newsletter
- Information specific to your industry
- Tips and resources
- Free pass to event
- White paper
- Podcast

You must include a call to action in your communications. This will give your new contact, a way to reach you and a way to stay engaged.

4th Tool: Leveraging, Affiliate Programs and Joint Ventures

What does *leveraging* people mean? It means collaborating with someone to have reciprocal access to each other's warm markets. For example, if I have 1,000 people on my list and you have 1,000 people on your list, now we collectively have 2,000 people to connect with. A win-win-win, as you get to collaborate and share the responsibility of communicating to the community.

Affiliate programs are when an online merchant, website or individual pays an affiliate website or landing page to their site/product/service, a commission to send them traffic. The most common types of affiliate programs include pay-per-click, pay-per-lead, and pay-per-sale. Affiliate programs can earn you some extra money and give you access to other networks.

Another way to grow your business is through a joint venture. This is when two or more organisations come together to promote products or services that go hand in hand. A simple example would be merchandise companies partnering with McDonalds Restaurants to provide toys for their McHappy Meals.

5ᵗʰ Tool: Podcasting

What is a podcast?

A podcast is a digital audio or video file made available through the Internet for downloading to a PC, tablet or mobile device. It is usually available as a series or as new instalments which can be received or downloaded by your subscribers automatically and usually for free. I have seen businesses and brands grow to over 375,000 subscribers and over one million downloads in the first year of launching a podcast. They also received invitations to speak internationally, and offers to be an affiliate partner, all because of this worldwide exposure.

WOW! Can you imagine what this can do for your business if you had thousands of people following you on a podcast?

- Exposure
- Generate leads
- Opt-ins on your website or landing page
- Increased sales
- Added credibility

It is so inexpensive to learn how to create a podcast and to deliver a podcast. You can do it for free, just by having a podcast on iTunes. Hosting your podcast can be expensive; some sites charge $12/month USD to start. Previously I have paid over $80 USD per month, I have since switched my podcast hosting over to www.mypodcastworld.com and it only costs me $99 USD per year.

One requirement is that you will have to create a piece of artwork that represents your podcast show. This can be created on www.fiverr.com inexpensively, or you may choose another source that can create a nice graphic for you.

Having an intro and outro for each of your podcasts with a call to action can increase your leads and sales directly from your podcast. If you would like to see samples of an intro and outro, please view my podcast show www.empowermentradioshow.com

A podcast can be of any length, from a few minutes to an hour or more. I suggest one interview or topic per podcast; this will help you generate numerous podcasts for your show.

Topics for your podcast can be created from life situations, subjects that inspired you, business topics, interviewing people and so much more.

When you start your podcast you will not be perfect, so don't worry about that. The more podcasts you create, the more comfortable you'll be with the process, and you will become more proficient in podcasting. You will become the expert, so don't worry how you got there, just start the process.

Your subscribers can download the podcast and listen to it on their time, while driving, working out, going for a walk, working on their computers, etc. You will be viewed as a celebrity when you have your own podcast show; people will look up to you as the expert and credible. This is an incredible growth opportunity, especially if you are in sales or want to speak on stages to groups of people.

Giving a presentation to an audience, whether it is one-on-one, in a group, or a room full of people will elevate you as a speaker. Podcasting speeds up that process. You may be asked once in a while to be on a stage, but you can be on stages multiple times per day when you podcast.

If you would like access to a set of videos that will illustrate the steps to set up, create, and deliver a podcast, send your paid receipt for podcast hosting on www.MyPodcastWorld.com to podcast@empoweringwomentosucceed.com. The videos are free to you and I'll email you access to them, a $499 value.

6th Tool: Online Marketing - Online Courses

There are websites which host online courses that have established audiences from the thousands to the millions of users, and these are users who want to learn. You can upload your online courses to these platforms, and in doing so you get access and engage with the site's already established audience. In using this tool, you will not have to do nearly the hard work to build and acquire your own audience.

Between 2005 & 2009 my friend was working with a company that generated 29 million in sales through online courses. What could that do for your business? You would be able to reach mass audiences that will pay to learn from you and gain exposure to students that would otherwise never have known about you. You could earn thousands of dollars by sharing on these sites.

There are specifics as far as audio and video quality that you will have to adhere to. It is best to work with a team that is familiar with these criteria to ensure you publish a high-quality product that will be accepted onto these sites. If you are interested, you can connect with me directly at podcast@empoweringwomentosucceed.com and I will have a 15-minute chat with you to discuss how you can go forward.

You can use this tool to direct individuals to the next step, enrolling in your next course or program.

7th Tool: Book Writing

Sharing your story is a permanent record of your thoughts, your experience and your wisdom. There are different versions you can create: paperback, hardcover, or electronic versions.

Books are created for many purposes, including:

- Self-healing
- Healing others
- Educating on a topic
- Leaving a legacy
- Empowering others
- Building your business
- Adding credibility to your brand
- Elevating your status
- Establishing yourself as the expert

If you wish to be part of a compilation, you can view information on www.empoweringwomentosucceed.com and www.365empoweringstories.com

What does having a book do for you?

- ❖ Creates passive income
- ❖ You can get bulk sales of your book
- ❖ It can be licensed
- ❖ Generates leads
- ❖ Brings more traffic to your website
- ❖ More referrals
- ❖ Media attention
- ❖ Elevates you as a business person or expert in your field
- ❖ Adds credibility
- ❖ Turn it into other products that you can educate others on and earn money from
- ❖ Opens up opportunities that were not there before
- ❖ Respect and prestige in your industry
- ❖ More income from speaking engagements
- ❖ More joint Venture partners interested in working with you
- ❖ More ideal clients for your programs
- ❖ Letters after your name :) A.U.T.H.O.R.
- ❖ Have an add-on benefit at your speaking engagements
- ❖ Get connected with key influencers – reap the benefits!!
- ❖ Deliver more value to your customers and connections
- ❖ Stand out from your competition
- ❖ Have an ongoing marketing tool
- ❖ Build your brand
- ❖ Be able to raise the price of your services
- ❖ Build a revenue stream even while you sleep

Books are not just books. There are so many spin-off products that can be created and sold from having a book:

- Programs
- Live Events
- Products
- Services
- Movies
- Podcasts
- Courses
- Webinars
- eBook
- Audio programs
- Video programs
- Coaching programs
- Workshops
- Seminars
- DVDs
- Tele-seminars
- Workbooks
- Newsletters
- Memberships
- Kits
- Manuals
- Train the trainer programs

You can use your book as a gift to your clients or people you wish to do business with. You can receive invitations to gatherings you would never have been invited to. A book is a vehicle that will promote you, bring attention to your brand and generate business for you.

Think big. You can do this!

Imagine what it would be like when you have that book and see your story in it. Think…

- who you can share it with
- what you can do with it
- and more importantly, how you can make money with it
- and build your business.

Who would you want to share your story with? Whose life could you change?

I am so proud to tell you that I have produced well over 200 podcasts and have created 40 #1 international bestselling authors to date. I have helped numerous people create an online course and helped people generate thousands of new leads.

My business has exploded exponentially by implementing the steps we have discussed in this chapter, and you can do it too! Please reach out to me. I would be happy to help you take your business to the next level.

Draw a crowd to you and your business. Do something that we have discussed to generate exposure and leads to increase sales for your business. Tap into other networks to gain exposure to groups that you have not connected with or met. That tool opens doors to people who wouldn't look at you before, wouldn't do business with you. Speak on stages because you are now a published author. Connect with certain speakers or C-level executives; they will now look at you because you have published a book.

Think about using all these different pieces of marketing, which are not expensive, and will generate immediate results for you.

Just imagine the possibilities!

RANDI GOODMAN

Randi Goodman is a mom of four beautiful boys, a 4th Level CMA, a second Dan in Shotokan Karate and has an incredible passion for business as well as sharing tools and resources to help entrepreneurs take their business to the next level. She is the author and co-founder of the *Empowering Women to Succeed* book series and events, co-founder of globally renowned business conferences, workshops, and podcast show, including Toronto Women's Expo, Action Think Tank Academy, Empowering Women to Succeed Conferences, Business Wealth Summits and the Empowerment Radio Show. She is a caring, heart-centered entrepreneur who nurtures her networks with an altruistic view for the betterment of all in growth and prosperity. Randi's vision for this book series is driven by her dedication to empowering the success of all women, and men, worldwide.

CHAPTER 27

How to Find the Magic that's Inside You

BY TIM BANSAL

Each of us has a uniqueness within that will never be replicated in the future, nor has it existed in the past. Many of us, we live our entire lives without knowing what that magic is.

We get caught up in our daily lives, living the dreams of others, paying our bills and living a mediocre life.

All around us, we see famous people in sports, business, entertainment, and industry who represent the epitome of success and happiness. They seem to have some magic formula that eludes most of us. We assign them as receiving luck or some special circumstance, like having good genes or being born into privilege.

We currently live in the most extraordinary time in history, which offers many unique circumstances and the opportunity to achieve a great deal. There are so many avenues that offer all of us a chance to be successful, from creating viral YouTube videos or podcasts; selling products on the Internet, eBay, or Amazon; creating high-tech inventions like Tesla cars or meditation apps; to writing hardcover books or ebooks.

"If you try to do your best at every task, you'll see big changes in all areas of your life."

— Tim Bansal

Today, there are so many gurus and motivational speakers that provide so much great information online and in person. However, you have to beware, as most do not provide any solid direction or instruction that is concrete enough to actually follow. What you really need is real steps that can lead to lasting change, a new direction, and discovery of your "sweet spot." In all of us lies great abilities and skills, and for the most part, they lie dormant unless you have been lucky enough to discover them.

The goal is to find one or maybe two things you are good at, interested in, and generally excel in. Then, sharpen those strengths to see how you can be better than most. I'd like to provide a number of actions you can start taking today to help you find out what your strengths are and avoid a life of regret. Conversely, I'd like you to live an extraordinary life.

Discipline

Understand that whatever you do, whatever your ability, <u>discipline</u> is a key element to achieving any kind of success.

While we see many examples of success around us in the media, we never see the elements of discipline, because those are done behind the scenes. We see the awards ceremonies and never see the day-to-day training and practice that is required. For most of us, discipline is a concept, an idea, but not a daily ritual.

My challenge to you, to get you on your way, is to choose a small discipline to start with. It could be waking up an hour earlier, adding 10 pushups each day, making small dietary improvements, or reading 10 pages a day of a book. Make any small change that you can stick with for at least 60 days and track your progress.

These small changes, over time, will yield big results. More than that, they'll provide you with the building blocks of confidence, and you'll start to understand that there are very few limits.

Most people try too many things at the same time, and they end up giving up. The key is to start small and celebrate each day as a "win." Try just one new discipline at a time and build from there. Your brain is programmed to resist change, and it will fight you all the way. So be strong. Once this becomes a habit, it will become easy.

Discipline challenges our "comfort zone," so what was once uncomfortable soon becomes the norm. Similarly, if you try to do your best at every task, you'll see big changes in all areas of your life. So, as we implement discipline in one area, it affects all other areas by strengthening your belief in what you can accomplish.

The truth is, everything matters.

How you do one thing will affect everything else. We tend to go through our lives and save our effort for things we like, while we "half-ass" other things that seem unimportant.

My challenge to you is to take another 60 days and put your best effort into everything you do, from the most menial task to the most important. This means everything. If you're going to wash your car, do the best job you can. How you perform your tasks represents who you are and reflects an attitude of pride and success.

Another critical element of success and learning is documenting your life. The documenting can be done in a few different forms: pictures, videos, or writing. Writing, for me, has always been therapeutic. As a kid, math was the enemy, but writing has always been a pleasure. Even if you are not a writer, <u>keeping a journal</u> can provide benefits on so many different levels.

Writing helps you save good ideas. I know that we all carry around cell phones that have note pages, and I've used these as well. The problem is that every time I get a new phone, those notes are misplaced or worse, forgotten. The journal becomes a written record of a date and time that I can go back to, to learn from, reflect, write down my goals, and see patterns in my thoughts and behaviours. If we save those journals, they become a day-to-day record of who I am as I develop.

Together, these journals can provide great insight and be passed on to our loved ones as a record. I would have loved to have journals from my parents to go through. Despite its "old school" nature, I would definitely recommend keeping a journal and customizing it to your personal needs. It will become a great learning tool.

It's all been done before. Most of us don't realize that all of our hopes, dreams, aspirations, and goals have most likely been documented somewhere. There's a book written somewhere, by someone, on the exact same problem or issue you are dealing with. Correction: There's a book, podcast, blog, vlog, or rant on that issue. All the information is out there, and at this exact time in history, the world is smaller than it has ever been.

We can share information with people all over the world with the press of a button.

"Your attitude predicts your altitude."

—Brian Tracy

Be a continual student, a lifelong learner.

We have easy access to the largest body of information in history. As you turn your attention to learning, different avenues will open up. For example, by reading biographies and autobiographies, you can learn from the mistakes and successes of others. This can be of great value. While books are not the only method of learning, find the method that works best for you. Media (such as YouTube) provides great learning videos. From learning guitar to French, many people make great progress.

Join clubs and groups that meet regularly with like-minded people. Mentoring and having one-on-one coaching have been great sources of inspiration and direction. Regardless of the method of learning, having the idea that learning is a critical path to becoming more skilled is very essential. Just the very act of understanding that we need to learn more puts us in a position of seeing opportunities that we may have not been aware of before.

Learning to add value has been a big theme in business and, on a personal level, everybody wants to add some kind of value. For most people, they have no idea how they can add value or be more valuable to the world at large. This is where learning new skills and expanding your mind connects you with what you can offer.

If you focus attention on certain of your skills and interests, this type of self-discovery can have big dividends. People often overlook their interests and passions because they have a hard time relating it to a career or a direct way to monetize something. However, start with things that really interest you to the point where you could do that activity without having to worry about getting paid because it brings you so much joy and fulfillment. These types of hobbies and activities turn into great careers.

Let's look at some examples.

Learning a new language can be a great value-added skill, and it can open opportunities that didn't exist before. It can create travel opportunities and open up new cultures, qualifying you for employment and access to business that would have otherwise been limited.

There is a host of new travel photographers and videographers earning a great living making videos, combining two passions to create a great lifestyle. Have a close look at the things that really drive you, and this will help turn something you love into a career, such as teaching a language, creating art, doing photography, making videos, sharing skills, travel writing, translating, being a food critic, etc.

Being a lifelong learner is really the <u>mindset</u> of people who understand that we can all get better and need to be students our entire lives.

An essential element of any kind of success starts with your beliefs; particularly, your beliefs about who you are and what you can accomplish. In looking at some of the most accomplished individuals, we see that in the face of adversity and obstacles, successful people go back to the belief of who they are. It determines their ability to keep on persisting.

It is believed that 90% of what we accomplish externally comes from us internally. That means that our <u>mindset,</u> internal beliefs, and internal dialogue relates to how well we will do, particularly when facing challenges. As stated by Brian Tracy, "Your attitude predicts your altitude."

As you continue to improve and look for opportunities, be careful what's going into your mind that might be undermining your confidence and self-belief.

Many would argue about those in our society who are born with talent. The belief is that without a positive mindset, discipline, or continuous learning, those few will triumph no matter what. However, despite your level of talent, all those elements are essential for any kind of success. Having talent or intellect is no guarantee of success. I am sure you know brilliant, talented individuals who achieve very little, despite having so much to work with. Talent, without grit or hard work, is no guarantee.

Most of us are born with moderate amounts of talent and need to rely on hard work. The good news is that hard work trumps everything else. If you're willing to put in the work, there is very little that can hold you back. Alternatively, without hard work, very little is possible, and relying on luck is a guarantee for disappointment.

Tied to hard work is integrity.

Success is generally empty without it.

A key downfall of many people is internal and external negativity. Some of the people closest to us will be our greatest dream killers. It may be your mother, father, relatives, or close friends. You taking a risk scares them, so they will discourage you.

Most people are terrified to pursue something new or risky. Watch out for these people, as they will easily and politely drag you down to inaction.

Similarly, many people are their own downfall. Whenever they start something new, they can, and often do, talk themselves out of success because of fear. This relates to many of the points I have covered, and this is particularly relevant as these people hit obstacles. There is no question that obstacles will arise. This should be expected. The obstacles provide a test of one's fortitude and commitment.

While you explore your interests, go wide and deep.

People often limit themselves to what they think is popular, or they get caught up with popular trends. Look at things you are naturally drawn to. It may not make sense right away, but as you explore them further, many opportunities can arise. Talk to people who know you best. Ask them what they think your skills may be. Personality surveys can often be enlightening.

Many successful business ideas or companies develop out of solving a problem or helping others in some way. I am hoping that by providing this information to others, it helps me to refocus and renew the information, as I am on the same quest.

There is a big push for business and entrepreneurship, a push to start your own company or venture.

I want to highlight that running a company is not for everyone.

You can follow your dreams with a small-scale operation, a consultancy, or an organization limited to one. There are a number of what I call new careers, designed to create a certain lifestyle. I think this is a very important element of following your dreams. Design the life you want, focusing on the important things to you. It could be travel, family time, or having the biggest building on the block.

When determining who you are and what you want, make sure to spend some time to consider this. Follow your dreams as opposed to those prescribed by someone else. It may even be a worthwhile exercise to think back to your childhood to look at your interests. Children are unencumbered by the limitations. It's not until we get older that the baggage slows down our creativity and imagination.

There are opportunities all around us. We just need the foresight to see them.

Try and expose yourself to as much as possible. There is so much great information out there. And, remember that someone has probably already given some great advice that can really help get you started.

As Jim Rohn says, "Nobody gets out of here alive," so give it your best shot.

Everything you need to succeed is already inside of you. Try some of these tips, explore who you are, and you'll find the one thing you can develop and be great at. In no way will it be easy, but the payoff will be worth it.

TIM BANSAL

Tim Bansal was born and raised in Toronto, Canada.

He received his BA in Political Science from York University in 1992, his B.Ed from Brock University in 1996, and his MBA from the University of Birmingham, UK, in 2000.

Tim worked in finance with top financial institutions until after getting his MBA. After that, he fell into sales, which became his career for the following 17 years.

Tim was an investor for almost 20 years, and eventually went into real estate as an investor and finally a real estate agent and success coach.

Keep your eye out for upcoming publications, and reach out to Tim at Tim.Bansal@century21.ca.

CHAPTER 28

"Grow Happiness in the Workplace: An A-to-Z Guide for Companies to Create Supportive Environments That Employees Thrive In."

BY MARK KERWIN.

Organizations and companies that want to win in the marketplace today require their entire work culture to be engaged in the pursuit of excellence. Finding best practices to create thriving work environments and grow happiness is at the heart of this A-to-Z guide for the company interested in outshining the competition.

A is for Audit

Look around your spaces – where your employees work and the spaces that serve as communal areas – do they feel inspired and creative to you? Create an ongoing wish list of all the aspects of these environments that you would improve. For our space at KLINK Coffee Inc., one low-cost solution has been working with local design students at Ryerson University. Partnering with schools can allow you to involve people at the beginning of their interior design careers and have them work on your spaces as part of their real-life projects for school.

B is for Brave

One must be brave to go beyond just wanting supportive space, but to actually go ahead and create the supportive space that you and your staff need. Don't wait for permission. Don't assume someone else will do it. When I first started at KLINK, I needed to create something that would foster inclusive space and herald a fresh start. I went ahead with a community mural project that had not entirely been approved of by the person filling in for my boss who was on medical leave. I saw the value and believed in what I was doing, so I went ahead with the project and it really turned out beautifully for all who participated. Fortunately, when my boss returned, she approved the project and recognized the value in what I was attempting to create.

C is for Community

The greatest need we all have is to feel a part of something larger than just ourselves. Building community is fundamental to supportive environments. One of KLINK's customers in the United Way gave herself the title Chief Coffee Procurement Officer, and began organizing coffee socials for staff members. This was such a hit that it grew into impromptu group visits to coffee shops nearby to explore coffee further.

D is for Diversity

Diversity is strength. Accepting, allowing and encouraging diversity is a deep part of supportive environments and can lead us to learn and grow. At KLINK, an easy, low-cost diversity-friendly addition to the workspace environment I started right away was to post a gender-neutral bathroom sign. Many people comment on the proactive and positive sign and say that it makes them feel welcome, no matter how the person self-identifies.

E is for Energize

Supportive spaces are all about energizing and elevating. Tune in to your workplace - do the colors, textures, smells, tastes, visuals, sounds in the space inspire you? Inspired by my visit to an eBay office, I learned to personalize my workplace no matter where I am. I love showing off my

Hulk action figure or my Marvel superhero posters, alongside posters of heroes Terry Fox and Muhammad Ali as well as comic book art by Lights. Allowing staff to personalize space is energizing and motivating and can create a place of calm that leads to great work.

F is for Fun

At KLINK Coffee, staff is encouraged to find and share positive, motivating videos and music and discuss why it inspires them during two recess breaks we have per day. Having fun creates a positive learning environment and builds trust between those that work and play together. One of our best clients is the renowned Centre for Social Innovation – they do an amazing job of creating regular social events for the community to participate in and share – we are proud to serve our KLINK Coffee at fantastic spaces like CSI that promote fun for the community as part of their social mission.

G is for Genuine

Google "Zappos Ten Core Values" to get a great sense of how a company can create a workplace culture that allows for authenticity and personality to shine through. I love what they are doing at Zappos to allow people to bring 100% of themselves to work. At KLINK Coffee Inc., our dress code is two words: Look Awesome. I find that allowing people to express themselves through their clothes allows them to bring their genuine self to work and allows us to stay focused on the quality of our work as opposed to formal dress codes.

H is for Hero

We all have a hero within us, one that wishes to conquer our fears with bravery and help others overcome their own inner challenges. At KLINK, I try to bring out that heroic quality in staff by having team huddles at the beginning and the end of the workday. We repeat out loud "The Titan's Declaration" *by Robin Sharma* – this builds up energy and enthusiasm and helps us keep focused on the tasks at hand with a shared sense of purpose. It is more fun and exciting to be a part of a movement and a mission than just a job or work, so finding creative ways to bring our heroic sense of purpose out in everyone is fundamental to leading supportive spaces.

I is for Integrated Planning

Supportive spaces must not only address individual needs, they also must integrate the learning and sharing that comes from those individual needs among the collective. At KLINK, we love using big white boards (inexpensive; easy-to-use technology to share and integrate perspectives) to display people's long, medium and short-term goals and plans. Seeing the shared individual goals publically is motivating and supportive.

J is for Joy

Supportive spaces contribute to the growing joy in incremental, daily ways. I once worked at a sales office that would play a personalized song whenever someone made a sale. Everyone in the office would hear that song and know who made the sale, and everyone could easily share in the victory dance celebration of running a lap around the office. We have a small budget at KLINK, but we still have quarterly staff retreats and use local cafes to meet at so we can enjoy reviews as a joyous occasion to learn and grow.

K is for Kind

Satya Nadella, the CEO of Microsoft, talks about how supportive environments and work culture in which employees thrive can insulate organizations from the disruption of technology. The heart of KLINK is about creating empathy and kindness, even while we try to become a better coffee company, and finding creative ways to embed kindness in our supply chain is critical to our success. Search for ways to add social enterprises to your supply chain – this is an easy start in creating more kindness in your company through the products and services that are used throughout your business. Buy Social Canada is a great resource to source social enterprises for your supply chain.

L is for Love

Love is the most important quality in the universe, and also the one we need and wish for the most. Feelings of love are very healthy and contribute to our longevity and wellness. Make sure to schedule time for staff to be around people, places and pursuits that fuel passion and saturate space with care. Making time to deeply think about bringing love into the workplace is critical for the well-being of your company and staff.

M is for Messaging

Collaboratively deconstructing and simplifying whatever message is at the core of your work can help you redefine your work environment and create a sense of unity. It was time consuming, but KLINK invested in several days of examining and redefining our core Mission, Vision and Values with everyone on staff participating. The process of defining the heart of our movement helped everyone commit to a more clearly communicated message.

N is for Never-Ending (Improvement)

Investing in regular, scheduled and ongoing education for yourself and your staff is key to keeping your organization in the flow of never ending improvement. I highly recommend looking at events in your local area that allow groups to participate in. At KLINK, I regularly scan Eventbrite for low-cost or free events that we can participate in as a company – this allows us to build more rapport amongst staff but also keep learning.

O is for Outreach

Dan Kershaw, Executive Director at Furniture Bank, has taught me that a leader must strive to surround her/himself with people who are better at aspects of the business than they are themselves. When I reached out to Dan for some help in onboarding into the social enterprise industry, he generously agreed to meet me quarterly for breakfast and share with me many of his strategies to help grow leaders within his own company. Make sure to invest in opportunities for staff to engage with different leaders within your industry as well as outside of it. Having outreach to fresh perspectives is critical to keeping your organization thriving.

P is for Playful

Even the military is using play and games to strengthen skills and build collaboration among groups of leaders. Creating regular opportunities for your staff to play at problem-solving issues can make overcoming obstacles fun and interesting, rather than confusing and aggravating. The brand Geek Squad encourages online gaming for its employees as a way to share resources and solve work-related challenges in a relaxed setting, leading to informal skills sharing and collaboration.

Q is for Question

Don't be afraid to question. I have a No Stupid Rules policy at KLINK Coffee Inc. that encourages anyone in our organization to email me stupid rules (like having to wear uncomfortable shoes) and then we review the rules and/or do away with them. We care about results. Not silly dress codes. Policies and procedures should always be changeable and questioned if they don't lead to better results. Many companies are doing away with rulebooks altogether in favor of more participatory structures and guidelines.

R is for Reward

Building up morale starts with regular, daily recognitions and rewards. Some innovative companies like Zappos have gone and created internal currencies that staff members can reward other staff members with for great work. Creating an environment where we all feel empowered to congratulate others for great work is part of a winning culture.

S is for Self -Care

We rarely schedule self-care. Encouraging your organization to invest in self-care tools will help improve performance. I recently was at an Immigrant Women in Business event and purchased Karlyn Percil's excellent *Success Planner: Making Time For What Matters Most* for all of my staff. It was a great gift but also one that will provide excellent returns for the staff using it. Actively promoting tools for self-care sets a positive tone and supportive environment for everyone to invest time in renewal and reflection.

T is for Trust

Tim Ferriss' book The 4 Hour Work Week motivated me to create systems at work that help people feel like they are trusted. Empowering decision making into the design of the workplace encourages staff to be proactive in using their own judgment and discretionary powers. I suggest setting a monetary amount where anyone can make a decision without management if the stakes are valued at $1000 or less. This also encourages calculated risk-taking, something that is critical for fostering the creative process of business development.

U is for Universal

FoodShare in Toronto is one of my favorite social enterprises. They offer healthy food in generous portions for lunch as a perk for all staff and volunteers, regardless of income or status. This benefit builds community and levels the economic differences between people, making sure everyone can eat well. These are the kinds of experiences that lead to supportive environments that are equitable and accessible for all. We all need to put time and focus into creating these kinds of universal benefits in our workplaces.

V is for Victory Talk

I encourage my staff to share out loud their positive victory talk every day with phrases like "I can do this," or "I am committed to finding the best solution" when faced with challenges in the day. Creating a sports team feel to our daily operations at KLINK allows us to engage in victory talk—like our Thank God It's Monday (TGIM) where we proudly wear Toronto sports team clothing and give shout outs to the #6ix in our social media. Victory talk is contagious and helps create a supportive environment.

W is for Welcoming

When we design our supportive spaces with warmth, and inclusive principles, we set up those that enter that space, including ourselves, for success. One of my staff members put together a statement for honoring First Nation lands, something we aim to read before any events or gatherings at the KLINK office. Putting in an effort to truly welcome all has a powerful impact on empowering thriving work cultures.

X is for X-Factor

Supportive environments allow us to contribute our unique X-factor to our workplace. The "Je ne sais quoi" aspect that makes us so unique in the world also helps us be extraordinary and give all we have with authenticity. People are what sets your business apart – putting people first must also include your employees. We brainstorm once a week at KLINK Coffee Inc. (www.drinkklink.com) on how we can continue to improve customer service by adding our own unique X-factor to our roles. This personalized service also allows staff to be authentically engaged and increase happiness in the workplace.

Y is for Yes

Saying yes to partnerships and collaborations with other agencies and brands is why social enterprise is influencing the marketplace towards more shared projects where all can win more than they put in individually. When creating the Alleyway of Dreams, I worked with the local BIA (business improvement area) to find ways for the whole community to feel the positive impact of laneway improvements and be on board for the project. Look for ways to get people to say "yes" and empower partners to improve spaces, staff and activities, allowing all to feel engaged and participate.

Z is for Zeal

Nothing beats zeal in achieving excellence and success in our lives. Enthusiasm grows outward in waves and impacts the spaces where we work. For an example of zeal, go to the awesomeeh.ca website where you can see the inspiration of a group of "moonshot" visionaries and how they all want to have a positive impact on Canada and the world. At KLINK Coffee, the supportive space has infused staff with genuine excitement for our story, product and company and the work zeal is contagious. Putting thought, effort and resources into creating zeal for your company's mission will reap long term results well beyond the investment.

Thank you for reading this chapter. If you are ready to reap the benefits of a supportive environment and create a happy, thriving work culture, please contact me today at markkerwin@gmail.com

MARK KERWIN

Mark Kerwin is the Executive Director of KLINK Coffee Inc., a non-profit social enterprise dedicated to supporting those coming home from prison with mentorship, life skills, employment and supportive environments. Mark is also the Creative Director of the community- supported street art project, the Alleyway of Dreams. As a global ambassador to Team Diabetes, Mark has raised over $100,000 for Diabetes Canada and supported many with health and wellness improvements. His goal of completing fundraising athletic events on all 7 continents will be completed in 2020 in Antarctica. Mark is available for consulting, coaching, keynote addresses, retreats, panel discussions and more. For more information on transforming your staff, spaces or organization, and how to design supportive environments, please contact Mark at markkerwin@gmail.com or visit his LinkedIn profile at https://www.linkedin.com/in/markkerwin.

CHAPTER 29

The Power of Decision

BY RALSTON POWELL

Doing the impossible is possible. Despite the ups and downs in life (and there may be many), you can come out ahead of the game and have the massive wealth, joy, and health that you want.

How do I know? I did it.

Faith is a Healer

I was born in the parish of Manchester, Jamaica, and grew up poor, but with a fairly normal life until the age of 16. At that time, I began losing my sight. It became so bad that I couldn't even read my own Bible.

> *"Determination opens doors."*
> —*Ralston Powell*

As things got worse, I could hardly go outside because the glare of the sun was overwhelming and painful. It was dangerous to walk. I could go a few feet, then try to cover my eyes, and go a little farther with my eyes closed before opening them again for a quick glimpse.

Over time, I was almost completely bedridden. I didn't know what was wrong with me, and a doctor gave me some paste to put in my eyes and said I had iritis. Nobody I knew had ever heard of it. We had nothing to go on but faith.

I decided to open myself up to help in the way of prayer. I had people come to my home to pray for me 1-2 times per week, and I was healed miraculously by the power of God through prayer after 2 months.

When you make a decision to persist instead of accepting failure, you magnetize good results. When you have faith, you can stay on the path to recovery.

You can't waver from your decision. You must be determined.

Faith Can Get You Through Hard Times

I migrated to Canada in the late 1960's. My wife and I had jobs and were renting, but at some point, we decided to invest in a home and set a deadline of six months. We made immediate cutbacks, set aside money every month, saved up a down payment, and bought a home within six months using pure determination.

We succeeded in buying the home, but we still didn't know enough about investing.

Shortly after buying our first home, we bought a second so we could rent it out. I could glimpse my dream of massive wealth, but we hadn't reached the end goal yet.

"Never give up. Never give up. Never give up."
—Winston Churchill

Unfortunately, like I said before, you'll have ups and downs. In 1989, a number of events led to us losing both homes.

The housing bubble had burst in Toronto. I wasn't expecting it. Although it was crushing at the time, things got even worse. Our marriage started to flounder, and we separated.

Now, when I look back, I can see that this huge loss was just one more step on the path to achieving a vision of wealth and financial freedom. Indeed, as the years went by, my old desire to manage real estate stayed with me.

A Trip to the Holy Land

When I went to Israel in 1988, I had a chance to walk where Jesus walked and visit his empty tomb, the place where angels declared that He had risen. I had a chance to experience first hand some of the places he'd been and talked about, deepening my understanding. It was eye-opening to not only read these things in the Bible, but to see these places with my own eyes.

Jesus came into the world to show mankind how to live, love, and learn. He went about doing good, not killing people.

He was born poverty-stricken in a manger, yet the three wise men came from the east to present him with gold, Frankincense, and myrrh. They treated him as royalty, and, as a King, he rules his Kingdom today.

Unlike many of the kings on this planet, Jesus chose to shower love and resources on the people.

One of the first parables he told people was to encourage them to be prosperous. Just like any farmer, when we sow seeds in fertile soil, we're provided with an abundant harvest. One seed in the ground, once sprouted, can be plucked at maturity and provide many more seeds in that one stalk. Imagine planting a single seed of wheat, and the resulting stalk producing a bountiful harvest, a 30-fold, 60-fold, or 100-fold yield.

This is what we are meant to do for ourselves and the rest of humanity.

Planting a spiritual seed of kindness produces the fruits of the spirit: love, joy, peace, gentleness, goodness, and faith. That's what we are meant to do.

Jesus Christ was personified to be the mediator between God and mankind. In other words, a direct line to help people find and connect with their spiritual source. He also showed us how we are to live.

"We have known Ralston since 2002. Over the years, we have come to appreciate him as a man of character and integrity. He has deep insights into the issues of life that have come out of years of reflection and study."

— Dr. Dan and Carol Silehi, Senior and Associate Pastors of the Access Center, Greater Toronto Area

Be Willing to Start Over

A few years ago, I started studying again. I invested in myself by attending a talk given by Robert G. Allen, who became famous for teaching people to invest in real estate with no money down. I knew that if I surrounded myself with successful people and learned from them, it would pay off.

In fact, it was because of that investment that I met Sunil Tulsiani and became part of the Private Investment Club. I was lucky enough to travel to Robert G. Allen's home in San Diego and spend time there, which was extremely inspiring. I felt surer than ever that with the right education, the power of decision, good connections, and faith, I'd be back on the right path again.

Be Determined

This is the story of my life. I had to face extreme obstacles, but I had the insight that success is a decision. If you have faith and courage, you can do anything.

You have to be determined to do whatever it takes and have the willingness to help others along the way. In fact, giving is the biggest indicator that you will be successful, not just financially, but spiritually, too.

My faith in Jesus has taught me a great deal of compassion for others. That's my core value. Growing up in Jamaica, I can see that the problems of poverty are all over the world, and I feel a very strong desire to help.

Throughout the world, many people can't even find clean water to drink. There are charities giving them food, but if the wells are full of polluted water, the food won't do them any good.

I believe in five kinds of health, and they're all important.

Five Distinct Kinds of Health

Spiritual Health: The most important thing anybody can do is to get their spiritual house in order. When you're out of touch with God and try to do everything yourself without spiritual guidance, it's like you're drawing water out of a dirty well. You might do all the right steps, but your results won't be the same.

Take some time each day to pray and meditate on all the gifts God has given us. When you do, you'll be much more joyful and feel more peace. It will help you get your day off to a good start and help you sleep better, too.

You're meant to be an instrument of your Maker, so make each day count.

Physical Health: People can't function properly when they're in pain, sick, or unfit. So much of what's fun in life depends on having a healthy body that can play, dance, and work productively.

So many people suffer from bad lifestyle choices that eat away at their well being.

Listen to the great doctors out there. Value and appreciate your health. There are experts ready to help you, people who have traveled a similar path to yours. It's just a matter of finding them and not giving up.

Mental Health: My faith in Jesus Christ is unshakable. And, on a personal level, I'm self-motivated. Like a man baking a cake with all the right ingredients, I cannot fail as long as I maintain the effort.

When your mind is cluttered up with feelings of worthlessness or confusion, it's hard to be your best. And yet we're called to help the poor, love our neighbors as ourselves, and serve God to the best of our ability. When you know your true purpose in life, it helps you to be at your best.

Emotional Health: Being angry all the time can only bring you ruin. Even if sad things happen to you in life or people have done you wrong, you only hurt yourself when you carry bad feelings against other people. Instead, recognize that there are many good people in the world, and try to forgive the others.

Financial Health: It's so important to be mindful of money. Pay your taxes, keep good records, and keep your financial house in order just as you'd keep your physical, mental, emotional, and spiritual houses in order.

We're meant to shine our lights to the world, not hide them under bushels. Accumulating wealth is one way that you can do great good for the world and have plenty to use for the benefit of the poor and needy.

I would love to see clean water brought to desperate countries, peace brought to war-torn territories, and plenty of food and medicine for the people who need it. I know that this dream can come true, but we must all start with ourselves first.

My Purpose Resurrected

My new motto is, "Helping you find the diamonds in your backyard."

As Pastor Silehi says, God has purpose, and we all have a destiny to do great things. The good pastor also says that we have to have the desire to find our purpose, be determined to fulfill it, and take action to accomplish it. That's how God does his work. He gives you the talent and the purpose, and you have to use your power of decision to carry it out.

To the very fiber of my being, I feel that purpose, and I'm grateful that I do. My purpose and desire is to help people spiritually, physically, and financially.

People miss the opportunities right in front of them while searching far and wide. There is medical help for you 24/7, so I let people know where it is. There are people suffering expensive conditions, not knowing they are caused by simple vitamin deficiencies.

Not knowing is like having acres of diamonds in your backyard but dying as a pauper. All the information in the world is available to us now. It's my life's purpose to distribute it.

Take Action

If you have dreams or goals, don't be dormant. The trials that you experience will give you insights that you wouldn't have had otherwise.

When you're on the right path, you see value in all your experiences, even if they're painful, and your path unfolds as part of the perfect plan.

"Ask not what your country can do for you. Ask what you can do for your country."
— **John F. Kennedy**

When I was afraid that I would lose my sight forever, it was terrifying. When I lost my own residence and the rental house I had, it was frightening. When I lost my wife, I was devastated. Yet, my desire to share with humanity and my love for Jesus Christ are what kept me moving forward.

When you think of it, it's not lack of food or medicine that keeps people homeless, poor, or sick. It's lack of love. Greedy people suffer from emotional discord: blaming the poor and being afraid that the poor will rob them. It leads to the emotional sickness of greed, which is as thick as a concrete wall and keeps people stuck whether they're wealthy or poor.

To really prosper, don't worry so much about money. Even the lilies are beautifully dressed, and money without generosity is more like a cancer than a blessing.

Generosity Heals

When Jesus was on the earth, he was moved with compassion and made it his business to heal the sick, the blind, the dead, and the broken-hearted. That's love. And his disciples did the same. One of the first things Jesus did was to sow seeds of humanity and use them as a lesson in true prosperity. Imagine if countries drop-shipped food instead of bombs. Just think how much more prosperous the entire planet would be.

Some people hoard knowledge. I like to associate with people who are generous with information, because I believe that sharing knowledge is a major way to help the world.

Learning and teaching keep the brain healthy and can offer so much hope. Education is very powerful in getting people on the right path to healing their physical bodies and every other area of their health. Even young people can get heart disease or cancer of the blood, and it's devastating.

There is a time and a season for everything under the sun. Jesus was a giver and so am I. I'm not ashamed of it, and I want to help people get on the right path.

What Can We Do to Help?

"Mr. Powell lays out a clear roadmap to recovery for the millions of people needlessly suffering from physical, spiritual, or financial pain. He provides you with recommendations for change, in this case, diet supplements and environmental, to assist people dealing with and even reversing heart problems. Mr. Powell gives you both knowledge and solutions. You just need to apply them."
— *Francis K. Long, DDS*

Think of it this way: "For God so loved the world, that He gave His only begotten Son." If Jesus was a gift of love, then Love must have Greater Power than we know.

Take care of your own health, spiritually, physically, emotionally, mentally, and financially. Then, in a spirit of love, spread the wealth and goodness far and wide. You'll be blessed, I promise.

If there was one thing I could tell you to help ease your pain, in any area of life, it would be that you don't have to stay the way you are. There is help. Associate with and get to know people who speak from the heart and want to help you.

Thank you for reading my chapter and considering my words. My biggest motivation in writing this chapter is to help people. I would love for everybody to enjoy the health and well-being that I found, and I would love to provide support for anyone wishing to benefit from my experiences.

As my life enhances and expands, my cup overfloweth, and the overflow is for sharing. To get in touch with me, reach me at www.boosthearthealth.com.

RALSTON POWELL

Ralston was born in Jamaica, West Indies. He discovered the power of faith when he lost his sight due to a rare infection and was healed through prayer. At age 17, he studied English, math, and chemistry at Dinthill Practical Training Center.

When he was in his early twenties, his mother moved to Canada, and he followed six months later. He continued his studies at George Brown College, and later at Jarvis Collegiate Institute, and studied real estate at Seneca college. He lives in Toronto, Canada.

He loves all sports and enjoys swimming, playing soccer, and cricket. He knows what it's like to have a serious ailment, and therefore feels compassion for people with heart disease and cancer. He's also very concerned about lack of clean water in developing countries.

Ralston has one purpose in life, and that's to help others. His passion is helping people physically, spiritually, and financially.

You can reach Ralston at his website, www.boosthearthealth.com.

CHAPTER 30

11 Steps to Building Wealth with LinkedIn

BY NAVEEN BAHAR SUJAN

Did you know that using social networking to advertise your business is not only fun, but profitable? And do you know why LinkedIn is the best platform to use?

There are over ½ billion people on LinkedIn, and many of them are looking to do business with you right now.

I continuously use LinkedIn to bring high-paying clients to the Private Investment Club and build its brand equity.

In my view, LinkedIn is more important than even our website because it brings new blood to our business and builds credibility at the same time.

The Difference Between LinkedIn and Other Social Media

Other social media platforms are meant for people to connect, keep in touch, and socialize. Although they offer business pages and advertising, there's a world of difference with LinkedIn: it's specifically created to connect businesses.

How Linkedin Can Generate Massive Wealth for You

Last month, one of my clients asked me, "Is it true that I can make money from LinkedIn?" Of course, we all know the answer to that.

"Yes."

You see, in any business, whether you're an accountant, real estate professional, mortgage broker, marketer, coach, speaker, author, or in virtually any business – you need one thing. You need a supply of paying clients who want to work with you.

And, LinkedIn has millions of potential clients right now who may do business with you if they know about you and trust you.

The main thing to understand is this: Whether you're looking for private investors to fund your real estate project, help raise money, connect with CEOs, find joint venture partners, or locate buyers for your product, LinkedIn has the traffic for you to tap into.

And, it can be set up at absolutely no cost.

I'm going to go over the 11 steps to building your wealth and how to set yourself up on LinkedIn, so people actually find you and want to do business with you.

11 Steps You Should Take on LinkedIn

1. Set up Your Profile Properly

This is really critical. It's where people will look for you.

Make your profile exciting. You should have a distinctive photo and a description of what you do so that people get a good idea of who you are, what you offer, and what you stand for.

If you want investors, have a fully rounded personal brand, backed up with substance, and indicate where the link will lead. If you want speaking engagements, add pictures and link to your past speaking gigs.

On your showcase page, you can have a link to your one-sheet description of the types of talks you do. Interested organizations can download it there. You can link to articles in your field and link to articles you've written. Everything you can do to deepen the visitor's experience with you is good.

Here's a screen shot of a good LinkedIn Profile that you may want to model after.

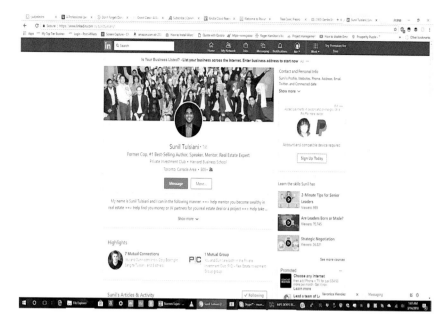

If you're blogging on LinkedIn or sending InMail to make contacts, people will naturally check your personal page to see who you are. You've got to make an impact if you expect them to connect with you or give any credence to your business.

Always write your personal profile in first person. Saying "him" or "her" when talking about yourself makes it sound impersonal and distant. You want people to relate to your profile personally.

You might want to use keywords to attract attention to your business or personal name. For example, a headline like, "Smith and Jones Real Estate, Serving Toronto, Canada," is much better than "Smith and Jones Real Estate." Put a lot of thought into your headline and test it by changing it from time to time and searching your keywords to see where you're ranked.

In the example above, Sunil Tulsiani uses his name alone, but uses keywords throughout his headline (under the name), tagline (specific business proposition), and location/industry. Using keywords will make people want to click to learn more. Brainstorm the best keywords to use, which don't have to match your current title exactly if you've done the equivalent work.

Make sure your summary is terrific. Use testimonials and videos. Show awards, achievements, interests, and personality. Make sure to highlight articles you've written on LinkedIn.

The value of a personal brand is that you can use it to find and retain candidates to work in your business, find and retain customers, promote awareness of your business, get access to people in your market, make people aware of your events, and find more opportunities to speak and write.

Find some way of making yourself stand out. The personal page helps your company page and vice-versa. To give you an idea of a great profile, go to LinkedIn and search for Sunil Tulsiani's (www.linkedin.com/in/suniltulsiani).

When you have a paid LinkedIn account, you can find out who's viewed your profile, company page, blogs, etc. Reach out to those people, as it's much more effective than cold calling.

2. Your Company Profile

If you have a company or organization, you may want to have a separate company page. Your company page should be vibrant and interesting, which means a lot of pictures, accomplishments, Mission and Vision Statements, and links to testimonials and events.

Both the company profile and the personal profile count; they both need to tell your target market that you can give value. And, you have to know your market: where the prospects are located and what motivates them.

3. Choose Keywords Carefully

Use keywords that relate to your business. If you don't have content and keywords on your business page, you're pouring business down the drain.

You should sprinkle your articles and personal profile with keywords, too. Remember that you're trying to present a cohesive picture of what you do and your area of expertise. Use keywords in your content, speech titles, pages, blogs, comments, etc.

Do keyword searches on a regular basis and see if your articles come up. This will help you track your progress in the rankings. Are you going up or down over time?

Also, LinkedIn supplies analytics on LinkedIn. From your homepage, just click the "Me" icon, then Manage, and then Company Page. After that, click the Analytics tab and select Visitors, Updates, or Followers from the dropdown menu.

4. Shared Posts

You need to be multidimensional, so curate other people's posts on your pages. It encourages people to come to your site for input about your industry, not only about you. Besides, it shows people that you are not only in business, but that you're keeping up to date on industry issues.

Shared posts don't sell you; instead, they invite visitors to engage with your page using likes and comments. They make your page interesting to visit. The longer visitors dwell on your page, the better for your ranking on the LinkedIn search engine, Google, and others.

5. Blog Posts

If you're blogging on your business website, that's great. Consider posting those blogs on LinkedIn, too. That's because it adds dimension to your LinkedIn page and gives unique information about your area of expertise. Visitors to your website are looking for hours, prices, and other information like that. If you hide your blog posts on your business page, you're missing a huge opportunity to connect with other business professionals and prospects on LinkedIn, where lots of them are looking.

When you blog on LinkedIn consistently, you'll become an Influencer and become easier to find in searches. It also gives you a chance to use keywords that attract people in your target market. And, people will probably like, comment on, and share your content, which makes you easier to find and more credible.

You'll be more than a vendor with a simple sales page, prices, and order form, and people on LinkedIn appreciate that more in-depth view of your business. They're business oriented, but want to connect with interesting human beings, too. Blogging gives you some depth and individuality.

By the way, blog on a regular basis. If your blog is haphazard, you're representing yourself as a haphazard person. And, update your blogs from time to time to show that you're on top of changes.

Make sure to write on Pulse, the timeline you see when you log in, on a regular basis. Millions of business professionals on LinkedIn are looking for engaging business content, and they're also looking for comments on their content. And, LinkedIn will notify you automatically every time someone comments, so you can respond and engage.

Use a 1:1:4 ratio in your content. Use one hard sell article, one soft sell article, and four relevant industry-related posts just for engagement.

The best content generates likes, shares, engagement, and advocacy.

6. Commenting

Make contributions to the thought in your industry. Use the opportunity to plant seeds of thought about you and your own business while you make relevant, useful comments. Keep the spotlight on the author, but if you've accomplished something like making a speech or breaking a personal or company record, feel free to share it, especially because it might help others.

7. Showcase Pages

Have up to 10 showcase pages. These are places where you can create depth and purpose to your activities and experience. For example, you might have one for your public speaking, one for your books, and another for your investment opportunities. Use background pictures, pop-ups, or anything else that makes your pages interesting.

Remember, LinkedIn is the world's largest publishing platform, so take advantage and use everything it has to offer.

8. Sales Navigator

Sales Navigator is a paid tool you can buy on LinkedIn. It allows you to see your network in more depth and search with more detail. It helps you identify companies that you might want to develop a relationship with, and that will help a lot when it comes to finding and developing leads.

9. Connecting via InMail

Do an advanced search using your keywords, such as investors, real estate agents, investments, properties, money, accountants, coaches, etc. You can even scan the most commonly used keywords in your category, and narrow by location or distance.

Develop many first connections so you can have more second and third connections, because first connections can introduce you to others. Be very diligent about answering all your InMail.

Pick 10 Influencers who have at least 500 connections, but look for those with 10,000-100,000 when you can. That's because once you connect with these Influencers, you can only reach out to their first and second connections, so look at their profiles and make sure it's worthwhile according to your business interests. Look for relationships that will most likely be mutually beneficial.

When you send a contact request or send InMail, be sure to personalize your message. People sending the stock, done-for-you contact requests that LinkedIn supplies don't generally get very good results. You might indicate that you're considering their services or that you want to connect because some of your students might be interested in what they have to offer.

You can offer a gift, such as a free book, and link the offer to an opt-in page to get their email when they download the book. After that, you can email them. When you do, make sure to say something about yourself, remind them how you met, and tell them why you're interested in connecting. When they've responded, and you've begun to reach out regularly, contact them by phone to share something of value to them: news about real estate trends in their area, a new investment opportunity, market news, etc.

If you can connect personally over coffee, via email, or Skype. Appreciate your contacts and use LinkedIn as a catalyst to meet them in some other area if possible. Everyone who's been in business realizes how important personal relationships are, but everyone needs their time respected, too. Strike a balance and focus on providing value for the other person.

It's much easier to connect on a business basis on LinkedIn than it is in other social media, due to the very nature of LinkedIn. You'll need to follow up consistently and add value to the relationship, and you can even hire someone to do that for you.

Again, hopefully you've done your homework and done a great job developing your profile page, company page, blog, and shared posts. If you're a multidimensional person and represent a company with achievements, goals, and purpose, you're much more likely to develop meaningful contacts that will pay off in the future.

10. Timing

Fix all your basics before you start marketing, including personal and business profiles. You don't want to start a lengthy marketing campaign and draw in lots of new prospects when all the basics aren't covered.

Write a marketing plan before you start sending InMail, joining groups and discussions, making comments, and updating content about your industry.

11. Advertising

Buy the advertising on your own page. There is no point in letting your prospects consume your content while finding someone else's ads on your page. This will not only give your page a more unified appearance but will allow people to check out your offers.

Now that we talked about what to do, let's go over some of the most common mistakes so many business owners make.

The Most Common Mistakes

1. Spreading yourself too thin by listing everything you know how to do in life. You need a robust profile, but your content should primarily relate to your business without too much clutter.

2. Failing to get a professional writer's help to build a personal or business profile. If you need someone's help to bring out the best in you…it's worth it.

3. Forgetting to use pictures, links, content, and updates.

4. Failing to engage when people interact with you. You want to build depth into your relationships; otherwise, you might come across like a spammer. Be sincere and direct, just like you would in any business relationship.

5. Letting your profiles fall out of date. People won't be open to your friend requests and InMail if you do.

6. Ignoring criticism or complaints.

7. Forgetting to ask your past clients or people you know to write recommendations every 2-3 months.

***

Remember, most professional people on LinkedIn are open to doing business with you if they find you interesting, engaging, well informed, and competent. No matter what your field is, people can find you on LinkedIn. It's a gold mine for attracting quality, high-paying clients, students, and investors. At the same time, it's the best place to network with CEOs, Presidents of large companies, authors, speakers, joint venture partners, and lot more.

I hope you dig deeper and take immediate action using this amazing platform to grow your business to the next level.

If you've not grabbed my exclusive report, "7 Ways to Identify Your Ideal Clients," please do so by going to PrivateInvestmentClub.com/Nav.

NAVEEN BAHAR SUJAN

Naveen received his MBA in 2000 and went on to assist software clients develop robust businesses in the European Union and Africa. He developed acclaim as a marketer for real estate brokerages and now serves as Marketing Manager for the Private Investment Club.

Naveen's specialties are finding properties; growing memberships; branding, finding and attracting high-paying business clients; and helping people become authors, speakers, and mentors through his cutting edge social media strategies.

While he works with all social media marketing platforms, his unique understanding of LinkedIn has brought solid business wealth to his most prestigious clients. According to Naveen, "Because of its unique standing as a business site and a social connection site, LinkedIn offers the best business connection solutions by far of all social media."

His passions are personal growth, yoga, and helping others achieve success and wealth. Naveen can be reached at +1-905-488-4033, or naveen@ privateinvestmentclub.com

CHAPTER 31

How I Bought 600 Doors

BY ROBERT ELDER

Congratulations on making it to the end of this book!

Two of the most important traits to being successful in the real estate business are the ability to get started and the ability to follow through to the end. You have succeeded on both counts!

I bought my first property, a duplex, in 1981 when I was 18 years old. I was absolutely the most inexperienced and unknowledgeable real estate investor possible. I was working as a part-time janitor and had no credit history.

My first two properties and first seven years in the real estate business were only about providing me with free housing.

As the market entered a downward cycle, I realized that if my earlier investments were good, additional investments would have to be much better. So I began to acquire additional rental properties as a way to build a portfolio and take advantage of bargain pricing.

Over the next 15 years, I dealt with some issues and challenges as a young adult. I had a family, got divorced, went back to school, and struggled with business failures. I struggled to find my ideal business and my ideal investment vehicle.

I was fortunate enough to meet and be mentored by legends like Brian Tracy, Tony Robbins, T. Harv Eker, and other wonderful mentors. It was at a mastermind event with T. Harv Eker in 2004 when I embraced two challenges.

The first was to simplify and focus on my business activities. At that point, I had 12 different business ventures going, including rental houses, two multilevel marketing businesses, partnerships with friends in small side businesses, an effort to perfect stock market trading, a hotel, and a part time law practice.

The challenge that I embraced was to eliminate every business except the one that I chose to be my single primary business.

Within three months, I had narrowed my focus to only acquiring, rehabbing, and renting single-family homes.

What a relief it was to be in only one business. It was also a little scary because those other businesses had provided emotional security and distraction even though they provided little economic benefit or promise.

The second challenge was to commit to a really BIG goal. I welcomed this challenge by setting a six-year goal to grow my real estate portfolio from $2.5 million to $25 million.

Today, I own 400 properties and 600 doors, and I have far exceeded my big goal.

Since then, I have not only grown my own real estate business but have mentored others to do the same. I realize that I have a unique system that anyone can plug into to become wealthy.

For example, one of my students who has done very well is a gentleman named Bob.

Bob and his wife were in their late 20s when we met. My first contact with Bob was at a local real estate investment association meeting that I was hosting.

After attending a few of the monthly meetings, Bob signed up for my coaching program.

Although Bob and his wife both had jobs, they had very little in savings, and because they had two young children they were also limited on time.

As I coached Bob, I realized what his two biggest issues were: a lack of support and enthusiasm from his spouse, and fear that any mistake would leave him open to criticism.

The training that Bob was getting with me was designed to help brand new investors buy their first rental property and be successful from Day One. Due to Bob's fear of having to report any type of problem to his wife, it was critical that his first property be a home run, which meant: it had to make money.

With my help, Bob decided to start with a very simple investment property.

It was easy because the property was in a working-class neighborhood but not in a war zone. It was built in the mid-70s, so it did not have all the construction and updating issues of a house built before 1950. The property needed repairs such as paint, flooring, new roof, and heating and air conditioning repairs.

Focusing on a house that had simple repairs made it highly unlikely that his remodel project would have any significant cost overruns. Although new roofs and HVAC equipment can be expensive, that work is always performed by a professional, comes with a guarantee, and requires little supervision during the work.

One of the key principles I teach everyone who invests in Oklahoma, or almost anywhere, is that the house has to have a positive cash flow after all expenses.

When I calculate my expenses, I take into account the mortgage payments (principal and interest), insurance, taxes, vacancy allowance, maintenance costs, and management fees. I also insist that the loan be repaid in 15 years instead of the usual 30.

Even with a 15-year amortization, the house has to have a positive cash flow after all the expenses.

This means that your tenants are expected to make your house free and clear in 15 years while giving you monthly income.

Obviously, there will be tenant issues along the way and some unforeseen expenses. This is why I recommend putting aside some emergency funds.

The great news is that Bob's house was repaired to be rent-ready on time and on budget. He immediately refinanced his investment property and got almost all his initial money back, which meant that he ended up buying this property with very little money out of his pocket.

Of course, the side benefit in Bob's scenario is that his wife was really happy, and they both decided to buy more properties to build their financial nest egg together as a couple.

As you can imagine, Bob has continued to grow his business by pursuing the idea of using section 8 money from the government to help pay the majority of his rent. The idea of using these government rent subsidies is something that I have mastered over the last 30 years and teach as a way to improve the stability of rental income from low-to-moderate rental housing.

Bob took my idea a step further by insisting that in his business, his section 8 rentals would be the absolute best, nicest, and newest section 8 houses in the market, which means that his properties get rented fast and he tends to attract better renters with a lot fewer headaches.

Another example of a success story is when I met Anthony at my monthly Millionaire Possibilities REIA meeting.

Anthony was a real estate investor with six properties and wanted to take his real estate business to massive levels.

Anthony decided to become part of my coaching program.

During the goalsetting session, Anthony decided that he wanted to buy 50 cash-flowing rental properties in seven years.

Now, not every mentee of mine wants to buy 50 properties, as this requires a lot more commitment, focus, persistence, and direction. One of the main challenges with Anthony was that he had maxed out on the number of conventional mortgages he could get. The bank would not lend him money anymore.

So, as his mentor, I decided to help find all the money he needed to fulfill his dream of becoming wealthy.

I coached Anthony to approach locally owned small banks that had up to six branches located within 100 miles and asked him to call the vice president(s) of these relatively small financial institutions and ask the following questions:

Q. Does your bank make loans for investment real estate?

Q. Which loan officer makes these kinds of property investment loans the majority of the time?

Then, Anthony was to schedule an appointment with that person.

Now, this is really important. When Anthony was calling or meeting the loan officer, he needed to have the mindset that he was making a sales call. He was selling them on the idea that he had a great business plan and that the bank should lend him the money.

In addition to normal documents Anthony needed, he also had a clear written plan for the house he wished to finance. He explained in detail exactly what he was going to do with the money. He talked about the recently sold comps, the repairs (including written estimates from contractors), how the property would be managed, the expected ongoing expenses, the expected rental income, and the after-repair value of the property.

During the meeting, remember to dress well, be prepared, and ask questions. Ask questions like:

- "Do you do in-house appraisals or use certain appraisers?"
- "What kind of properties do you like to lend on?"
- "Which areas do you like?"
- "Which areas do you not lend in?"
- "How can we build a long-term relationship?"

One of the things I helped Anthony do was to ask for five-year balloon notes. Even if the bank was willing to do a three-year note, this was good news. You see, most people are worried about what will happen when the note comes due in three or five years. They think that the bank is going to come back at that time and ask for all their money back.

Well, that's not what happens in most cases. Banks actually want to continue to lend money because that's the business they are in. If anything, banks want the opportunity to adjust the interest rate at the end of three or five-year term. All you need to do is pay on time and take care of the property.

And before you know it, the property is paid off by your renters.

The amazing news is that Anthony did end up finding the money he needed for 50 properties and more.

My favorite and most important student is Linda, who is now my wife.

Linda and I met in a high-end mastermind and I discovered that she had some big goals in real estate investing.

Linda was new to the country and on an investor visa. She had limited command of the English language, no connections, and no real estate experience in the USA.

The positives were that Linda had amazing real estate experience in her country Brazil; had been a real estate broker; and was the owner of a construction company that built homes and over a dozen high-rise apartment buildings (in the latter years, focusing on eco-friendly high-rise buildings).

Initially, Linda decided to buy properties below market value, fix them, and flip them. Although she made some money flipping in a short period of time, she had a much better goal: She wanted to build a real estate business that would bring in lots of cash flow on a monthly basis.

One of my jobs when coaching Linda was to convince her to buy rental properties so she could build the wealth she wanted.

I explained how I buy properties discounted, fix them (make them rent-ready), get a renter in, and have my established management company manage them. I explained to her that one of the main advantages I had was that I had been operating a management company that could look after these rental properties.

This brings us to an extremely important topic: property management. It's the holy grail of building your wealth through rental properties. I know it sounds like everyone should know this, but getting a good management company should be one of your highest priorities.

Please do your due diligence, make sure the management company has an office in the same city as your properties, get some referrals from other investors, attend your local REIA clubs, live events, masterminds, etc., and ask around.

Anyway, back to Linda. I explained to her in detail that my business model of buying houses produces monthly positive cash flow with little to nothing out of my pocket. Basically, I buy properties discounted, fix them up, and refinance them using the after-repair value (ARV).

I was happy to see Linda getting excited about this proven moneymaking system. Now, I had two goals. One was to help her grow her wealth, and the second was to marry her.

Linda agreed to move from Dallas to Oklahoma City (where I live and invest). I researched on how a non-US citizen can borrow money from banks, and I connected her with my group of banks. I've spent years building good relationships and using these bankers for loans.

The amazing news is that Linda just purchased an 84-unit apartment building in Oklahoma using creative financing strategies and connections.

I'm also delighted to report that I did close the sale on the marriage, and she is now Mrs. Linda Elder. I'm really a lucky guy!

In summary, the best way to become wealthy or financially free is to:

- Write your goals.
- Educate yourself.
- Attend trainings and local REIA meetings.
- Connect with like-minded people.
- Build your team.
- Buy properties below market value.
- Buy cash-flowing properties only.

- Learn to raise money.
- Join mastermind groups.
- Get a mentor who is successful.
- Don't give up until you've reached your goals.
- Take immediate action, even if you're scared.

What to Do Next

Obviously, this book is a starting point. It is important that you take action despite your current situation, setbacks, or experience. The good news is that anyone can become wealthy in real estate despite gender, background, education, or even location.

My mentees and I are living proof of the fact that if you truly put your mind on becoming wealthy and take the necessary steps, it is actually not that hard to become financially free.

Whether your goal is to make a certain amount of money per month, become a millionaire or multi-millionaire, take care of your parents, send your kids to certain schools, travel the world, buy the finest things in life, have more quality time with your spouse, or donate for your causes, it's important that you do this now.

If you ever have a chance to meet wealthy people and ask them what is the one major attribute that differentiates successful people from unsuccessful people, they will tell you that by far, the most important thing you can do right now is to take timely action whether you are ready or not.

As I end this, I want to gift you a special ebook that goes into detail about my processes, how I find properties, how I raise money, and how I've bought over 600 doors. You can get your copy by going to http://www.millionaireinvestmentclub.com/FreeGift, and you can reach Robert at robert@millionaireinvestmentclub.com

ROBERT ELDER

In 37 years as the top real estate investor and founder of the biggest REIA club in Oklahoma, Robert Elder has built an impressive portfolio of over 600 doors.

He is an author, mentor, lawyer, and a public speaker who has shared stages across North America with well-known trainers, including the legendary Robert G. Allen.

Robert has a simple, yet very powerful, motto: "When investing your hard-earned money, buy properties below market value and make sure it produces positive cash flow."

Robert currently helps his clients and members attain financial freedom through mentoring and speaking at the Millionaire Possibilities REIA club, Millionaire Investment Club, as well as offering professional real estate coaching.

With easy-to-understand, simple language, Robert has put together this life-changing ebook for anyone wanting to master the game of real estate investing and building massive wealth. You can get your copy by going to http://www.millionaireinvestmentclub.com/FreeGift.